2.99
Ld history
27

To: Carole, Paul, ~~~~ ~ ~~~

I would like to use this opportunity and thank you for all your help and support all these years.

With lots of love & kisses,

Elahe.

20th November 1993;
London

IRAQ, THE GULF CONFLICT AND THE WORLD COMMUNITY

Also available from Brassey's

BROWN
The Strategic Revolution

CDS
London Defence Studies Papers

CLARKE
New Perspectives on Security

IISS
Military Balance

IISS
Strategic Survey

NAVIAS
Going Ballistic: The Build-up of Missiles in the Middle East

ROGERS/DANDO
A Violent Peace

SAYIGH
Arab Military Industry

TAYLOR
The Fanatics

IRAQ, THE GULF CONFLICT AND THE WORLD COMMUNITY

Edited by
James Gow

Centre for Defence Studies

BRASSEY'S (UK)
LONDON · NEW YORK

First English edition 1993

UK editorial offices: Brassey's, 165 Great Dover Street, London SE1 4YA
orders: Marston Book Services, PO Box 87, Oxford OX2 0DT

USA orders: Macmillan Publishing Company, Front and Brown Streets,
Riverside, NJ 08075

Distributed in North America to booksellers and wholesalers
by the Macmillan Publishing Company, NY 10022

Library of Congress Cataloging in Publication Data
available

British Library Cataloguing in Publication Data
A catalogue record for this book is
available from the British Library

ISBN 0-08-041780-9 Hardcover

Typeset by Florencetype Ltd, Kewstoke, Avon
Printed in Great Britain by BPCC Wheatons Ltd., Exeter

Contents

THE MAGREB, MEDITERRANEAN AND GULF AT THE TIME OF THE SECOND GULF WAR

Chronology

1988

18 July   Iran accepts UN Security Council Resolution 598 calling for a cease-fire and withdrawal of troops to the internationally recognised border and a commission to decide responsibility for the Iran/Iraq War.

1989

February   Arab Co-operation Council formed by Iraq, Egypt, Jordan and North Yemen.

May   Non-aggression pact between Iraq and Saudi Arabia.

15 September   Farzad Bazoft, *Observer* journalist arrested in Baghdad.

10 March   Bazoft condemned to death for spying. Executed 15 March.

1990

22 March   Dr. Gerald Bull, inventor of Iraq's 'supergun', murdered in Brussels.

28 March   British Customs seize American-made 'kryton' capacitors destined for Iraq.

10 April   British Customs seize pipes destined for 'BABYLON', the Iraqi supergun project.

27 May   Arab summit, Baghdad. Saddam Hussein criticises Gulf oil over-production.

9 July   Gulf oil ministers meeting in Jeddah.

14–15 July   Arab foreign ministers meet in Tunis. Iraqi Foreign Minister Tariq Aziz accuses Kuwait of syphoning Iraqi oil from the Rumailah oil field.

17 July	Saddam Hussein attacks Kuwait and UAE policy of over-producing and pushing prices down.
25 July	American Ambassador to Iraq April Glaspie visits Saddam Hussein. Appears to give the Iraqi President a 'green light' to invade Kuwait.
26 July	OPEC conference, Geneva. Agrees $21 per barrel oil price for member nations.
31 July– 1 August	Kuwaiti and Iraqi representatives meet, Jeddah. Kuwaitis take intransigent stance and talks break down.
2 August	Iraq invades Kuwait in early hours. UN Security Council passes Resolution 660, demanding an immediate Iraqi withdrawal to 1 August position and calling for the two countries to begin immediate and intensive negotiations for the resolution of their differences.
4 August	European Community (EC) imposes economic sanctions on Iraq.
6 August	UN Security Council Resolution 661: imposes sanctions on Iraq.
8 August	US 82nd Airborne Division begins deployment in Saudi Arabia. Saddam Hussein annexes Kuwait.
9 August	Arab League meets in Cairo, splits into two factions. Iraq orders all Western embassies to close and their staff to leave the country.
10 August	Arab League summit in Cairo, decides to send Arab forces to Saudi Arabia.
14 August	US holds discussions with other permanent members of UN Security Council on establishing joint military command structure under UN to enforce sanctions.
18 August	UN Security Council Resolution 664: demands that Iraq permit and facilitate immediate departure of all foreigners from country, that Iraq takes no action to jeopardise security of nationals of third countries, and rescinds 9 August orders to embassies. Iraq removes 60 American, British, German and French citizens from Kuwait to Iraq.
19 August	Saddam Hussein offers to release detainees if US forces are withdrawn from Saudi Arabia and sanctions are lifted; says foreigners will be used as shields against military aggression.
21 August	Iraqi troops begin to round up Western citizens. Tariq Aziz offers talks without preconditions; US responds that there is little to discuss whilst

Western citizens are detained and demands compliance with Resolution 660.

22 August   EC member states reject Iraqi deadline for closure of embassies.

23 August   EC announces $1.3m aid to countries whose economies have been significantly damaged by the crisis.

24 August   US makes $1m available to Jordan to help meet urgent humanitarian needs. 25 foreign missions in Kuwait do not comply with Iraq's demand for closure. Soviet President Mikhail Gorbachev signals that he is prepared to support additional measures to strengthen UN sanctions against Iraq.

25 August   UN Security Council Resolution 665: authorises necessary measures, including military action, to enforce sanctions.

26 August   Soviet Foreign Minister Eduard Shevardnadze says Moscow will not object if other countries use military means to support sanctions.

28 August   Iraq formally absorbs Kuwait into its administrative structure as its 19th province.

5 September   Saddam Hussein calls for Islamic Holy War against US forces in the Gulf and to overthrow the Saudi king.

7 September   EC approves aid to rescue economies of countries hardest hit by crisis – Jordan, Egypt and Turkey. Jordan announces that 600,000 people have fled Iraq and Kuwait since 2 August; up to 25,000 refugees a day have been entering Jordan.

10 September   Presidents Bush and Gorbachev meet in Helsinki, warn that they will consider unspecified further steps against Iraq if it does not heed UN demand for withdrawal from Kuwait. Iran and Iraq renew full diplomatic relations.

11 September   President Bush tells US Congress that 'new partnership of nations . . . will not let this aggression stand.'

13 September   UN Security Council Resolution 666: sets procedures for determining extent of humanitarian need for food supplies among the civilian populations in Iraq and Kuwait. US announces $28m humanitarian assistance for displaced persons fleeing Iraq and Kuwait.

16 September   UN Security Council Resolution 667: condemns Iraq's violation of diplomatic premises in Iraq

	(Iraqi soldiers had invaded Moroccan, Belgian, Dutch and French diplomatic premises.)
23 September	Iraq says it will launch all-out war against multinational forces in Gulf if it judges that sanctions are about to strangle Iraqi people, identifies Israel and Middle East oilfields as targets
25 September	UN Security Council Resolution 670: requires each member state to impose air transport embargo against Iraq and occupied Kuwait. World Bank emergency assistance programme announced to help resettle refugees fleeing Iraq and occupied Kuwait.
27 September	EC and Gulf Co-operation Council foreign ministers, meeting in New York, reaffirm co-operation to restore peace, legality and stability in the Gulf.
3 October	President Gorbachev sends special envoy Evgeny Primakov to visit Baghdad and Amman. Organisation of the Islamic Conference foreign ministers' meeting at the UN, demands that Iraq abides by UN resolutions and expresses full support for Kuwait, Saudi Arabia and other states in the Gulf who asked foreign forces to defend their lands.
5 October	Primakov meets Saddam Hussein, delivers letter from President Gorbachev. US Defence Secretary Dick Cheney reports that Iraq has over 350,000 troops in Kuwait and that twenty-five countries have contributed to the military deployments in the Gulf, now involving over 300,000 personnel.
26 October	CIA Director William Webster says Gulf cannot be secure as long as Saddam Hussein rules Iraq and that destruction of Iraq's arsenal may be necessary. Pentagon announces up to 100,000 additional troops and 700 tanks to be deployed in Middle East by year's end.
29 October	UN Security Council Resolution 674: demands immediate end to hostage taking and calls on Iraq to ensure immediate access to food, water and basic services for Kuwaitis and third country citizens in Kuwait; declares Iraq responsible for Kuwaiti losses caused by invasion; stresses urgent need for Iraqi withdrawal and restoration of Kuwaiti government. US Secretary of State James Baker warns that Saddam Hussein must realize that there is a limit to the international community's patience.

4 November	Iraq's information minister, Latif Nassiff al-Jassem, says Kuwait no longer exists and world should forget about it.
5 November	Italian Treasury Minister Mario Sarcinelli announces $13bn aid for those worst affected by the crisis from the Gulf Crisis Financial Co-ordination Group – comprising Austria, Belgium, Canada, Denmark, Finland, France, Germany, Greece, Ireland, Italy, Japan, Korea, Kuwait, Luxembourg, the Netherlands, Portugal, Qatar, Saudi Arabia, Spain, Sweden, Switzerland, the United Arab Emirates, the United Kingdom and the United States. Beneficiaries include Jordan, Egypt, Turkey, Syria and Morocco.
8 November	President Bush orders deployment of further 200,000 military personnel and their equipment to the Gulf, saying that the further deployment is necessary to make the force credible. Saddam Hussein sacks Chief of General Staff Lt. Gen. Nizar Khazraji; his replacement is Saddam's son-in-law Hussein Rashid. Baker and Shevardnadze agree that partial solution to Kuwait's occupation is unacceptable.
9 November	General Committee of UN General Assembly refuses Iraqi request to label US forces in Gulf a threat to Arab and international peace and security. Committee, instead, labels Iraq as threat.
10 November	Baker, at the end of a week-long tour (embracing Bahrain, Saudi Arabia, Egypt, Turkey, the Soviet Union, Britain and France) to reinforce the international coalition, says there is full agreement that there can be no partial solution.
12 November	Arab Maghreb Union, after a foreign ministerial meeting with the EC, announces intention to try to persuade Iraq to receive UN delegation to discuss third country citizens detained by Iraq; all five member countries have maintained constant contact with Baghdad.
15 November	Iraq announces deployment of further 250,000 troops in Kuwait.
21 November	President Bush makes separate visits to the exiled Kuwaiti Emir al-Jabber and the Saudi Arabian King Fahd in Jeddah.
22 November	President Bush visits US troops in Saudi Arabia.
24 November	President Bush meets with Egyptian President Hosni Mubarak in Cairo.

27 November   UN Security Council discusses 'inhuman' practices of Iraqi occupiers in Kuwait.

28 November   UN General Assembly Resolution: 148–1 vote condemns acts of violence against diplomatic and consular missions, singling out Iraq's actions in occupied Kuwait; calls for immediate end to violations, citing earlier Security Council resolutions. UN Security Council Resolution 677: condemns Iraq's efforts to alter the demographic composition of the population of Kuwait, authorizes UN General Secretary to take custody of copy of Kuwaiti population register current at 1 August 1990.

29 November   UN Security Council Resolution 678: authorizes the use of all necessary means to force Iraq to withdraw from Kuwait if Iraq does not withdraw by 15 January; demands full Iraqi compliance with UN resolutions.

30 November   Iraqi government calls Resolution 678 illegal and invalid, rejects UN's 15 January ultimatum. President Bush announces invitation to Tariq Aziz to come to Washington, and suggests that Saddam Hussein reciprocate by receiving James Baker at a mutually convenient time between 15 December and 15 January.

3 December   UN General Assembly's Human Rights Committee votes 132–1 to condemn Iraq's violations of human rights against the Kuwaiti people and third country citizens.

5 December   Baker tells the US Senate Foreign Relations Committee that delay in forcing Iraq from Kuwait could help Saddam Hussein to destroy Kuwait. British Prime Minister John Major rules out negotiations with Iraq. Iraq formally accepts President Bush's proposal for a top-level exchange of visits. Defence ministers of the Gulf Co-operation countries meeting in Riyadh undertake to help liberate occupied Kuwait.

6 December   Saddam Hussein asks Iraqi parliament to approve freeing of all foreigners held in Iraq.

7 December   Iraqi parliament approves decision to free all foreigners held in the country. Iraq's Ambassador in the US, Mohamed al-Mashat, apologizes for his country's detention of foreigners and says Iraq expects nothing in return. US State Department

insists that the dates for both the planned high-level US-Iraq visits must be agreed before the first one takes place.

10 December Iraq's Information Minister, Latif Jassim, says suggestion of Iraqi withdrawal is wishful thinking. Indications that Iraq is preparing partially to withdraw to the northern part of Kuwait. Kuwaiti government-in-exile says it will not cede an inch of Kuwaiti territory to Iraq.

13 December Saddam Hussein replaces Defence Minister Saidi Tumah Abbas with Lt. Gen. Abd al-Jabbar Khalil Shanshal. Iraq announces setting up of 370 civil defence training centres in Baghdad and orders building of air-raid shelters. US Federal District Court Judge Harold Greene turns down request from a group of Democratic congressmen for an injunction to prevent President Bush from initiating offensive action against Iraq without authorization from Congress.

14 December President Bush says that the high-level meetings are 'on hold' until Iraq agrees to receive James Baker before 3 January, saying that Baker is available to go at any time until that date. Algerian President, Chadli Bejedid, ends a diplomatic mission to Baghdad without success. Last staff leave US Embassy in Kuwait, although the mission officially remains open but not staffed.

15 December Iraqi announcement that Tariq Aziz will not fly to Washington on 17 December as had been provisionally agreed and that Iraq alone will set a date for Baker to visit Baghdad. EC heads of government call for complete Iraqi withdrawal and restoration of Kuwait's sovereignty and legitimate government.

17 December President Bush meets ambassadors from Coalition countries and reports afterwards that none wants war, but that none will accept partial solution. Saddam Hussein orders all able-bodied thirty-three-year-old men to report for military service. US officially repeats Baker's offer to meet with Saddam Hussein any time between 20 December and 3 January. North Atlantic Council foreign ministers, meeting in Brussels, reiterate demand for complete withdrawal; Baker warns them that Iraq may make partial withdrawal to create division in

Coalition. British ambassador and consul, last Western diplomats in Kuwait, return to London. Britain advises British subjects in the Gulf region to leave before 15 January.

18 December   UN General Assembly votes 144–1 condemning Iraq's violations against Kuwaiti people and third state citizens, adopts ten point resolution. Saddam Hussein says he has ruled out peace talks with United States if US only wants to re-read the UN Security Council Resolutions already rejected by Baghdad.

19 December   Amnesty International issues extensive report on human rights violations in Kuwait.

21 December   Baker and Prime Minister Major meet, express preference for peaceful outcome, but Major stresses that Saddam Hussein's only hope for a peaceful outcome is complete withdrawal from Kuwait.

23 December   US Defence Secretary Dick Cheney and Chairman of Joint Chiefs of Staff Colin Powell end five day inspection of US forces in Gulf, report that Iraq has 500,000 troops in Kuwait, and that US forces are ready to fight. Later, in Cairo, Cheney says international Coalition may soon have no other option than to use military force to achieve its objectives.

25 December   GCC countries meet in Doha, agree and complete security arrangements to guarantee regional and national security of members. Meeting stresses need for complete and unconditional withdrawal of Iraqi forces from Kuwait.

26 December   Soviet Union sends two high-ranking envoys to Baghdad in hope of securing evacuation of almost all the 1,700 experts and advisers still in Iraq before the 15 January deadline.

1991

2 January   NATO Defence Planning Committee authorises deployment of aircraft from Belgium, Germany and Italy to south-eastern Turkey.

3 January   President Bush says he would be willing to send Baker to meet Tariq Aziz in Geneva.

4 January   Tariq Aziz agrees to meet Baker in Geneva on 9 January.

8 January	James Baker and Tariq Aziz arrive in Geneva. In the United States, President Bush calls on Congress to adopt a resolution supporting Resolution 678, including the use of all necessary means.
9 January	US and Iraqi foreign ministers meet in Geneva for six and a half hours. Afterwards, Baker regrets that he has heard nothing indicating Iraqi flexibility about compliance with the Security Council resolutions and that Tariq Aziz refused to accept a letter from President Bush to President Saddam Hussein. Saddam Hussein says that Americans will swim in their own blood if war starts.
12 January	US Congress passes joint resolution giving President Bush full authority to use armed forces to evict Iraq from Kuwait. US publishes Bush letter to Saddam Hussein returned by Tariq Aziz; letter says war can only be ended by full compliance with Resolution 678. American diplomats leave Baghdad. US orders Iraq to reduce its Embassy to four persons, including the ambassador.
13 January	UN Secretary General Javier Perez de Cuellar meets Saddam Hussein in Baghdad, emerges from talks unable to report progress. Egyptian President Hosni Mubarak indicates to Baker in Cairo that his country's forces would join in offensive actions against Iraq if necessary.
14 January	Iraqi parliament votes by acclamation to go to war rather than accept UN demands. EC foreign ministers decide not to send a last-minute peace mission to Baghdad and agree to discourage individual missions.
15 January	UN Secretary General Perez de Cuellar makes final appeal to Saddam Hussein to avoid catastrophe. US Ambassador to UN, Thomas Pickering, speaks of 'pause for good will' to give Iraq last opportunity to comply now that period for compliance has come to an end.
16 January	US leads multinational military offensive to end Iraqi occupation of Kuwait, under the label DESERT STORM. The US and others formally notify the UN Security Council of the allied strike.
17 January	Iraq launches first Scud missiles against Israel and Saudi Arabia; US Commander of DESERT STORM Norman Schwarzkopf says missiles had 'insignificant results'.

19 January	US announces deployment of PATRIOT air-defence units to assist Israel.
28 January	Iran officially informs UN Secretary General Perez de Cuellar that Iraqi military planes and personnel have flown into Iran and that Baghdad will not be allowed to use them.
29 January	James Baker and new Soviet Foreign Minster, Aleksander Bessmertnykh, issue joint statement in Washington saying that cessation of hostilities would be possible if Iraq were to make an unequivocal commitment to withdrawal from Kuwait.
6 February	Baghdad government announces decision to break diplomatic ties with Egypt, France, Italy, the United Kingdom, Saudi Arabia and the United States.
7 February	Reports that Iraq has set fire to oil wells in Kuwait.
13 February	Soviet Union advises US that Evgeny Primakov is visiting Baghdad to tell Saddam Hussein that he must comply with UN Security Council resolutions.
14 February	UN Security Council begins formal discussion on Gulf crisis in closed session. Iraqi government decrees that all seventeen year-old males report to conscription offices between 15 February and 20 March.
15 February	Saddam Hussein makes first offer of withdrawal from Kuwait on condition that all cases of occupation in the region be resolved simultaneously and all foreign troops should be removed from occupied territories. Allied countries say withdrawal must be unconditional.
18 February	Tariq Aziz meets President Gorbachev in Moscow, Gorbachev presents him with plan. President Bush says Soviet plan falls short of compliance with UN resolutions.
22 February	President Bush gives Iraq until 1700 GMT 23 February to begin immediate and unconditional withdrawal if ground offensive is to be averted.
23 February	Allied leaders order use of all forces, including ground forces, to eject Iraqi army from Kuwait.
24 February	Coalition troops begin ground offensive.
25 February	UN Security Council meets at request of Soviet Union to discuss proposed peace plan in compliance with Resolution 660 which would set date for withdrawal and a short withdrawal period and

nothing else. Security Council members conclude that they cannot do anything unless Iraq officially notifies the UN of its compliance. Baghdad radio announces leadership's agreement to withdraw in accordance with Resolution 660. US says Iraq must abide by all 12 UN Security Council resolutions.

26 February   Iraq's army in full retreat.

27 February   UN receives and releases letter from Tariq Aziz in which Iraq accepts three out of twelve resolutions (660, 662 and 674) on condition that the Security Council calls for an immediate cease-fire. Security Council rejects Iraqi offer, demanding unconditional, explicit acceptance of all resolutions. President Bush announces that coalition forces will suspend assault at 0500 GMT 28 February to allow Iraq opportunity to arrange formal cease-fire.

28 February   UN Security Council meets to discuss further letter from Tariq Aziz in which Iraq agrees to comply fully with all resolutions. Saddam Hussein orders his troops to cease fire, begins discussions on permanent cease-fire.

1 March   New US Embassy staff arrive in Kuwait.

2 March   UN Security Council Resolution 686: lays down framework for permanent cease-fire, requires Iraq to rescind purported annexation of Kuwait, accept liability under international law for war damages, release all Kuwaiti and third country citizens, return all seized property, cease hostile and provocative actions, release prisoners of war.

3 March   Coalition and Iraqi commanders agree on how to stop hostilities.

6 March   President Bush in an address to the US Congress outlines US effort to build lasting peace in Middle East. Foreign ministers of GCC member states, Syria and Egypt meet in Damascus, affirming new spirit of Arab co-operation and creation of Arab peace-keeping force to guarantee safety and security of Arab states in the Gulf region. EC announces $4.5m aid to war ruined Iraq and Kuwait.

11 March   Iraq renounces annexation of Kuwait in letter to UN Secretary General.

13 March   President Bush, meeting with Coalition leaders in Ottawa, says Iraq's use of helicopters against armed rebels violates temporary cease-fire.

15 March   General Schwarzkopf sends warning to Iraq's military command that continued use of Iraqi aircraft could jeopardise cease-fire.

17 March   EC announces $6.5m for help to civilian victims of conflict, particularly in Iraq.

22 March   UN Sanctions Committee eases restriction on humanitarian food supplies to Iraq; other restrictions remain.

25 March   Iraq submits copy of resolution by its Revolutionary Command Council declaring all Iraqi decisions regarding Kuwait to be null and void to the UN.

27 March   Permanent members of Security Council reach general agreement on resolution for permanent cease-fire.

1 April   Leader of Kurdish guerrillas, incited to rebel against Iraq by President Bush, calls on US, UK and France to protect Kurds against genocide at hands of Saddam's forces.

3 April   UN Security Resolution 687: establishes terms for permanent cease-fire, these include turning Iraq into a largely demilitarised state.

5 April   UN Security Council Resolution 688: condemns Iraqi government's repression of its civilian population, names Kurds, demands that Iraq removes the threat to peace in the region posed by this repression. NATO accuses Iraq of massive violations of human rights, warns Baghdad to stop attacks on Kurds.

6 April   Iraq's parliament accepts Resolution 687.

7 April   Iraq sends letter to UN Secretary General complaining that terms of Resolution 687 are unfair, but it has no option but to accept. Formally the Gulf war ends.

8 April   James Baker visits Kurdish refugee camp on Turkish border, calls for quick and effective international response. EC endorses British proposal to create protected Kurdish enclave in northern Iraq (this will become 'Operation Provide Comfort', involving 12,000 US, British, Dutch, French, German, Spanish, Canadian and Turkish troops working to give aid to refugees in the mountains on the Iraq-Turkey border.

9 April   UN Security Council authorizes UN Iraq-Kuwait Observer Mission (UNIKOM) to be deployed in

demilitarized areas along Iraq-Kuwait border to monitor cease-fire.

11 April   Formal cease-fire goes into effect to end Gulf war in accordance with Resolution 687.

Glossary

ACC	Arab Co-operation Council
AFCENT	Air Force Central Command (US)
Ahl al-Thiqa	Saddam Hussein's inner circle of confidants
Al-Jihaz al-Khass	Iraqi 'tribal militia' who, with the Republican Guard, put down the revolts which followed Iraq's defeat in the war.
April 7 Group	Libyan terrorist organisation responsible for attacks on economic targets in the early 1980s.
ARCENT	Army Central Command (US)
ATP	Allied Tactical Publication
AWACS	Airborne Warning and Control System
Baydan	Northern Moorish
BCR	Battle Casualty Replacements
BFME	British Forces Middle East
CAP	Combat Air Patrol
CBG	Carrier Battle Group
CENTCOM	Commander United States Central Command
CIA	Central Intelligence Agency (US)
COMBFME	Commander British Forces Middle East
DESERT SHIELD	US code-name for the operation to protect Saudi Arabia from the Iraqi threat.
DESERT STORM	US code-name for the Coalition attack on Iraq to liberate Kuwait
$/b	Dollars per barrel (oil)
EPC	European Political Co-operation
EW	Electronic Warfare
FDP	German Free Democratic Party
FLN	Libyan National Front
FIS	*Front Islamique de Salut* (principal Islamic Fundamentalist group in Algeria)
FOB	Forward Operational Base
GCC	Gulf Co-operation Council

GFCCG	Gulf Financial Crisis Co-ordinating Council
GNP	Gross National Product
GRANBY	British code-name for the operation to support the UN in the Gulf
Haratin	Former slaves in Mauritania
IEA	International Energy Agency
IFF	Identification Friend or Foe
IGC	Intergovernmental Conference
Ikhwan Muslimin	Islamic Fundamentalist groups in Egypt
IMEMO	Institute of World Economy and International Relations (Moscow)
IMF	International Monetary Fund
Inqath	Libyan National Salvation Front
Intifadah	Shi‹ain›i revolt in Southern Iraq
JCS(US)	American Joint Chiefs of Staff
JFC	Joint Force Command (Saudi commanded Arab forces)
JHQ	British Joint Headquarters (High Wycombe)
JSTARS	Joint Surveillance and Target Attack Radar System
LAS	League of Arab States
LNF	Libyan National Front
MARCENT	Marine Central Command (US)
MATS	Military Sealift Command (US)
MCMV	Mine Counter Measures Vessel
MEF	Marine Expeditionary Force (US)
MSR	Main Supply Route
NAVCENT	Naval Central Command (US)
ODI	Overseas Development Institute
OECD	Organisation for European Co-operation and Development.
PDRY	People's Democratic Republic of Yemen
PLO	Palestine Liberation Organisation
PLOD	Pipeline Over the Desert (UK)
RAS	Resupply at Sea
RFA	Royal Fleet Auxiliary
RIIA	Royal Institute for International Affairs (London)
ROE	Rules of Engagement
SCR	Security Council Resolution (UN)
SEA	Single European Act
Shari'a	Islamic religious law
6 plus 2 Group	GCC States plus Syria and Egypt
SLCM	Submarine Launched Cruise Missile
SLOC	Strategic Lines of Communication

SOCOM   Special Operations Command
SPD   German Social Democratic Party
TACON   Tactical Control
UMA   *Union Maghreb Arabe*
Wild Weasels Defence suppression aircraft (US)

Contributors

Anoushiravan Ehteshami	is Lecturer in the Department of Politics, University of Exeter.
Lawrence Freedman	is Professor of War Studies, King's College, University of London.
James Gow	is Research Officer in the Centre for Defence Studies, University of London.
Jo-Anne Hart	is Lecturer in the Department of Politics, Brown University, Rhode Island, USA.
George Joffe	is a member of Centre for Near East Research, School of Oriental and African Studies, University of London.
Elahe Mohtasham	is Research Fellow at the International Institute for Strategic Studies.
Trevor Salmon	is Jean Monnet Professor of European Integration, Department of Politics University of St. Andrew's.
Julian Thompson	is an Associate of the Centre for Defence Studies, University of London.
Charles Tripp	is Lecturer in the Department of Politics, School of Oriental and African Studies, University of London.
Susan Willett	is Research Officer in the Centre for Defence Studies, University of London.

Introduction

James Gow

Iraq, the Gulf Conflict and the World Community, perhaps needs more definition than might at first glance seem to be necessary. The book itself is an attempt to provide a case study of one instance in which world order was starkly in question, not only in terms of what happened, but in relation to the way in which many of the actors perceived and described what they were doing. The volume is not, therefore, a collection of essays on the Iraqi invasion of Kuwait on 2 August 1991, but a set of case studies, written within a few months of the ending of hostilities between Iraq and the coalition that evicted it from Kuwait. They are intended to reveal the differing perspectives which shaped the international response to the Gulf conflict.

Our major interest is with the sum of those perspectives, with the world community, and the way in which it handled the invasion of Kuwait as a question of international order. This requires us to establish an understanding of terms such as 'world community' and 'world order'. As will be shown below, these may be subject to differing interpretations, which may, of course, depend on differing perspectives, underlining the fact that the global community is primarily a community of states. The labels 'Iraq' and 'Gulf conflict' also have variants which require some consideration.

It needs to be made clear, for example, that although Saddam Hussein survived the initial post-conflict months, as well as the conflict itself, far better than his people, the Iraq at the heart of this book is indisputably Saddam Hussein's. The world did not react against the Iraqi people, nor did it seek to add to the punishment of living under Saddam's rule. In this regard, it is notable that UN Security Council Resolution 674, which raised the possibility of war crimes, specifically referred to individual, not collective crimes; the state would not be held responsible for what had happened. In the event, what happened penalised the Iraqi people more than the individual responsible for it all.[1] Yet, in international law, it was Iraq, the state which was guilty of transgression, rather than Saddam, its leader.

The distinction between Iraq, the people, and Iraq, the synecdoche for its leader and his régime may be obvious, but it has consequences for understanding 'the Gulf conflict'. The label 'Gulf conflict' focuses on Iraq's behaviour towards Kuwait and involves the position taken by the United States. But, the term's content depends on how far Saddam Hussein is regarded as its initiator. It also depends, in part, on when the conflict is judged to have begun.

Discussions on the launching of the anti-Iraqi coalition's air attack in January and its ground attack in February made reference to 'going to war'. In these terms, the 'war' began on 17 January, when the American-led campaign began: the Americans were starting a war with Iraq. However, whilst a true statement, this interpretation was limited. To Saddam Hussein and, perhaps, others, there was evidence that the United States and some other western countries had been conducting a duplicitous, anti-Iraqi campaign from February 1990.[2] The State Department's preoccupation with the Soviet Union at that time was such that contradictory signals could have been as much a product of inattention as of dissimulation. This would weaken any assertion that Saddam had been 'set up' or 'double crossed' by the Americans.

Others would argue that the Gulf conflict of the 1990s was conceived during – or even before – the Gulf conflict of the 1980s.[3] Saddam Hussein, it could be argued, had intended to dominate and control the Gulf region through the use of military might from the fall of the Shah in Iran, onwards. Plans for the total control of Kuwait and at least partial occupation of its territory had been finalised during the Iran-Iraq war. Whether these were assumed to stem from the historical legacy of 'lines in the sand' subject to dispute, or whether they are taken to be reflections entirely of Saddam Hussein's immediate designs (or a combination of both), there is clear evidence that Saddam had ambitions with regard to Kuwait long before he ordered the invasion. Yet, ambitions, plans and intentions are not necessarily the same. Because Saddam and his generals had thought of controlling Kuwait, it is not possible to deduce that this determination was enough for them to attempt to realise the thought – even for someone judged widely to be unstable and a 'true psychopath'.[4] Yet, the invasion of Kuwait came at a specific moment, in response to a specific train of events.

That train began the day after the Iran-Iraq war finished.[5] On 9 August 1988, Kuwait took a decision to increase its oil production, to a level in excess of those agreed within OPEC. That decision involved further exploitation of the Rumailah oil fields, long time subject of an Iraqi territorial claim. As a result of Kuwait's action, Iraq's economic situation declined dramatically, its oil income falling by $7bn, whilst its annual interest repayment on the debt incurred during the war with Iran grew to the same amount. Kuwait's wealth augmented as Iraq's diminished and the Iraqi leader's position weakened. This factor contributed directly to the invasion of Kuwait, which was the culmination of two years of argument and threat.

Nonetheless, if the Gulf conflict opened as the Iran-Iraq war closed, it remains indisputable that the key event was the invasion of Kuwait on 2 August 1990. The decision to invade was Saddam's and was made to the amazement of a world which, in spite of all evidence, did not believe Saddam would really do it. In this sense, whatever the role of the Kuwaitis, the Americans and others, the Gulf conflict was Saddam's: he initiated armed hostilities. However, he did so within the context of a limited, local dispute over levels of oil production. That context restricts the regional dimensions of the confrontation to the Gulf itself. The conflict, despite its ramifications throughout the region, was not Middle Eastern in nature. This means certain things for the present volume. Israel, for example, was not included for specific study, whereas the implications of the conflict for it would have necessitated its inclusion in a study on the Middle East as a whole.

In the context of Middle Eastern security, it is inescapable that Israel, regionally, was both a major beneficiary of the outcome of the war and, to some extent, a loser. The war disabled the only military machine in the region capable of presenting Israel with a serious threat. In particular, it removed Iraq's developing nuclear capability. This guaranteed Israel's military and nuclear supremacy in the region. However, the fact that Iraqi missiles hit Israel was a warning for the future. Despite Israel's buying some credit through not complicating American relations with the Arab countries (by not retaliating against the missile attacks), the events in the Gulf also made what had seemed to be the case before overtly clear: under Bush and Baker, US foreign policy was no longer so benign towards Israel as it had been in the past. The results of the Gulf conflict created conditions in which Israel could not avoid edging towards a regional peace conference, because what had happened was treated as a question of world order.

The United States and the Soviet Union together sponsored efforts to hold a Middle Eastern peace conference. This was one aspect of concerted activity by the two superpowers, begun before August 1990, to work together to solve regional disputes and, so, create a more secure world. The international handling of the Iraqi invasion of Kuwait must be seen in this context. The ending of East–West competition meant the dissolution of a particular order in international relations, one which had been the crucible of most international security matters for forty years. International reaction to the invasion clearly and consciously perceived it to be a matter of global portent. The big question raised by the Iraqi-Kuwaiti dispute, at least, for many people at the time, was this: how much of the energy released, as disorder replaced the old Cold War order, could be harnessed in the creation of a new and better one?

The invasion of Kuwait was, in itself, a far-reaching question of international order: whether or not one state should be allowed to interrupt the territorial integrity of another. However, questions of order and disorder were raised on a higher plane by President George Bush's vision of a 'new world order'. He couched the US-led international rejection of what Iraq had done in these terms and this phrase characterised the international treatment of this breach of international order even before its utterance in September 1990.

Bush's position depended on the mobilisation of support around the globe to demonstrate that this was 'not, as Saddam Hussein would have it, the United States against Iraq. It is Iraq against the world.'[6] The American objective according to Bush, was to create a 'new world order . . . freer from the threat of terror, stronger in the pursuit of justice, and more secure in the quest for peace, an era in which the nations of the world, East and West, North and South, can prosper and live in harmony.' This world would be one in which 'the rule of law supplants the rule of the jungle . . . nations recognize the shared responsibility for freedom and justice, a world where the strong respect the rights of the weak.'[7]

Many missed the relative aspects present in Bush's initial discussion of 'new world order': 'freer . . . stronger . . . more secure'. These were readily taken to be absolutes: free, strong, secure. There can be little doubt that the Bush Administration generated a great deal of optimism, grounded largely in the inclusion of justice as a key to a better world (see Lawrence Freedman's chapter on page . . .). However, as the Americans worked out a definition of the 'new world order' during the conflict and after the ending of hostilities, statements by the President and other members of the Administration toned down the more positive visions of a better world.

In this respect, in a speech by Bush in April 1991, the 'new world order' merely meant 'new ways of working with other nations to deter aggression and achieve stability, to achieve prosperity and, above all to achieve peace'. This was clearly a scaling down of any sense of an overarching order; nonetheless, it might be easier to establish. At the same time, Bush described the 'new world' as 'no more structured than a dream; no more regimented than an innovator's burst of inspiration.'[8] This both dismissed the extreme optimism engendered by talk of 'new world order', made clear that there was no fixed definition to the term and yet it still retained some of the optimism the phrase had provoked. The 'new world order' was a vision, not a programme.

The bulk of Bush's April speech had concerned East–West relations as an aspect of the new world. Indeed, it emphasised that central to any new world order was not so much co-operation in the Gulf, *per se*, but the co-operation between the Soviet Union and the United States which had characterised the previous few years. In the September speech which introduced the 'new world' vision, Bush reported that he had shared that vision with his Soviet counterpart, President Mikhail Gorbachev at their Helsinki meeting. But, it is not entirely clear that Bush shared a single concept of world order with others, especially the Soviets.

The term 'new world order' itself was not new. It had been coined most recently by Gorbachev five years earlier. Bush had adopted it as his own, yet, it had been Soviet 'new thinking' which had made it possible to think in terms of 'world community'. Of course, there was no shared definition of 'world community', either. These 'words misunderstood' recalled the possibility that the two superpowers had had distinct interpretations of 'détente' at an earlier stage.[9]

Within the Soviet Union there were at least two ideas of what was meant by 'world community'. When Professor Sergei Blagovalin of IMEMO wished the Americans a 'crushing victory',[10] he added that the Soviet Union's only chance of survival was to become part of the world community. By this, of course, what he really meant was to become part of the West. This version, more or less accepted by the Soviet Foreign Ministry at the time of the invasion, corresponds with the American view of the world community. For others, including, probably, Gorbachev, 'world community' meant something else.

For Gorbachev, it meant, *inter alia*, security through co-operation and use of the United Nations (UN) to find political solutions to international problems; this was predicated on the assumption that the use of force to resolve problems was unacceptable. Although Bush obviously had a commitment to using the UN, as well, the two ideas of a 'new world order' diverged on the question of using force. The UN was actively engaged, probably for the first time, in something resembling the way it was intended to operate. However, it cannot be ignored that American and other troops were originally deployed under Article 51 of the UN Charter. This gives countries the right to self-defence and to call on others for help in self defence; the initial deployment of American troops was not as a UN force but at Saudi Arabia's request for assistance in self-defence. Moreover, the active engagement of those forces in military combat seems to be easier to justify in terms of that Article, applied with reference to Kuwait, than of the Security

Council resolutions passed in the course of the crisis.

Although Resolution 678, which allowed for the use of any means to ensure that Iraq left Kuwait, was widely taken to be the justification for use of force, it was a 'rubbery' resolution. As the Yemenis mocked, it permitted 'persons unknown to use means unspecified to achieve goals unstated'. As the only legal foundation for the anti-Iraqi coalition's operations it would have been questionable. But, in the end, it did add extra respectability to what happened.

Although the committment of the UN to this operation was indispensable, its involvement was subject to criticism from the Soviet Union, and other countries, that the UN was being hijacked by the Americans for their own purposes. Questions on that score came to the fore in the debate surrounding the use of force. The difference in views between the superpowers was a source of tension as the crisis developed, leading the liberal Soviet newspaper *Komsomolskaia Pravda* to suggest that the end of US-Soviet co-operation was nigh, as 'after the Gulf, Moscow and Washington will never trust each other to the degree that such co-operation requires.'[11]

Whether or not the degree of superpower co-operation witnessed in the Gulf episode would be repeatable, and the fact that it was a global rather than a regional issue, are matters deserving special consideration. There were, in fact, several areas in which the continuation of that co-operation would make progress towards the resolution of regional disputes. Partnership over Kuwait and Iraq catalysed prior efforts into a concerted campaign to bring long-standing conflicts closer to settlement. Because the focus of this collection is on global order, the present volume does not concentrate on the Middle East. However, the Middle East is one of the key regions in which international co-operation and pressure was being used before the Gulf conflict and in which it was renewed with vigour afterwards – although in terms of the world community, co-operation was as asymmetrical as it had been during the conflict itself. In short, the world community was primarily an American responsibility and would be shaped by America's might.

However, if that world was to depend on America's might, it would also depend on other countries' wealth. The US-led military operations in the Gulf did not come cheaply, costing $80–100bn. The United States was fortunate that there were a handful of wealthy countries ready to finance the commitment. These included Saudi Arabia and Kuwait, both oil-rich and with an immediate interest in seeing Saddam Hussein's Iraq countered. Those bankrolling Deserts Shield and Storm also included Germany and Japan, both of which had been constitutionally neutered in the military domain after their defeats in 1945. Unable to contribute militarily, they were looked to for financial support, which was forthcoming.

The Gulf conflict prompted questions, however, on changing those two countries' restrictive constitutions, as well as raising doubts about their ability and willingness to repeat their beneficence. It also catalysed pre-existing concerns about the UN Security Council. There were grounds to argue that the world's strongest economic powers should be given more say in big UN decisions. The 'no taxation without representation' principle could not be avoided with Germany and Japan being expected to pay for decisions to which they were not necessarily party. 'Can't pay, won't pay', could well be the plaintive cry should a situation similar to that in the Gulf arise again.

That refrain would reflect the importance of two factors in any consideration of world order: states have particular interests which influence their behaviour and every government's behaviour is conditioned especially by domestic determinants. The combination of these two, somewhat overlapping, factors means that any attempt to generate concerted international action in particular circumstances is always going to be restricted by the friction it causes. This conclusion emerges from the studies presented here, although it is an aspect which is more central to some of them than to others.

Charles Tripp identifies the link between Iraq's internal situation and its external 'myopia'. It was, he argues, the 'singularity of the political processes within Iraq' that explains why Saddam Hussein ordered the invasion of Kuwait, why he defied the threats of the international community and why, initially, at least, his régime seemed resilient enough to survive enormous defeat. Saddam and his 'inner circle' had the exact measure of Iraqi society and what they could do within Iraq. This created a confidence that the world outside Iraq conformed to the same rules. Both the invasion of Kuwait and that of Iran a decade earlier, were products of Saddam's régime and its 'fears, ambitions and delusions'. In terms of world order, it is likely that there will always be rogue régimes like his with which the world community will have to deal.

If the world community has to deal with problems of this or any other kind, responsibility will lie with those who have influence and power. In particular, in the present context, this means the United States. Any notion of world order depends on the strongest not only acknowledging that they have responsibilities to others, but behaving responsibly in their execution. In the instance of the Iraq-Kuwait dispute, the American role was paramount. There had clearly been ambiguous signals from American sources before the invasion – gestures sufficient to make the Iraqis think they could invade without offending the State Department. As Jo-Anne Hart writes, American concern about Iraq was not great before August 1990 – the US 'did not perceive a serious Iraqi threat'.

Yet, once the Iraqis had initiated the conflict, the American response quickly became massive, as it led a mobilisation of international action through the United Nations. Memories of Vietnam undoubtedly had a big influence on US behaviour in the second half of 1990. The scale of the American response reflected these memories. The US military widely had interpreted failure in Vietnam as a result of not using sufficient force soon enough. They were determined not to fail again: should it be necessary to use force, they would be fully prepared.

Of course, this revealed a concern about public opinion and the likely impact of a difficult war on the American electorate. Jo Anne Hart certainly indicates that domestic concern about the electorate influenced policy. It cannot be insignificant that the gear change she identifies in American policy was made after the Congressional elections in November. Hart clearly suggests that the domestic impulse of the next Presidential election campaign was a major element in shaping that change, as well as the policy which followed it and the timing of actions thereafter.

In the regional context, many Arab states regarded the dispute as intra-Arab. Yet, the friendship of other Arab governments, notably the Saudis and the Kuwaitis, with the United States was at odds with this. Anoushiravan Ehteshami demonstrates that the political complexion of individual Arab countries gives them interests which contrast with those of other Arab countries. Although these differing Arabs have a more or less common position with regard to Israel and the Palestinian question, their other concerns predominate and so prevent them from taking united action on a front which would radically alter the Middle East balance of power. Ehteshami also points out that the inability to arrive at a common position on the Iraqi-Kuwaiti affair amplified the tendency to follow particular interests at the expense of pan-Arab ones – 'intra-Arab differences multiplied as a result of the Kuwait crisis'. Those differences were added to by the impact of emergent democracy in a group of Arab countries. The development of pluralist institutions in those countries, particularly in North Africa, generated ambivalence in the then governments' behaviour.

George Joffe emphasises the impact of popular opinion in some of those same countries within the regional framework of North Africa. One impression that emerges is that, even though the governments of different Arab countries may have different interests, there was broad, possibly pan-Arab, support at the popular level for Saddam Hussein in many cases. This clearly had a major influence on policy in those countries and had a role in creating an informal, loose alliance of North African states. Yet, these governments were in ever weaker positions after the crisis as popular pressures created tensions within many of the North African countries. This, Joffe suggests, could only mean increased democratisation or muslim fundamentalism. Both were the foci of movements seeking to break the 'diplomatic stagnation' in the region. He argues that perhaps the most significant feature of the Gulf conflict in North Africa was the shift in political ballast from governments to autonomous groups within society. Those groups, although created to channel popular anger at what was happening in the Gulf, intensified 'the growth of civil society in North Africa'. That development was likely to alter the nature of the region and had implications in terms of Mediterranean security and co-operation, including relations with southern Europe.

North African relations with Europe would depend not only on developments in the former, but on the evolution of the latter. Although the events in the Gulf demonstrated some kind of desire or need for common action by the members of the European Community, it also lucidly displayed their inadequate preparation for such action. As Trevor Salmon writes, the 'Europeans and the European Community did not cover themselves with glory during the Gulf crisis'. He shows the effect of different domestic pressures and concerns, capabilities, interests and intentions on the member governments of the EC which constrained its actions.

In many ways, the diversity within this Community which had specifically set itself the aim of co-operation was a microcosmic herald of the problems to be encountered when trying to secure international co-operation on a wider scale or on an *ad hoc* basis. 'It is difficult', asserts Salmon, 'to gainsay the argument that if unity is impossible on such a clear-cut issue then it will be incredibly difficult to reach a common position on a whole range of matters'. Most of all, the differences between EC governments reflect the importance of domestic politics in 'determining reactions' and the limitations imposed by internal divisions.

The significance of internal considerations also emerges from Elahe Mohtasham's analysis of Iran's perspective on the conflict. She identifies two main groups as religious moderates and religious extremists and describes the way in which Iran became a main beneficiary of the Gulf conflict because its foreign policy was controlled by the religious moderates. The moderates were able to control foreign policy because they shared key aspects of domestic policy with the extremists. The absence of internal strife left those in charge of external policy with room to manoeuvre.

The re-establishment of ties with western countries was just one of the successes which could keep the extremists at bay. Co-operation with the West was the best antidote to the extremists' ideological enmity. The conflict provided Iran with the opportunity to clarify its position in the international system and enhance the 'process of moderation' which, although it had begun well before the crisis, was 'accelerated' by it. The importance of a strong but moderate Iran for regional and global politics was paramount, not least with reference to that country's support of terrorist groups in the past.

Whereas a measure of domestic harmony between extremists and moderates contributed to Iran's position during the Gulf conflict, the opposite was true for the Soviet Union. The Soviet Union's stance was the most important of any, apart from those of the main protagonists, Iraq and America. The US strategy was only possible because of the Soviet Union's position. As the chapter by James Gow argues, the existing Soviet policy when the Gulf conflict began was determined by the country's domestic disorder. The Soviet Union's behaviour throughout the crisis stayed within the rubric of 'new thinking'. However, there were obvious shifts in emphasis or interpretation which damaged the Soviet-American alliance. Those deviations were a product of pressure from domestic sources.

Military operations would have been virtually impossible without Soviet support, even if there was no participation. Indeed, it was perhaps beneficial in practical terms that the Soviet military did not join the anti-Iraqi coalition. Julian Thompson's chapter on the military coalition identifies the many problems created by coalescing a force with so many components, each of which has its own equipment which is incompatible with that of its allies. In this respect, the particular coalition in the Gulf benefited from the experience of some of its members co-operating within NATO.

To this must be added the 'friction' which impedes co-operation – for example, jealousies between component forces and, particularly, 'the effect of domestic pressures and aspirations on each coalition member'. Such pressures bore on operation Desert Storm, despite the basis for success it had in the 'well understood and practised procedures, exercised over a number of years under the NATO Alliance'. What this means in effect is that any similar military operation would require American participation, or, at the very least, backing.

If the Americans bore the physical burden of the military action against Iraq, then the 'main burden' was borne by the 'least privileged sections of the world's population', maintains Susan Willett. Those countries most heavily engaged in the war were not those who paid for it. Germany and Japan apart, payment for the Gulf operations 'intensified' the established flow of capital from the southern hemisphere to the northern one. Many Third World countries suffered large scale reductions in their national incomes as a consequence of 'subtle but profound' changes in the Global economy caused by the Gulf crisis. The US, however, received in excess of $50bn direct capital inflow. In spite of this enormous capital transfer, the US economy did not benefit as indirect costs of the conflict helped tip it into recession. There emerged a danger that any 'new world order' would be characterised by even greater insecurity than anything which had gone before, as 'immiseration of vulnerable economies precipitates instability and volatility'. Economic insecurity would be a poor foundation for any attempt to create a better world.

If any 'new world order' will necessarily rely on the role of the US, then economic considerations must be paramount. America's position in such an order would rest on its having become the only superpower. Yet, as Lawrence Freedman points out many features of the Gulf conflict, particularly the economic need to 'pass the hat round to partners who were not able to contribute in any other way' revealed that the US was 'not *that* super'. It was significant that those most in need of US assistance – Kuwait and Saudi Arabia – could pay for it. It would be a mean 'new world order' that would only benefit those who could pay for American protection, in the right circumstances.

These considerations are reason to be cautious in addressing notions of 'new world order'. Freedman makes clear that the initial, elevated expectations of what a 'new world order' might mean were misplaced. There was never likely to be a world characterised throughout by 'peace, stability, justice and prosperity,'. Perhaps the one new element to emerge from the Gulf conflict of lasting consequence was the preparedness, ultimately, to intervene in Iraq's internal affairs to give 'safe haven' to some of those subject to Saddam's wrath. This is what Freedman calls a 'movement away from the assertion of the rights of states to the rights of individuals and groups'. He recognises that this is controversial and could not easily be achieved, which leads to the low-key conclusion that 'the new world order may have gone as far as it can go'. Put otherwise, this might mean simply that it never had anywhere to go.

Such conclusions reflect a general lowering of expectations. Only months after the cessation of armed hostilities, doubts, where none had been present earlier, about the point and value of what had happened were obvious. *Time* marked the anniversary of Iraq's incursion into Kuwait with a cover story headed 'Was it worth it?'. The magazine was not in any way unique in expressing this sentiment. What, in January, had appeared to be a glamorous turning point in history, as television beamed the first-ever, blow-by-blow, on-screen war around the world, by the summer, looked far less important and impressive. This was especially so as the re-ordering of the world embraced the aftermath of events in the Soviet Union. Yet, what had happened remained a unique example of international co-operation. However, whereas it had initially raised expectations of what might happen in other cases, the indications very quickly appeared to be that the case would remain unique.

Looming large among the various reasons for this are the internal dynamics of states and their particular external interests, identified throughout the present volume. Less emphasis on the rights of states and more on humanitarian intervention might be a welcome feature of any new world order. Certainly there were signs that international co-operation to resolve regional disputes, begun before the Gulf conflict, but spurred by it, might become a permanent feature of world politics. That would be, in a limited sense, a new world order worth the name, particularly if its problem solving included humanitarian questions.

Attention to humanitarian issues arose in part because of the sense of promise created at the popular level by the notion of 'new world order'. The phrase created a great feeling of promise throughout the world, but especially in the industrially advanced countries. For, 'new' indubitably meant *better*. This meant raised expectations, at the popular level in the West, at least. These were that, when something awful happened, the international community would do something to stop it, put things right and perhaps improve on what had been before. It was this kind of impulse that resulted in UN 'safe havens' for the Kurds in northern Iraq, when, to Western public opinion, it looked as though Western governments had incited a Kurdish rebellion and then left the Kurds to Saddam Hussein's malignity. The 'safe havens' were areas in which international forces operating on behalf of the UN provided relief and protection from Iraqi forces. The policy resulted from popular pressure on western governments to 'do something'. That pressure, of course, was a repercussion of the television age.

Before long, the Kurds were again left, more or less, on their own, as international troops pulled back, although certain missions, such as overflights by the British air force from Incirklik in Turkey continued. Intermittent harassment by Saddam's men (who avoided western opprobrium by low-key, small scale operations) and later aerial attacks from Turkey could have done little for Kurdish faith in a better world. Nonetheless, some idea of an improved world order lingered elsewhere; there were clearly raised expectations in populations in the west of action by governments and international agencies in situations which appeared to deserve it.

Most of all, Iraq was a source of disorientation for those who had placed belief in the human justice Bush included in the 'new world' dream. Saddam Hussein's retention of power was hard to reconcile with a diplomatic and military campaign which, despite official disclaimers, had been waged by the US and its allies in personal terms – albeit that it was Iraq as a whole which suffered. Indeed, Iraq's position was another blot on ideas of a better world, as details of the damage done to Iraq's people and its economic infrastructure emerged. The protraction of the Iraqi people's human miseries by continuing international economic isolation, caused by Saddam's ever-presence in power, presented humanitarian challenges avoided by those who wrought devastation.

By May 1991, according to one study conducted by Harvard University, published in October 1991, '55,000 additional deaths of Iraqi children occurred because of the Gulf crisis'.[12] The study added that 500 children a day were dying from disease, malnutrition and inadequate medical care and that 'at least 170,000' children would die in the following year. One consequence of the US-led operations was the crippling of 18 out of Iraq's 20 power plants. This and the damage done to water purification, sewage and hospital facilities created conditions in which disease thrived, in particular, cholera, which spread epidemically. The continuation of UN economic measures against Iraq ensured that neither disease, nor the other hardships faced by the population could begin to be dealt with.

This situation raised questions in the humanitarian sphere. The 1977 Protocol I Additional to the 1949 Geneva Conventions, article 54(2), states that:

> It is prohibited to attack [or] destroy . . . objects indispensable to the survival of the civilian population, such as foodstuffs . . . drinking water installations and supplies . . . for the specific purpose of destroying them for their sustenance value to the civilian population

Whilst this protocol clearly leaves scope for argument that the types of installation in question were not destroyed because of their sustenance value to the civilian population, but for their sustenance value to Iraq as a whole, including its military, it does suggest that consideration should be given to the position of the civilian population and that the aim of any such operation should be very clearly defined. It is not self-evident that 90 per cent of the Iraqi infrastructure could in fact be tied to the military other than in the most general sense. Whether such destruction was necessary and proportionate could only be established in the light of full evidence and the hindsight of history.

As far as this might raise doubts with regard to humanitarian values in international action, it certainly demonstrates that, in this operation, the assertion of state sovereignty – Kuwait's – remained more important than maintenance of humanitarian values. Any concerted international action in the domain of humanitarian issues would inevitably disturb the internal dynamics of states. Such action, in favour of the rights of individuals and groups, could only be accomplished at the expense of the rights of states and governments.

Indeed, if humanitarian values were to be emphasised at a cost to those of statehood and sovereignty, this would create a dilemma: if the international community chose to use force in a similar situation to the Iraq-Kuwait dispute, how far could similar hardships be justifiably inflicted on people not necessarily responsible for what had happened? Would a specific campaign to be rid of Saddam Hussein as President of Iraq have been any more acceptable? The Americans, whether or not they were in earnest,[13] persistently stressed that their aim was to eject Iraqi forces from Kuwait and rejected talk of a 'decapitation' strategy, which could only be a precedent for some states getting rid of leaders they did not like in other states by similar means. Ideally, of course, the Iraqi people would have overthrown their leader. But those who tried this did not receive support – because that would have been 'interference' in internal affairs. That brings us back to the place of internal politics in the world community.

A shift towards weakened sovereignty, to enable greater concern for humanitarian matters, would radically alter the nature of internal politics. Governments would lose some measure of control. For this reason, they would be reluctant to accept emphasis on humanitarian affairs. In certain cases, Iraq among them, the 'interference' of humanitarian concerns might break the circle which has permitted internal omniscience to turn into external myopia on more than one occasion. However, only the subjection of all governments, like that of all citizens within a democratic state, to an independent judiciary with powers of enforcement could prevent manipulation of a 'right' to go beyond state sovereignty.

A limited, initial move in this direction was the 1987 treaty between the member states of the Council of Europe. This set up a body with the right intrusively to inspect all locations where people were deprived of their liberty with a view to preventing abuses – by private recommendation or, if necessary, public disclosure. A greater shift towards human values in relations between and within states would radically alter both the internal and external politics of many countries were it to be achieved. That in itself seems to make it unlikely. However, seeking to move in this direction, even a short distance would be a positive way of trying to use the energy released by the end of the Cold War.

The Iraq-Kuwait dispute is the core subject matter of this book. But, it really concerns the end of the East-West conflict and the possibility of harnessing the energy released by the passing of the old order for useful and positive purposes. From the disorder of that collapse, there could be a better re-ordering of the world. However, there will always be problems judging whether or not a better order has really been achieved. There is no scale. Politics and physics share an interest in questions of order and disorder. One difference between them in this respect, however, concerns entropy. Entropy is a measure of disorder, or inaccessible energy, in physics. Politics, however, has no equivalent for measuring either order or disorder. The existence of an equation to do this might enable a more conclusive assessment of the subjects dealt with in the present volume than is possible.

The essays presented here concern one instance in which disorder and order at global level were immediate concerns. They provide a set of case studies, written within a few months of the ending of hostilities between Iraq and the coalition which evicted it from Kuwait, which will be a foundation for future study of both the Gulf conflict of 1990–91 and issues of world order. Time alone will tell if order and the world community are what the events dealt with in this book were really about.

Notes

1. US Deputy Secretary of State, Robert Gates, in an address made in Vancouver, on 7 May 1991, made clear that American policy was toward 'Saddam Hussein and Iraq while he may remain in power'. That is, the Iraqi people would continue to be punished for being prisoners of their leader.
2. Pierre Salinger and Eric Laurent, *Guerre du Golfe: le Dossier Secret*, Olivier Orban, Paris, 1991, pp. 11–13, suggest that contradictory signals from the US State Department appeared to be proof to the Iraqi leader that he was subject to American double-dealing,
3. Adel Darwish and Gregory Alexander, *Unholy Babylon: the Secret History of Saddam's War*, Gollancz, London, 1991, p. 229.
4. Hosni Mubarak, President of Egypt, cited by Salinger and Laurent, *op. cit.*, p. 21.
5. *Ibid.*, pp. 7–9.
6. President George Bush, 'Toward a New World Order' Address to joint session of Congress, Washington DC, 11 September 1990.
7. *Ibid.*
8. Speech at Maxwell Airforce Base War College, Montgomery, Alabama, 13 April 1991.
9. See Michael MccGwire, *Perestroika and Soviet National Security*, Brookings Institution, Washington, 1991, pp. 96–7.
10. Dev Muraka, 'A winter of discontent', *The Middle East*, April 1991, p. 24.
11. Cited by Judith Perrera, 'Relations Unscathed', *Middle East International*, 8 March 1991.
12. Quoted by Edward Pearce, 'Death and indecency in a time of cholera', *The Guardian*, 25 October 1991.
13. *Cf* the speech by Robert Gates cited above.

1

Iraq and the War for Kuwait

Charles Tripp

The Iraqi invasion of Kuwait on 2 August 1990 took most of the world by surprise. Quite apart from the particular preoccupations and distractions of various governments at the time, there seems to have been a fundamental reason why few could believe that Iraq's visible menace would be transformed into outright invasion. The Iraqi threats were seen as little more than the common currency of international pressure, designed to extort some advantage from Kuwait and the Gulf states. No-one doubted Iraq's military potential, but the disastrous consequences of using it to invade a fellow Arab state and member of the United Nations were thought, by those outside Iraq itself, to be so obvious, that they would act as a deterrent to the Iraqi leadership.

As the events of 2 August showed, however, they were not sufficiently obvious to deter Saddam Hussein. Clearly, his calculations of advantage and risk were based on a very different set of assumptions from those of the governments with which he was soon locked in conflict. During the months of crisis which followed, this fact became ever clearer, as the initial strategic miscalculation of the invasion was compounded by a series of miscalculations which led inexorably to war and defeat. These were the disastrous consequences which in general, if not specific form could have been foreseen as likely to follow the invasion, occupation and annexation of a member of the United Nations. The fact that Saddam Hussein failed to foresee this and was thus undeterred by the prospect when considering the use of force against Kuwait, is an indication of the singularity of the political processes within Iraq. Understanding these processes and the structure of power in which they operate, may help to explain both Saddam Hussein's decision to invade and the strategies he devised to deal with the consequences of that invasion. They may also explain in some degree the extraordinary resilience of the régime in the aftermath of so massive a defeat.

During the past fifteen years or so, Saddam Hussein has constructed a system of power in Iraq founded on a small inner circle of men whom he can trust, if not absolutely, then more than any others in Iraq. These, the *Ahl al-Thiga*, are bound to him, in the first place, by links of blood, originating as they do in the related families of the al-Majids, the Ibrahims and the Tulfahs, of the same clan grouping within the larger entity of the Al Bu Nasir tribe. Beyond these individuals are others, unrelated to Saddam Hussein, but who also come from Saddam Hussein's home town of Tikrit or from similar towns of the Sunni Arab northwest of Iraq. They can be expected to share a similarity of outlook and, in some important respects, an identity of interest. In addition, Saddam Hussein has used his patronage to reward long-standing associates in the Ba'ath party, who may come from quite different ethnic, geographical or religious backgrounds, but whose complicity, subservience and personal loyalty have been put to the test periodically during their years of association.[1] Each of these men has his own descending network of patronage which he sustains with the rewards made available through his intimacy with Saddam Hussein himself. This, in turn, makes such people more valuable to Saddam Hussein as his agents of social control and surveillance.

The advantage of this system for Saddam Hussein has been that it has given him nearly absolute power in Iraq for longer than any other Iraqi ruler. However, the disadvantages inherent in this narrow, cohesive circle have been all too evident in the Iraqi leadership's strategic thinking. Whilst the like-mindedness of the inner circle gave its members a clear idea of what they could realistically achieve within Iraq itself, it induced a peculiar self-confirming myopia when trying to judge the world beyond Iraq. So absolute had been the success of both diagnosis and prescription within the confines of the state, that to disagree with – let alone to challenge – similar inner circle consensus on regional or international strategies was either genuinely unthinkable, or highly dangerous. It was unthinkable because the most influential of the inner circle come from provincial backgrounds so similar to their leader's that their outlook is much the same as his own. At the same time, it is highly dangerous to contradict him since to disagree with an autocrat is the first step towards treason.

Consequently, those who had the license to disagree, were those least well equipped to do so. Conversely, those who were able to distance themselves sufficiently to see disaster looming, were by that very token less likely to be fully integrated into the inner circles and would, therefore, be suspected of disloyalty if they voiced their dissent.

Such a system is only threatened when doubts begin to surface within the inner circle of the régime and its descending networks of patronage about the capacity of the leader to guarantee their continued privilege and survival as a ruling elite. A number of signs might alert such suspicions in the case of Saddam Hussein: indecision or vacillation; inability to arbitrate effectively among the various factions of clan and community; inability to deliver the kinds of privileges expected as a reward for loyalty, whether in the form of present pay-offs or of future access to the resources of the state; the erosion of his authority through the refusal of other states, especially those in the Arab world, to recognise Iraq's dominant role in the region.

The Prelude to Invasion

These were precisely the kinds of development which were becoming visible in the years following the end of the war with Iran. During 1988 and 1989 clannish conspiracy in the armed forces and simmering family feuds were both symptoms of malaise and indications to others that the inner circle was possibly cracking up. On the economic front, Iraq was burdened with massive debts, amounting to roughly $80 billion by 1990. Worse still, at a time of falling oil prices and high international interest rates, the debt grew larger, while Iraq's revenue dwindled. Frustration in the economic sphere was compounded by lack of progress in the talks with Iran. The Shatt al-Arab was still unusable, 60,000 Iraqi prisoners remained in Iran and the promised demobilisation of the Iraqi armed forces had never materialised. Although Saddam Hussein was determined to claim that the war with Iran had ended in a splendid victory, it was becoming very clear not only to the people of Iraq generally, but also to the privileged élite that the fruits of that victory were very meagre indeed.

The slow, corrosive effects of these frustrations were dangerous for Saddam Hussein. Rather than appearing heroic, he now seemed simply incompetent. Furthermore, a series of events in the first quarter of 1990 may have suggested to him that he was facing not only potential internal conspiracy, but also an externally inspired plot to weaken the country and to overthrow him. Criticism of the Iraqi government's human rights record in the US Congress and the threat of economic sanctions were followed by similar criticism in Europe. This led to closer scrutiny of Iraqi arms purchases and the seizing of the parts of the 'supergun' and of the 'atomic triggers' in March and April. At the same time, the major coalitions of the Iraqi opposition – Kurds, Shi'i, Arab Nationalist and disgruntled Ba'thist

– met in London to sign a joint statement calling for the overthrow of the régime in Baghdad.[2]

Employing a strategy he had used often enough before, Saddam Hussein sought to highlight the seriousness of the external danger in order to drive home to wavering domestic constituencies the fact that they were all under attack – as Arabs, as Muslims, as Iraqis, as Ba'this, as Takritis or, more intimately still, as sons of the Al Bu Nasir. He expected them, therefore, whatever their motivation, to rally round the standard of Saddam Hussein, as the only effective protector of their interests. In short, he was seeking to transform a mundane plight of economic hardship and regional disregard into a heroic struggle of epic proportions, worthy, therefore, of the uncritical solidarity of the years of war with Iran. With Saddam Hussein at its head, Iraq was posing in the Arab world as the Arabs' champion against its historical enemies.[3] This bore a strong resemblance to the Iraqi thesis advanced during the war with Iran and for very similar reasons: the Arab states were expected to support financially their military protector, Iraq.

In 1990 roughly half of Iraq's $80 billion debt was owed to other Arab states, chiefly to Saudi Arabia and to Kuwait. The writing off of this debt and the renewal of subventions to Iraq to allow it to finance its ambitious reconstruction and rearmament plans without having to borrow further from the non-Arab states were central to Iraq's economic future. The non-Arab creditors of Iraq were now unwilling to lend any more, and this reluctance was complicating the Iraqi government's attempts to purchase the civil and military technology which only the industrialised world could provide. Financial assistance on the scale required by Saddam Hussein appeared to him to be crucial to the survival of the political order in Iraq. Failure to grant him his demands was, therefore, increasingly portrayed by him as betrayal, as testimony to the fact that his Arab creditors were in league with all the other enemies of Iraq.[4]

This equation explains much of the vehement rhetoric used by Saddam Hussein himself, following the disappointments of the Baghdad Summit in May 1990. He had failed to extort at that meeting the kind of financial aid he was coming to believe was his by right. Furthermore, as oil prices continued to fall, due – among other things – to overproduction by OPEC members, so the scale of Iraq's economic plight continued to grow. Saddam Hussein singled out the weakest links in his chain of oil-rich creditors: Kuwait and the UAE. It was the former which was soon receiving the full force of Iraq's denunciations. Geographical proximity, the memory of past conflicts and territorial claims, the still unresolved question of border demarcation and the stark imbalance in the relative strengths of the two states made Kuwait an obvious pressure point. In addition, the careful cultivation of the Iraqi leadership's image of ruthlessness, determination and capacity to use force in pursuit of its objectives lent an added seriousness to Saddam Hussein's talk of acting decisively if words failed to produce the required results.[5]

Despite some minor concessions on the question of oil production, Iraq gained nothing from its increasingly bellicose talk. Indeed, Kuwait appeared to be almost indifferent to the threats from Baghdad. This seems to have encouraged the Iraqi leadership's sense of exasperation and may have led to a belief that it could only be explained by the existence of some form of secret guarantee of protection which allowed Kuwait to adopt so intransigent and defiant a position. In the circumstances, the only possible source of such a guarantee would have been thought to be the United States. Whatever the verbatim truth of the encounter between Saddam Hussein and US Ambassador Glaspie in late July 1990, this meeting seems to have provided Saddam Hussein with the opportunity to discover that no such guarantee existed.[6] From his perspective, he had found out that Kuwait did not enjoy any protection whatsoever. He could conclude, therefore, that, although the US might object to the use of force, it was unlikely to do anything to prevent Iraq from using it. Consequently, the road to Kuwait was open, even if the Al Sabah seemed as yet unaware of the fact.

It is difficult to be certain about the precise nature of the future Saddam Hussein had in store for Kuwait at the moment of the invasion, since his subsequent declarations and actions gave the impression that he was seeking to dress up as coherent and thus determined strategy what was in fact a series of improvisatory moves. He might have been trying physically to eliminate the Al Sabah, in order to set up, under Iraqi auspices, a more pliant government which would give generously to Iraq – whether the gift involved territory or money. He might, equally, have had his sights set on the greater financial reserves of Saudi Arabia. Thus, the invasion of Kuwait might have been intended simply as a demonstration of Iraq's force and ruthlessness, in order to oblige the Saudi government to take Iraq's demands for financial aid seriously. It is also possible that the invasion of Kuwait was Saddam Hussein's attempt to realise a greater dream of expansion which would elevate him to an unparalleled position of dominance in the Arab world and assure him of a unique place in Iraqi history.

The boldness of the act and the economic resources that would have fallen into his lap, had the invasion been accepted without serious opposition, would certainly have had reverberations throughout the Arab world and beyond. However, the improvisation of much that followed, as well as the small part played in Saddam Hussein's political career by anything that could be called visionary or ideologically motivated if it did not coincide with the requirements of short-term political survival, suggest that more immediate considerations came into play in contemplating the advantages of invasion. These were intimately bound up with the material and other resources which he believed he needed to ensure his continued survival as autocrat of Iraq.

Facing the Consequences (2 August 1990 – 16 January 1991)

For these reasons, the self-reinforcing complacency of a ruthlessly successful autocracy remained the hall-mark of Iraqi strategy during the seven months of the Gulf crisis. To the very end, Saddam Hussein and his associates seem to have continued to believe that they could extract some advantage from the situation. Specifically, they hoped to extract from the regional states and from the world powers the material and diplomatic benefits which would justify the whole adventure by extricating Iraq from its predicament. In the eyes of the Iraqi leadership, this predicament related as much to the pre-2 August situation of the country, as to the post-2 August reality of economic sanctions and threatened military action. Thus, for most of the months of the crisis and even during the war itself, the underlying, if tacit, theme of Iraqi strategy seemed to be 'advantageous withdrawal'. It was, of course, in the nature of such a strategy that little or no direct reference could be made to the possibility of withdrawal itself, for fear that the coalition of forces ranged against Iraq might not take its leadership's resolve seriously. It is a testimony to the insulation and resilience of Saddam Hussein's autocracy that this strategy, and with it the belief that Iraq could expect concessions in return for withdrawing its forces from Kuwait, was only abandoned in the face of the unanswerable reality of military defeat.

The reactions at the UN and elsewhere to the Iraqi invasion may have come as something of a surprise to Saddam Hussein. However, in responding to them, he launched a series of initiatives which seemed to demonstrate that he always had two constituencies in mind. The actions he took, although part of a strategy aimed at securing some advantage from the international community, appear to have been motivated as much as anytime by a concern to maintain the morale of the inner circle through the projection of the image of the decisive and resourceful leader, still very much in command of his environment.

In both cases, Saddam Hussein clearly thought it necessary to give the impression of implacable resolve. As far as the outside powers were concerned, he seems to have believed that he would be facing them with the stark choice of either making concessions or using force. Since he seems to have convinced himself that the Americans and their allies were apprehensive of the prospect of war against Iraq, he thought that the more resolute, determined and inflexible he showed himself to be, the greater the rewards likely to come his way. Similarly, on the internal front, since he did not believe that war was very probable, or that, if it came, it would be easily manageable, any signs of premature vacillation or indecision on his part might feed directly into the suspicions of those who believed he was losing his touch.

It is in the light of these considerations that one should interpret the Iraqi moves which led to war in January. The formal Iraqi annexation of Kuwait on 8 August 1991 was scarcely designed to mollify international opposition to the original invasion. It had the effect not only of producing the first unanimous UN Security Council resolution (662) condemning Iraq, but also helped to harden attitudes against Iraq among the governments of the major states of the Arab world, as the Cairo Arab summit meeting a couple of days later demonstrated.[7]

In many ways, however, annexation seems to have been Saddam Hussein's way of raising the stakes in the game of bluff on which he was now engaged with much of the rest of the international community. It was as if he were making it clear that he expected very substantial concessions if he were ever to be persuaded to rescind a measure proclaimed so forcefully to be 'eternal'. It could, therefore, be seen as part of a series of moves aimed at gaining the advantages which Saddam Hussein believed would be his if he maintained his nerve and his resolve.

On 12 August, he indicated the nature of the advantages or concessions which he expected, when he suggested that he might be prepared to negotiate over the future of Kuwait if, prior to that, the Arab-Israeli question had been addressed, as well as the question of Syria's military presence in Lebanon.[8] On the one hand, Saddam Hussein evidently hoped that by linking the questions of Palestine and Kuwait he could cause confusion, especially among the Arab states of the international coalition. In addition, he sought to enhance his own authority by making it appear that his move against Kuwait had been motivated by his concern for the Palestinians. On the other hand, if he thought that the international coalition would go to great lengths to avoid using force to end the Iraqi occupation of Kuwait, he may have believed himself to be mapping out the future path of compromise.

By the light of this reasoning, the longer the process continued, the greater would be his prestige for having initiated it and the better his chances of arranging things in Kuwait such that he emerged with some substantial territorial or financial concessions. The immediate rejection of the idea of 'linkage' by the member states of the coalition, did not prevent it from being discussed at length and advocated by some parties as the ideal solution to the crisis. It also led some governments to talk in a more animated way about the need to address the Palestinian question. This may have been taken by the Iraqi leadership to suggest that a deal was being prepared.

These speculations continued right up to the last-minute French 'initiative' of mid-January 1991. That initiative may have stood little chance of success, but it was, nevertheless, based in some form on the idea of linkage between the two issues. The fact that the Iraqi leadership failed once again to respond in a way which would have made it difficult for the coalition states not to pursue it, reluctant as many were to accept its premises, suggests that Saddam Hussein felt that it was but the prelude to a substantial series of concessions more to his liking.[9] It is also possible that he saw it as a sign of weakness on the part of the coalition. He seems to have believed, until the launching of the allied air attack, that his attempt, begun in August, to link the issues of Palestine and Kuwait was having the desired effect. He was, of course, wrong. However, as in so many of his miscalculations, his belief was based on his own ideas about the weaknesses and insecurities of foreign governments, on his conviction that he had the winning hand and on the fact that nothing and no-one gainsaid him in Iraq.

Similar processes of thought or delusion could be said to have underpinned Saddam Hussein's offer to Iran on 15 August to cede to Iran's major condition for a peace treaty – the return to the terms of the 1975 Algiers Treaty which he himself had repudiated in 1980. This concession was evidently aimed at creating a kind of bond between the two countries in order to allow Iraq to escape from the economic embargo which now isolated it from any significant trading contacts with the world. In the short term, it permitted the repatriation of most of the 60,000 or so Iraqi POWs held in Iran. Beyond that, while the Iranian government welcomed the improvement in relations with Iraq, they had their own priorities. These were tied up with Iran's improving relations with the states of the industrialised west and the Iranian government clearly had no intention of placing these in jeopardy for the sake of Iraq. Much to the Iraqi government's chagrin these priorities shaped Iranian policy during the crisis and the war.[10]

A further notorious example of Saddam Hussein's wishful thinking and myopia in dealing with the outside world was the detention of Western residents in Iraq and Kuwait. Saddam Hussein may well have thought that the hostage question would create such concern in Western states that their governments would become paralysed, unable to think beyond the release of the hostages and would thus be willing to make any number of concessions to secure that release.

The fact that this was so obviously not forthcoming, may not have killed off all hope among the Iraqi leadership, given the amount of media coverage such public concern received.

Nevertheless, the detention of the hostages seems to have had a specific internal purpose as well. It was a move which made Saddam Hussein appear to be in command, seen to be not simply reacting to the outside world, but boldly and ruthlessly seizing the initiative. The procession of politicians and others who made their way to Baghdad to plead for the release of their nationals, the publicity devoted to their petitions by the Iraqi media and the fanfare which attended the President's 'magnanimous' release of hostages in batches – all of this was part of Saddam Hussein's strategy for reinforcing his authority within Iraq and maintaining the nerve of the inner circle. The messages which he appears to have succeeded in conveying to the Iraqis, were twofold. Firstly, the world was coming to him, on its knees, obliged at last to acknowledge the might of Saddam Hussein and, through him, of Iraq. Secondly, only the ingenuity and steadfastness of the President was preventing an all-out attack on Iraq by the evil-minded conspirators of the outside world.

The detention of the hostages undoubtedly hardened opinion against the Iraqi government, thereby making it easier to maintain the unity of the coalition against Iraq in the UN. However, it is unlikely that any of this was ever reported to Saddam Hussein. When, in December 1990, he characteristically let the remaining hostages go at a stroke, Iraq's predicament was, objectively, worsening, but as far as Saddam Hussein was concerned, the hostages had served their purpose and a new game was afoot. The 'new game' was created by the November decision to double the strength of American forces in Saudi Arabia and by the UN Security Council Resolution 678, sanctioning 'all necessary means' against Iraq if it did not withdraw unconditionally before 15 January 1991.

From the behaviour of Saddam Hussein and his government during the period leading up to the expiry of the UN deadline, it seems that he regarded the possibility of it being a strict military deadline as rather remote. As far as his domestic political considerations were concerned, the very existence of a deadline imposed by outsiders made his unconditional compliance very difficult, if not impossible. For Saddam Hussein to have agreed, unconditionally to withdraw from Kuwait before 15 January would have suggested to many in the inner circle that he had lost his nerve. It would also have suggested to them that the pretence he has maintained throughout his Presidency – that he has access to information which allows him to know better than any of them what is really going on – was indeed a pretence and that he was as inept as they sensed themselves to be when dealing with a world which they do not understand. Furthermore, the simple fact of unconditionally accepting terms imposed by outsiders would destroy the carefully calculated image of the decisive, ingenious leader on which much of his authority was based. Instead, he would merely be seen as a passive figure, obeying the commands of others and, if that were the case, although the commands today might emanate from the United Nations, a question-mark hung over the source from which Saddam Hussein might be intimidated into taking commands in the future. Such a leader would be not simply useless to the circles of privilege in the Iraqi régime, but positively dangerous to their interests.

Saddam Hussein had devoted most of his energies during the previous decade to the elimination of such doubts. Indeed, the very invasion of Kuwait itself could be seen to be partly due to his determination that such doubts should not arise. It was, therefore, inconceivable that he should have made a move at this stage which would have allowed them to proliferate, since it would have greatly increased the chances of his rapid overthrow. Compliance with the UN deadline seemed to be precisely such a move. As always in Saddam Hussein's strategy, his initiatives, or lack of them, were the product of a political system he had himself created, the perspectives it engendered and the priorities it imposed upon him as the person who attempted to manage it to his own absolute advantage. Consequently, the responses to outside initiatives were largely conditioned by his understanding of his domestic advantage. Successfully managing this aspect of his security was the *sine qua non* of everything else and, therefore, relegated considerations of the efficacy of his moves in the world beyond Iraq to second place.

War Strategy (16 January 1991–28 February 1991)

It is in the light of the above considerations that Iraqi strategy during the war itself must be judged. Even if the Iraqi leadership thought that some kind of allied military action might be expected after this date, it does not seem to have anticipated the scale of the air campaign launched on 16 January. Iraq had, in any case, no effective defence against this onslaught. As a result, the response of the Iraqi leadership was a political one: it launched the first of a series of Scud missile attacks against Israel. The belief was evidently that this would draw Israel into the fighting. Such a development would illustrate Iraq's argument that the crisis was really about the Arab-Israeli issue, causing confusion among the Arab members of the coalition forces and disrupting the allied war effort. However, none of these developments occurred. Israel failed to retaliate. Egypt and Syria declared that even if Israel did retaliate it would be acting within its rights. The Patriot anti-missile system from the United States was largely successful. Furthermore, the allied bombing campaign continued unabated. These developments did not prevent Iraq from continuing to launch Scuds against both Israel and Saudi Arabia for the remainder of the war, although neither their political nor their military effects seemed to be to Iraq's advantage.[11]

This makes one suspect that there was another logic at work simultaneously in Iraq's use of the Scuds. This had more to do with the reinforcement of the image of presidential command and resolve than with any external effect they might have had. In this respect, it was the very act of launching them that was important for Saddam Hussein. By this action he sustained the image of the ruthless, fearless and decisive leader which was so important for his authority, and thus for his power, in the inner circle of the régime. In this calculation, it did not matter very much what happened to the missiles once they were airborne, since their reported lack of effectiveness could always be claimed by Saddam Hussein – and may possibly have also been believed by him – to have been merely the propaganda of the enemy.

As the allied bombardment grew in intensity, the vulnerability of Iraq's armed forces became apparent. The quality of Iraqi military intelligence regarding the capacity of the allies to sustain their attack, is unlikely to have been very good. In these circumstances, Iraq's war strategy seems to have fallen back on some of the consolations of the war with Iran, however inappropriate this may have been as a guide. That war had been marked by a number of furious and intense offensives launched by Iran, during which the Iraqi forces kept their heads down, defended themselves as best they could and waited for the Iranian military effort to exhaust itself. This appears to have been more or less the tactic used by Iraq in 1991 prior to the land offensive.

Thus, within ten days of the beginning of the air attacks, reports emerged of Iraqi planes making for the safe haven of neighbouring Iranian territory. Saddam Hussein's practice of dispersing units of the Iraqi air force outside Iraq itself had been noticed during the Iran-Iraq war. He had publicly justified it at the time by stating that it was a way of keeping a formidable weapon in reserve for the time when Iranian land offensives were at their most intense.[12] Similar thinking may have dictated the eventual flight of nearly 130 of Iraq's aircraft to Iran. However, there may have been other motives at work which had more to do with the pilots' assessments of their chances and of their future than with any coherent strategy dictated by the Iraqi leadership.

As far as Iraqi ground forces were concerned, there was not much they could do, other than await the allied ground offensive. The limited operation on 29 January, when Iraqi forces seized the border town of Khafji for a couple of days, bears the stamp of Saddam Hussein's 'strategic genius' (the most obvious precedent here is the brief capture of Mehran by Iraqi forces in 1986).[13] Whatever the level of their information about the Allied forces, it is almost certain that the Iraqi high command would have known that such an operation would be futile, even if, in the short-term, some square kilometres of Saudi territory could be captured. However, it seems that it was necessary and important for them to proceed seriously with the operation (and, as far as one can gather, to plan follow-up operations), even in the knowledge that they were exposing their troops to allied air power.

They were possibly acting under the direct orders of Saddam Hussein, whose unmilitary imagination may have been seized by the apparent opportunity offered for Iraqi military action. Alternatively, the generals may have been under pressure from Saddam Hussein to produce some plan that would show that the Iraqi armed forces were not cowed by the Allied attacks. In any event, it gave them the opportunity to prove to the political leadership the difficulty they faced in taking any military initiative and to demonstrate that their inaction in the face of the Allied onslaught was due to the unequal balance of forces, not to malingering on their part.

Because of the speed, the direction and the overwhelming force of the eventual Allied ground offensive, it is difficult to tell how seriously the Iraqis intended to defend Kuwait by the time that offensive was launched. Most of their dispositions were made in the period preceding the Allied air bombardment, before it became clear that the Iraqis would be forced to fight the kind of war which they had never before experienced and for which they were ill prepared. By the first week of February the Allied bombing was rapidly reducing the capacity of their forces in Kuwait and the Khafji episode had shown what this meant in terms of planned military operations. Furthermore, the sustained destruction of all routes of communication and reinforcement to the south demonstrated the difficulty the Iraqi army would face in trying to sustain any prolonged defence of Kuwait, even if the Allied offensive were to come from the sea or directly from the southern front, as the Iraqis seemed to expect. Despite the defiant rhetoric, even Saddam Hussein must have been aware of the strong possibility of military defeat in Kuwait, were the Allied ground offensive to begin.

However, he may well have believed that his forces, even in defeat, could still inflict heavy casualties on Allied ground troops. Whether or not the Iraqi high command was prepared to use chemical weapons in the battle for Kuwait is a moot point. Given the speed and confusion of their defeat, as well as the sustained bombing campaign to which they had been subjected, it is possible that they were in no position to do so, even had they been ordered so to do by Saddam Hussein. He himself had hitherto sanctioned their use only against forces which could not retaliate in kind and he knew that this did not apply to the forces of the coalition. Nevertheless, the uncertainty about Iraq's capacity and the public voicing of concern about the possible use of chemical weapons against Allied troops was a highly visible and sustained feature of the media coverage of the crisis. It is possible that this exaggerated for Saddam Hussein the degree to which fear of casualties among the coalition members inclined them toward a diplomatic formula which would bring the war to an end before the ground campaign started.

It was at this point in the war, on 13 February, that about 300 people were killed after a direct hit on a Baghdad air-raid shelter. Interestingly, this was followed within a few days by an Iraqi offer to withdraw from Kuwait. The identities of those who were killed in the shelter are as yet unknown. However, it is possible that they may have been the families of members of what could be called the Iraqi 'nomenklatura' –[14] that is, of party and state officials, military officers and people connected more informally to the Iraqi leadership. If that was the case, then the cost of continuing to occupy Kuwait had been suddenly and terribly brought close to the centre of the very circles of power which sustain the régime of Saddam Hussein. It may have taken an event of this kind to cause the leadership to believe that the Allies would stop at nothing to achieve their war aims.

Whatever the truth of this incident and its effect on the thinking of the Iraqi leadership, there were other reasons for the Iraqi offer of withdrawal: militarily, the indefensibility of Kuwait was becoming each day more apparent; diplomatically, the visit of Primakov to Baghdad suggested to the Iraqi leadership that the Soviet Union would be willing to intercede in order to forestall a ground offensive. This, at least, seems to have been the message which Saddam Hussein derived from the visit. The result was the offer, in the name of the RCC, to withdraw from Kuwait on terms long rejected by the coalition powers. The offer to withdraw was taken as a new departure. In fact, it was merely the first public voicing, since the declarations of 'eternal annexation', of the underlying Iraqi strategy of 'advantageous withdrawal', first articulated by Saddam Hussein on 12 August 1990.[15]

The fact that the Iraqi leadership still seemed to believe that a withdrawal could be achieved on the terms suggested by the offer of 15 February is testimony to their difficulty in seeing beyond their immediate priorities and preoccupations. However, the week that followed appeared finally to convince them that the strategy of last resort – 'survivable withdrawal' – was the best they could hope for.

The Allies' rejection of the terms set by Iraq, the continuation and intensification of the bombing campaign and the discussions between Tariq Aziz and his Soviet counterparts appear to have driven home finally the fact that withdrawal would have to be achieved rapidly and on terms which Iraq would be unable to dictate.

It was this realisation which seems to have set in motion Iraq's scorched earth policy in Kuwait. The firing of Kuwait's oil wells and the destruction of power and water installations, as well as public buildings in Kuwait City, seem to have been due to Saddam Hussein's determination that he would at least gain one of the 'advantages' which his initial occupation of the country had been designed to achieve: the humiliation and spoliation of the domain of the Al Sabah. Within the inner circles of power in Iraq, for whose benefit these actions seem to have been chiefly designed, this was possibly regarded as an important achievement for Saddam Hussein.

Characteristically, the Iraqi leadership chose to ignore the American ultimatum calling for an agreement to withdraw unconditionally by noon of 23 February. A last Scud was fired at Israel and the destruction of Kuwait's assets was accelerated. In Moscow, Tariq Aziz produced a '6 point plan': all previous Iraqi conditions for a withdrawal from Kuwait were unceremoniously dropped and the only demand left was that the United Nation's sanctions should be lifted once the greater part of the Iraqi forces had been withdrawn.

By this stage, however, the initiative lay neither in the hands of Iraq nor in those of the Soviet Union. The Allies' ground offensive began in earnest. Driving through southern Iraq and cutting off the divisions of the Republican Guard supposedly held in reserve, the scale and direction of the offensive seems to have caught the Iraqis by surprise. Once it became apparent that their forces were overwhelmed, the strategy of the Iraqi leadership became that of 'survivable withdrawal' at its most crude. Principally, this meant putting as much distance as possible between its own troops and the advancing allies. In the case of the Iraqi forces in and around Kuwait City, this retreat turned into a rout. For the Republican Guard divisions it became imperative to battle their way across the Euphrates. This may have been to take up defensive positions against further allied onslaughts. It may also have been due to a sense of self-preservation which could be justified to the political leadership as preservation of their military strength to deal with the possible political consequences of defeat in southern Iraq. By the time they reached the river, they were in little shape – and, according to some reports, in little mood – to defend either their country or their régime.[16]

However, as far as the Iraqi leadership was concerned, the crucial question was how to organise things so that the régime could survive the repercussions of the defeat in the south. It was less the loss of

Kuwait that mattered than what else might be lost in the losing of it. It is here that Saddam Hussein's longer term, or underlying strategy of survival came into play, as has been borne out by the events in Iraq since the ending of the war for Kuwait. Indeed, the very smoothness of the transition from external military defeat to internal military repression suggests that by the end of February Kuwait – and the Iraqi forces trying to defend it – had virtually become an irrelevance in the strategic calculations of the régime. That strategy was now geared to the more familiar task of securing the political order against the attacks of internal enemies: crushing their open rebellion by force and re-establishing the networks of terror and surveillance which had briefly – and dangerously for Saddam Hussein – evaporated in the aftermath of the defeat in Kuwait.

Conclusion

All the Iraqi initiatives during the war had been marked by a double purpose: the Scud launches, the Khafji episode, the flight of Iraqi planes to Iran, the destruction wrought in Kuwait and even the kinds of troops stationed in Kuwait itself. They bore the stamp of a leadership which regarded the war as manageable, whatever the military outcome, as long as it was not permitted to touch on the underpinnings of the régime itself. The success, in the short-term at least, of this strategy on the internal front, despite its disastrous external consequences, is a testimony to the singlemindedness of those who devised it.

In the aftermath of the defeat in Kuwait, the inner circle around Saddam Hussein kept its nerve. Furthermore, although large numbers of Iraqi forces had been committed to the battle in Kuwait – and had been decimated there – sufficient coercive power remained in the hands of Saddam Hussein. The Republican Guard divisions stationed near Baghdad, as well as the units of the 'tribal militia' of Al-Jihaz al-Khass had come through the war unscathed. They were better organised and better equipped than virtually any other military unit in the country. They were certainly more than a match for the rebellions which followed the defeat. Faced by these revolts, Saddam Hussein immediately deployed his forces in a ruthless and coordinated way which succeeded in suppressing the widespread rebellions both in the Shi'i towns and villages of the south and the Kurdish areas of the north.

The fact that he could do so, with no hesitation and with an assurance that his orders would be obeyed, was due to the confidence he had in the very cement which has kept his régime together. The isolation of Iraq, the war itself and, finally, the widespread rebellions, paradoxically helped to increase the sense of beleaguered solidarity not simply among the kin of Saddam Hussein, but amongst all those who saw their privileges threatened by the disorder which seemed about to engulf them all. At such a critical time, there was a strong tendency for these people to rally round the leader and obey the commands coming out of central government, not necessarily through blind loyalty, but because they feared the alternatives more.

This was, ironically, exactly the heroic posture for which Saddam Hussein had been searching in the aftermath of the war with Iran. Equally, with the ending of the war in Kuwait and the crushing of the internal rebellions, the memories of such heroism will begin to fade again. Saddam Hussein will become vulnerable once more to the corrosive loss of faith in his capacity to govern in the interest of those who have hitherto benefitted from his style of rule. International mistrust, visible contempt and the casual infringement of Iraq's sovereignty bring home to many the invidious position of their ruler. Above all, the complete destitution of the country as long as Saddam Hussein remains in office will probably generate the pressures which will destroy him. His peril will be increased by the possibility that such pressures will come from those within the circles of power of the régime who are much better placed to act upon their resentments than the geographically, ethnically and politically remote Kurds or Shi'i.[17]

Whatever the immediate future of Saddam Hussein and his circle, the Iraqi invasion of Kuwait and its aftermath indicate the ways in which the patterns, developments and crises of Iraqi politics can disrupt any plan for regional order. The circumstances which allowed Iraq to build up its military capacity to the extent it did were peculiar to the 1980s, in that they stemmed from the eight-year war with Iran. Equally, the economic plight of Iraq was a consequence of that war. In that sense, therefore, both the means and the motive for the invasion of Kuwait were the products of a particular set of circumstances which are unlikely to be repeated. However, it should not be forgotten that the war with Iran which had produced these conditions was itself initiated by the fears, ambitions and delusions of the ruling circle of Iraq, led by Saddam Hussein.

Nevertheless, it would be unrealistic to believe that the events of 1990–91, or indeed of 1980–88, were simply due to the existence of one man. They arose partly from regional imbalances of power, from international complicity or neglect, but also from the unsettled nature of the politics of the Iraqi state. The system of power which Saddam Hussein had devised to master these political impulses and harness the resources of the state to his ambition has not eliminated the root causes of that restlessness. On the contrary, some would argue that where the present Iraqi regime has not simply 'frozen' social conflicts through repression, it has both exploited old social rifts and created the lines for new forms of contestation to appear. This will make it difficult to integrate Iraq into any form of regional order, regardless of the composition of its government. In a weak and fragmented condition, it has the capacity to invite the indirect intervention of regional powers, concerned about particular communities in Iraq, anxious of the advantages being gained by other regional states and fearful of the resurgence of an Iraq such as that of Saddam Hussein. As a militarily powerful and economically restored state, there is always the possibility that it will be directed once again by those in Iraq who feel that it merits a position of regional authority and power greater than that hitherto accorded to it.

The conclusions which may be derived from this, as far as long-term regional order is concerned, may not be very reassuring. However, the states of the region may take some consolation from the fact that the Gulf war has left two kinds of legacy which will restrict Iraq's capacity actively to compromise their security. Firstly, and most obviously, there are the legacies of material destruction. Iraqi military strength has been violently reduced, its economic infrastructure badly damaged and its financial capacities placed under severe restraint. Nor will there be much that the Iraqi government will be able to do in order to escape from this predicament in the short-term. Clearly, a change of régime and the downfall of Saddam Hussein will ease aspects of this situation, but it will not be able to restore Iraq militarily to the position it enjoyed in August 1990 or economically to the position of August 1980.

However, the prospect of a change in the system of power raises the question of the other, intangible legacy of the war and the crisis which led up to it. This is the degree to which the present Iraqi régime, or any future one, will be able to sustain the self-confirming myopia in its interpretation of the world beyond Iraq which led to Saddam Hussein's disastrous miscalculations. Whether or not Saddam Hussein himself has changed his view of the way the world operates is less important than the impact which the experience of the war has had on those who hitherto believed it in their interests to trust his judgment. In some respects, this could be said to be the single factor which led, perhaps more than any other, to the invasion of Kuwait and to the war which followed. The disastrous consequences of that war for Iraq will have shattered the foundations of that belief and it is unlikely that they will be reconstructed to such effect in the foreseeable future. That being the case, then even if the world does not necessarily have a better idea of Iraq's intentions, the Iraqi leadership should be able to form a rather more accurate view of the likely consequences of its own actions in the outside world. Being able to make this calculation with a fair amount of accuracy creates the inhibitions which so signally played no part in the Iraqi leadership's thinking during the weeks leading up to 2 August 1990.

Notes

1. A detailed picture of these people is provided by Amatzia Baram in 'The Ruling Political Elite in Ba'thi Iraq, 1968–1986: the changing features of a collective profile', *International Journal of Middle East Studies* 21 (1989) pp 447–493

2. E Karsh, 'Why Saddam Hussein Invaded Kuwait' Survival XXXIII/1 (Jan/Feb 1991) pp 22–24; *Le Monde* 12 February 1991 (2)

3. See Saddam Hussein's speech, broadcast on Voice of the Masses, Baghdad 2 April 1990 – BBC/*SWB ME/0730* A/1–4; also Tariq Aziz, as reported by INA 4 April 1990 – BBC/*SWB ME/0732* A/1–2; and the declaration by the Iraqi National Assembly BBC/*SWB ME/0740* A/4

4. See Saddam Hussein's speech to the Arab League summit of 30 May 1990, read out on Republic of Iraq Radio, Baghdad 18 July 1990 – BBC/*SWB ME/0821* A/1; also the declaration of the Iraqi National Assembly of 19 July 1990, reported in INA – BBC/*SWB ME/0822* A/2–3

5. Saddam Hussein's speech, Republic of Iraq Radio, Baghdad 17 July 1990 – BBC/*SWB ME/0820* A/1–4; also Tariq Aziz's letter to the Arab League Secretary-General of 16 July 1990, read on Republic of Iraq Radio 18 July 1990 – BBC/*SWB ME/0820* A/4–7

6. *International Herald Tribune* 17 September 1990 (1)

7. MENA 10 August 1990 – BBC/*SWB ME/0841* A/5

8. Republic of Iraq Radio, Baghdad 12 August 1990 – BBC/*SWB ME/ 0842* A/1

9. *Independent on Sunday* 13 January 1991 (15)

10. S Chubin, 'Post-war Gulf Security', *Survival* XXXIII/2 (March/April 1991) pp 144–5

11. IISS *Strategic Survey* 1990–1991 (Brassey's for IISS, London, 1991) pp 72–73

12. S Chubin & C. Tripp *Iran and Iraq at War* (I. B. Tauris, London, 1988) p 55

13. In a move heralded at the time as a mark of Saddam Hussein's military genius, Iraqi forces had been ordered to capture the Iranian town of Mehran as a kind of 'compensation' for the loss of the Fao peninsula to the Iranians. The Iraqi forces occupying Mehran found themselves in an uncomfortable salient which it was impossible to defend. Within a few months they were driven out by an Iranian counterattack.

14. This has been suggested by the fact that the shelter in question was sited in a Baghdad neighbourhood associated with such people, by the apparent military uses of the building above, thus restricting access to the shelter itself and by the notoriously small number of air-raid shelters in Baghdad, open to the general public

15. *The Times* 16 February 1991 (2)

16. IISS *Strategic Survey* op. cit., pp 76–79

17. *The Independent* 21 May 1991 (6)

2

American Objectives in the Crisis

Jo-Anne Hart

The Iraqi aggression against Kuwait completely reversed US policy.[1] The US did not anticipate Iraq's move. Within the American Administration the presumption held of an Iraqi bluff despite the tens of thousands of Iraqi troops deployed at the Kuwaiti border during the latter part of July 1990. Pre-invasion relations between the Bush Administration and Saddam Hussein's régime had been on reasonably good terms; the Administration called Saddam Hussein a 'force for moderation' in the region. From the moment of Iraq's invasion the American attitude toward Saddam Hussein was intransigent: the Bush Administration no longer felt Iraq could be moderate or moderated.

During the crisis and the ensuing war there was debate about American goals *vis à vis* Iraq and an evolving policy. The desire to evict Iraq from Kuwaiti territory was only one element in the set of American options. This chapter will trace the development of those options. It is contended here that the US Administration formed the view that a resolution of the crisis which expelled Iraq from Kuwaiti territory would not satisfy American interests. The elimination of Iraq's potential regional military power was a prime motivator of American decision-making and military operations. This has particular significance, beyond this crisis, for post-Cold War world politics.

The articulation and ranking of interests is clearly a linchpin of policymaking. In American decision-making during the Iraqi conflict, we can identify a political set of decisions (encompassing military options) which dominated the scene from the invasion in August until the start of the coalition offensive against Iraq in mid-January 1991. During the period where massive force was used, the Bush Administration faced a choice of military goals to pursue. Without suggesting a false dichotomy between political and military interests, since these are inherently linked, the distinction between political and military goals provides a framework within which to consider the development of ideas about these two sets of related problems.

In the first case decision-making focused on which political objectives to pursue and with what means. The original idea centred on containing Saddam Hussein politically and militarily. These choices included sanctions (as opposed to force), whether it was possible to be rid of Saddam Hussein, and what kind of Iraq would be tolerable. In the second case, following the decision to employ military force against Iraq, the remaining choices centred on which military objectives would guide operations – either to compel Iraq to withdraw from seized territories or to defeat Iraqi military power projection abilities. Some observers have labelled these 'implicit vs. explicit' goals and noted the disjunction between public and private statements made by key decision-makers during the crisis. Here we will analyse the form of these goals and pursue their logic and implications throughout the crisis.[2]

Pre-Invasion US – Iraqi Relations

The US was formerly concerned about potential Gulf instability at the hands of Iran, and the Reagan Administration chose to pursue Iraq as a 'balance' against those threats. In 1984 the US removed Iraq from its list of nations supporting terrorism and secretly supplied the Iraqis with American military intelligence and openly granted agricultural credits and Export-Import bank financing.

The basis of President Bush's policy in the Gulf derived from the October 1989 National Security Directive 26 which reaffirmed the 1980 Carter Doctrine by asserting that, 'access to the Persian Gulf and key friendly states in the area is vital to US national security' and again committed the United States to defend these interests with military force 'against the Soviet Union or any other regional power with interests inimical to our own.' While the Pentagon publicly acknowledged that the American defence posture for Gulf scenarios would no longer be preoccupied with the Soviet threat, the Bush Administration did not articulate a redefined set of threats beyond the vague notion of any regional power with adverse intentions.

In its Directive, the Administration noted concerns about Iraq's chemical and biological weapons and a potential Iraqi nuclear programme. Iraqi human rights abuses were also an acknowledged problem. However, these reservations were systematically played down in order to foster better relations with Iraq. The Bush Administration may not have liked or approved of the Iraqi régime but it felt that that was the best choice available to contain Iranian power. The intention of American policy was to use political and economic incentives to moderate Iraq's behaviour and to increase American influence. Specifically, US companies were encouraged to become involved in Iran-Iraq war reconstruction, especially in the area of energy. There were suggestions in Bush's Directive that US activities in Iraq might influence various segments of Iraqi society.[3] The Administration's position was that Iraq had emerged from war prepared to play a more constructive international role and that a positive relationship with the US would promote Iraqi good behaviour, thereby serving American interests.

In consequence, the US focused on the need to deter Iranian threats and, in the absence of better alternatives, chose to ally itself with Iraq. It was understood that Saddam Hussein represented some risk and the Bush Administration hoped to induce Iraq away from aggression. These assumptions raise certain questions: whether Iran needed to be deterred and the Iraqi 'balancing' was in fact required, and whether Iraq was 'appeasable'. In retrospect we can discern the path to an unintended outcome. What arguably followed from American policy was that American inducements, or appeasements, inadvertently encouraged Saddam Hussein to perceive that aggression was a viable option to solve his policy problems.

The positive relationship allowed Iraq increased buying power. From 1985–1990, it was permitted to buy $1.5 billion worth of advanced US products. In 1989, the US, imported $3.7 billion in petroleum products from Iraq and exported $1 billion in agricultural goods there. The Commodity Credit Corporation (CCC) guaranteed $500 million in credit to commercial banks who loaned Iraq money for the purchase of agricultural goods. The Export-Import Bank had a short-term revolving credit insurance programme of $200 million which insured exporters against non-payment. Iraqi rice sales alone accounted for a one-fourth share of American exports. The Washington Post listed $8.1 million in American military or military-related sales to Iraq.[4] House hearings in 1991 disclosed that the US Government approved 771 sales of technology to Iraq which included advanced computers, radio equipment, graphic terminals that could design rockets and analyse their flights, machine tools, computer mapping systems and imaging devices for reading satellite pictures. Much of the technology was sold to key government ministries including Defense and Interior.[5]

Policy with Iraq was closely monitored only in limited quarters. Trade incentives with Iraq clearly represented significant American business interests. The other source of attention to Iraq was from some Congressional members who were concerned, in addition to their connection to American business interests, about Iraqi violations of international law and its potential threat to Israel. However,

Iraq did not appear to rate high-level consideration from the Administration. From October 1989 until the Iraqi invasion, not one meeting of the National Security Council was convened to discuss Iraq, and the second-level Deputies Committee had only two meetings. 'Baker's total involvement', said an aide, 'could be measured in hours.'[6] Until Iraq invaded Kuwait, it was deemed a middle-range policy concern to be handled by middle rank officials like Assistant Secretary of State Kelly, not by the Bush inner circle. Kelly's first trip to Baghdad was in February 1990.

On January 17, 1990 Bush signed a presidential order declaring that expanded trade with Iraq, guaranteed by the Export-Import Bank, was in the American national interest. In the first half of the year, Saddam Hussein's actions and rhetoric drew media attention to Iraqi threats. A series of potentially ominous events evolved which included the Iraqi attempt illegally to import military electrical components which have nuclear weapons uses (krytons) as well as parts for a 'supercannon'; the Baghdad execution of a British journalist of Iraqi origin under charges of espionage; and Saddam Hussein's April speech in which he threatened to 'burn half of Israel' with chemical weapons in retaliation if Israel attacked with nuclear weapons. In response to these events, the United States Congress began to explore and consider American policy towards Iraq. Reports were filed in the spring and hearings were held in June. The Administration stated an unchanged Gulf policy. 'We remain determined to ensure the free flow of oil through the Straits of Hormuz and to defend the principle of free navigation. We also remain strongly committed to defend the individual and collective security of our friends in the Gulf with whom we have deep and longstanding ties.'[7] Positive relations with Iraq, it was believed, would create sufficient incentive to keep Iraqi behaviour within the parameters of American interests.

The American strategy towards Iraq was essentially unaffected by the Iraqi threats. In Congressional hearings, the Administration answered questions on Iraqi non-conventional weapons capability. The responses are particularly interesting in retrospect since during the Iraqi crisis much attention was devoted to assessing and defeating Iraq's military capability.

The Bush Administration testified: 'We believe that Iraq has the largest and most advanced chemical weapons programme in the Arab world, with a stockpile in the thousands of tons. Iraq can deliver chemical weapons using a wide variety of weapons systems, including artillery, multiple rocket launchers, mortars and air-delivered bombs,' and 'Iraq is actively engaged in the development of biological weapons . . . and either has already achieved or may soon achieve full scale production'.[8] Assistant Secretary of State Kelly testified that the Administration did not consider Iraq close to possessing a nuclear weapon. Furthermore, the Administration pointed out, Iraq's missile material was inspected regularly under the International Atomic Energy Agency which reported that there was no evidence of diversion following the inspection that took place in April 1990. The Bush Administration actively resisted efforts by Congress to apply any negative leverage against Iraq.[9]

Despite concerns over Iraqi actions at times during the year and the deployment of troops at the Kuwaiti border, the US continued business-as-usual with Iraq. On 1 August, the day before the invasion of Kuwait, with 100,000 Iraqi troops deployed at the border, the Bush Administration approved the sale of $695,000 worth of advanced data transmission devices to the Iraqi Government. Likewise, diplomatic channels apparently did not signal the seriousness with which the US would regard an Iraqi invasion of Kuwait. On 25 July, when US Ambassador April Glaspie met with Saddam Hussein to discuss the problem with Kuwait, she said that the US took 'no position on his border dispute with Kuwait.' According to summary cablegrams obtained by the American press, Ambassador Glaspie focused on President Bush's instructions to 'broaden and deepen (US) relations with Iraq.'[10]

It is clear that the US Administration did not pursue any action designed to *deter* Iraq from military adventurism or opportunism. The US did not perceive a serious Iraqi threat to the region. The expectation was that the Arabs would settle the primarily economic Iraqi-Kuwaiti dispute between themselves. The actual Iraqi military thrust was a surprise to the Bush Administration, despite some anticipation of it presented to the White House beforehand by American intelligence analyses.[11]

The Invasion Crisis

Once Iraq had crossed the Kuwaiti threshold to become a major aggressor, the United States appears to have ceased direct communication with Saddam Hussein. There was no initial period, following the invasion, when the resources of normal relations and significant economic ties between Iraq and the US were drawn upon in order to gauge Hussein's further intentions and/or to persuade him to reverse his course. The alacrity with which the Administration shifted its attitude toward Iraq is noteworthy. After tenaciously arguing Iraq's moderation and resisting condemnation of Iraqi atrocities prior to its invasion of Kuwait, including its invasion of another Gulf neighbour a decade earlier, the Administration was immediately unwilling to negotiate with Saddam Hussein. The White House seems to have felt that it was deceived by Saddam Hussein and in contrast to what could be seen as American conciliation prior to the invasion, the Administration chose a hardline response.

The first American steps in the crisis were focused on its Gulf allies. Upon learning of the onset of the Iraqi aggression, the United States began to support the Kuwaiti régime (and helped them to flee their country). Beyond condemning the invasion of Kuwait, the US was primarily concerned with the security of Saudi Arabia and deterring any Iraqi advance across Saudi borders. This issue engendered the first military component of the American crisis response. On August 8, 1990 elements of the US 82nd Airborne Division arrived in Saudi Arabia and Bush announced a 'purely defensive' deployment called *Operation Desert Shield*. The stated political goals were the 'immediate, complete, and unconditional withdrawal' of Iraqi forces from Kuwait, restoration of Kuwait's legitimate government, protection of the lives of citizens held hostage by Iraq and the restoration of security and stability in the region. Means were defined as a strong diplomatic, economic and military strategy to force Iraqi compliance. The immediate defence of Saudi Arabia and the protection of American civilians gradually receded as issues as the crisis progressed into the autumn.

On the diplomatic front, the Bush Administration sought international backing for its efforts by forging a multinational coalition and emphasising the role of the UN. From the very start, with Secretary of State James Baker serendipitously in the Soviet Union to meet with his counterpart there, Eduard Shevardnadze, the US was cementing international support, particularly with its erstwhile adversary. However much America was to set the agenda, it clearly judged that international legitimation was essential to carry it out. This was a marked change from the preceding era of the Reagan Administration.

Baker set out on constant tours of the globe to ensure broad political support and the advantages that it brought for military operations which the US would otherwise have been able to launch with the acquiescence of only a small number of states. These peregrinations also brought substantial financial backing for the American cause. Baker's diplomacy persuaded thirty three countries to contribute financially or militarily to the anti-Iraq coalition, as well as getting the assent of over one hundred states around the world. Baker was helped in his quest by peculiar international circumstances, of which Iraq's almost total isolation and Soviet co-operation and relative weakness were the most significant. This situation permitted the US administration to fuse its own programme with that of the international community. US interests could be expressed in terms of a 'new world order'; this both gave the Administration room for manoeuvre and acted as a constraint.

Although, in the run up to the use of force, the US was to use its room for manoeuvre, that constraint was clearest in the recourse to the United Nations throughout the initial stages of the crisis.

Bush and Baker actively sought a leading role for the United Nations. The Security Council immediately condemned the Iraqi invasion. Soon after that it unanimously approved the American-sponsored worldwide trade ban against Iraq. The sanctions resolution was only the third in United Nations history and appeared to signal a re-emergence of the international organisation in the wake of the decline of Soviet-American competition. The US, along with its coalition partners, was then given Security Council approval to enforce the economic embargo.[12] From the beginning of the crisis on 2 August, through November 1990, the Security Council passed twelve resolutions intended to press Iraq into withdrawing from Kuwait and compensating for damages. Aggressive US leadership was a major spur to the UN involvement and a significant feature of Bush's statements concerning the opportunity for this crisis to promote a 'new world order'.

The American objectives in the conflict with Iraq were never simply about Kuwait. Over the course of the crisis, Bush articulated American motives with various priorities. He spoke of: avoiding higher gasoline prices; the American 'way of life'; jobs; freedom of friendly countries around the world; Iraq's chemical and nuclear weapons threat; the 'new world order' made possible by the end of the Cold War; and the need to prevent Iraqi aggression in the future.[13]

In the early stages, the President clearly limited US aims to reversing the invasion: he spoke repeatedly of 'rolling back the Iraqi aggression.' Secretary of Defense Cheney outlined a defensive mission designed to support American Gulf allies and to enforce United Nations resolutions: 'Our military mission is clear cut. There is no confusion or doubt about it. Specifically, we were told by the President to deploy forces in order to deter further aggression by Iraq against other nations in the region; second, to defend Saudi Arabia and others should deterrence fail; and third, to use the military forces we have deployed to enforce the interception embargo or quarantine of economic activities with Iraq.'[14] However, by November the US had embarked on establishing an offensive military posture.

President Bush increasingly pointed to the need to be rid of Saddam Hussein; the man himself was the key to the problem of Iraq's bellicosity and intransigence. Administration statements made explicit the US desire to see Hussein assassinated or 'out of the picture.' This evolved into a more general notion of the threat from Iraqi power which needed to be destroyed. Congressman Les Aspin's conclusion about Saddam Hussein is illustrative of this perception, '(his) million-man army, biological and chemical weapons, and coming nuclear capability pose a long-term threat to the region. Iraq's military leverage in the region must be *neutralized* if security and stability are to be achieved in the Persian Gulf.'[15]

The presence of this notion of the larger Iraqi threat makes American intentions during the crisis more ambiguous. There is some question as to whether the Bush Administration was truly keeping its diplomatic and military options open or merely 'hitting right the marks' in order to appease dissenters and the international coalition along the way to an opportunity to nullify Iraq's aggressive power. The nature of the policy towards Iraq influenced both the crisis strategy and the eventual military operation. It is very difficult to discern with high confidence because the offensive military strategy of denial ie. to deny to Iraq its future potential for military aggression against its neighbours, can be seen to be concurrent with the strategy of presenting a credible military threat to induce territorial withdrawal from Kuwait. To resolve this problem, the evolution of American decision-making must be reconstructed in order to gauge which objectives dominated at which time.

Early on in the aftermath of the invasion, the Administration emphasized its orchestrated multilateral response. The international economic blockade was solidly keeping Iraq isolated and deprived. And the military strategy, the major force deployment to convince Iraq to withdraw, was rapidly being put into place. Bush stated he expected a peaceful resolution of the crisis and asked the American public to have faith and maintain united support. However, within three months of its initiation, the Administration moved to abandon the economic strategy in favour of mounting an offensive military campaign either to influence Saddam's withdrawal or to defeat his military power. Secretary Baker explained: 'It's just our view that (Saddam) is not going to retreat just because we've cut off his oil exports or just because we have cut off his financial exchange. His whole history as a dictator makes it clear that he is not uncomfortable in imposing extraordinary sacrifices on the people of Iraq.'[16] Why the Administration had reversed itself on the role of sanctions was not made clear. To many, its decision to shift the timetable was not convincingly justified.

The Administration made a judgement by late October, at least that economic pressures alone were not sufficient to induce Saddam's withdrawal from Kuwait quickly enough. The US then made what some characterised as a significant 'switch from a policy relying primarily on sanctions to one primarily relying on the threat of war.'[17] By the end of October, Baker was speaking to allies about 'a timetable for possible use of military force against Iraqi forces in Kuwait.'[18] During US-Soviet talks in October, discussions about an imminent deadline for military force may have begun: they certainly had by November.

Bush made several key policy decisions which promoted such a timetable and began the formation of the offensive option. The first was made in October and announced on November 8th, after the conclusion of the Congressional elections: the President doubled American force commitment to the Persian Gulf-region – to 400,000 troops.[19] He ordered this change without congressional advice or approval. Secondly, under Bush's order, the Pentagon cancelled the routine rotation of deployed forces. This was seen by some policy-makers to create more pressure to use the American forces soon since the troops could not sustain the 'ready' position indefinitely. Some members in Congress disagreed with this step because as Senator Nunn argued, it puts 'the US on too fast a track toward war . . . And unduly limits American options.' Senator Sarbanes drew a similar conclusion: 'I think two days after the election, the Administration undertook a new strategy. And I asked (the Administration) how long after you had an offensive force in the area, perceived to be capable of mounting an offensive attack, could you go without using it?' And lastly, Bush made a sustained effort at the UN to obtain an internationally approved deadline for the coalition to launch military operations against Iraq if it had not fulfilled the UN requirements for peace. The Bush Administration lobbied for a January 1st deadline and compromised on mid-month. On 29 November the Security Council passed Resolution 678 authorizing use of 'all necessary means' to secure Iraq's departure from Kuwait by January 15, 1991. The language was publicly considered a reference to the use of force. Throughout the months of conflict the US posture continually contained references to the coalition's determination to enforce the UN mandate. That mandate was clearly limited to removing Iraqi force from Kuwait and did not include the authorisation more widely to disarm Iraqi.

The pervasive query raised by this shift in the American agenda is 'what motivated the offensive policy?' In the absence of firm evidence, it is not possible to discern reliably the relative weight of the factors influencing the American Administration. However, at this stage we can identify a series of concerns which, taken together, could well explain American incentives. The international sanctions could have induced Saddam to concede Kuwait but they were not expected to defeat him or cripple his potential to do harm in the future. There was a powerful combination of American interests to be served by pursuing Iraq sooner, not later, and by defeating Saddam, not merely subduing him.

The Bush Administration feared that *time* would erode the solidarity of both the international coalition and American public interest in the anti-Iraq campaign. Time would also cost more money. Beyond the expense and localised economic opportunity-costs of military deployments, was the domestic and global economic effect of higher oil prices and fluctuations due to future uncertainties. (In fact, oil prices dropped as soon as the air campaign against Iraq began in January.)

Furthermore, a diplomatic solution could be messy, if not potentially risky. In a protracted international diplomatic approach, it was conceivable that wider issues of international compliance with United Nations regulations, especially Israel's occupation of Palestinian territories, would be included. The US did not want Israel nor any coalition partner embarrassed or pressured by diplomacy. Despite its determined effort to isolate the Iraqi transgression, the US implicitly recognised the element of linkage looming throughout the crisis by making promises to Arab coalition partners to commit American energy to the peace process once Iraq was defeated.

A military victory would have the virtue of a *decisive* as well as timely outcome. President Bush did not want to be embroiled in a Middle East military quagmire which would intrude upon the presidential election period. As long as military plans were designed to use overwhelming force and so to win the war quickly, Bush stood to gain without risking much. Brief and successful use of military strength has historically generated a rallying effect around Presidents. Presumably Bush would also have wanted to vanquish the hesitation and humiliation evoked by the last major use of American force, the 'Vietnam syndrome'. Furthermore, at the time of Iraq's invasion, the notion of a post-cold war 'peace dividend', or the reallocation of defence spending to the civilian sector, was alive in American domestic political debate. The Pentagon had strong incentives to define a salient role for itself, its weaponry, and its deployment abroad in the new security context.

The US ability to go after Iraq, unrestrained, existed partly because the US had beaten the Soviet Union in superpower competition. A decisive victory against Iraq offered double advantage. There was an opportunity to assert American preeminence in the Gulf region – the fruit of Cold War labours and a long-standing American pursuit. At the same time, the destruction of Iraqi military strength, the identified *bête noire* of the region, would further contribute to the security of Middle East allies. The intrinsic value which American foreign policy has traditionally attached to the guarantee of Israeli security was fortuitously combined with protecting Arab Gulf allies. Therefore as long as the military operation went according to plan, the US could gain substantially from a campaign not only to redress Iraqi aggression, but to eliminate it as a threatening player in regional politics.

Critics of American policy argued that the Administration was deliberately closing off its options with Iraq. Zbigniew Brzezinski commented that 'US diplomacy during the crisis often conveyed the impression of being dedicated to the prevention of a diplomatic solution.' The pursuit of a diplomatic option would have been directly related to what the Bush Administration considered a desirable outcome. There was a preeminent concern that Saddam Hussein should not retain any value from his aggression against Kuwait. The issue at hand was that any negotiation would involve compromise or a 'haggling' process which could consequently develop a face-saving device for Saddam Hussein. The objection was that anything of that kind would allow Saddam to claim victory and rally further political support in the Arab world. The Bush Administration never wavered from their demand for Iraq's unconditional withdrawal from Kuwait as a precursor for any negotiations. Such a stance left little room for a political settlement. If the diplomatic course – sanctions as well as other international means of containment – was under serious consideration then we would expect to have seen certain kinds of discussion, agenda issues, efforts to build a domestic consensus for negotiations, and gradations of response during the crisis. Furthermore, the extent to which the US appeared committed to reducing Iraq's military strength, irrespective of Kuwaiti territorial integrity could certainly have influenced Iraq's options in the crisis. Former Ambassador Battle pointed out that 'if Saddam thinks that we want to behead him and blow up his military equipment whether he gets out of Kuwait or does not get out of Kuwait, there is no real interest on his part in withdrawal . . . if we give the impression that the only goal is his demise and total collapse and we are moving in no matter what . . . I see no way to avoid war.'[20]

Negotiation specialist Roger Fisher testified to the Senate Foreign Relations Committee where he argued that a war represented a 'lose-lose game' in which no matter what happened, every country would be worse off. He argued that the purpose of negotiation would be to avoid disaster, to minimise total losses, and to see that Iraq does not benefit from perpetrating aggression. Fisher distinguished this from a 'win' in the sense of coming out with a positive gain.[21] He argued that Bush's decision to position the United States for an offensive campaign 'should not be allowed to preclude the option of maintaining sanctions if negotiations do not produce a quick result.'[22]

The argument for sustaining economic sanctions against Iraq had many adherents in the Congress. During the December hearings, Democrats almost unanimously supported giving sanctions more time to bring pressure on Iraq.

The consequences of the international blockade against Iraq were impressive. CIA Director William Webster testified that the sanctions denied more than 90 per cent of imports and 97 per cent of exports amounting to roughly $1.5 billion in monthly foreign exchange earnings lost.[23] The Senate was told that the hardship to Iraq was untenable yet it could take from six months to two years for the pressure to cause Iraq to capitulate. The pain inflicted on Iraq, as long as economic sanctions continued, meant that it was not profiting from its aggression. This provided an approach to the problem of eventually forcing Iraq's compliance – title and vigilance. While there was some hesitation that the coalition would be able to sustain sanctions over the longer term, the effectiveness of the embargo against Iraq relied essentially on Saudi Arabia's and Turkey's denial of overland oil pipelines. More importantly for discerning American motives, the sanctions approach to crisis resolution was preferable if the primary interest was that Iraq should not profit from its aggression and that the United Nations should function effectively. Fisher asserted, 'we do not need a war in order to "win".' However, that proposition depended on the desired outcome. If the Bush Administration wanted primarily to get Iraq out of Kuwait, then the role of force would be as a threat and if Fisher's conclusion was correct – the use of force was not imperative. If the objective of the US was punishingly to disarm Iraq, then a military offensive was indeed required. There was no viable political solution for the broader problem of further Iraqi aggression.

Once the Bush Administration *threatened* force there is an argument that to maintain a strategic reputation the US would be required to *use* force if the threat alone did not succeed in compelling Iraq. Otherwise, the United States could be seen as bluffing. However, whether or not that argument is persuasive, it does not dictate any military objectives beyond restoring the territorial integrity of Kuwait. The aim of a military campaign is logically distinct from the credibility dimension of the use of force.

It is important to emphasise here the distinction between the threat of war as a strategy to compel and the intention to wage an offensive disarming war. Clearly the two strategies overlap. The Bush Administration made the argument that Saddam Hussein needed to be convinced that he would face imminent attack if he did not accede to the United Nations demands. Such military pressure can *appear* the same as positioning to launch an offensive. Indeed that posture can boost military credibility and increase the compellence threat. To establish the American intentions accurately – as limited or offensive – requires evidence about the US deployment and military decision-making which is not publicly accessible.[24]

While it is perhaps impossible to establish with certainty that the Bush Administration framed its strategy around the desire to defeat Iraq's military strength, the case can be sustained on the basis of US policy and statements. In the first place, the notion of goals beyond the United Nations' resolutions, to include substantially disarming Iraq, was part of the landscape from early on in the crisis. As William Quandt described in his December testimony, 'disarming is on the agenda'. Secondly, evidence suggests that the Administration's officials despaired of losing the rationale for war against Iraq. And last, the war itself was an offensive drive to destroy Iraq's power projection. This must reflect back on intentions.

One month into the American deployment, Secretary Cheney was making the case for targeting Iraq's military strength beyond Kuwait. 'Over the long-term, Iraq would be much stronger militarily. Given its additional resources, Iraq could expand its vast arsenal of conventional weaponry – soon to include nuclear weapons. His military strength, coupled with enhanced economic and political power, would give Saddam Hussein even greater coercive power over his neighbours on oil and other issues.'[25] Iraq was characterised in expert testimony as a *malignant* problem. The existence of a political solution to the problem was labelled a myth. There were repeated arguments that if Iraq was forced to withdraw from Kuwait, but Saddam Hussein was not destroyed and the state not disarmed, then the US would have failed.[26]

Senator Sarbanes commented that it 'is just dreaming' that US military objectives should be limited actions to remove Iraq from Kuwait. 'I mean you are going to get to this other agenda. Not the explicit agenda, but the sort of implicit agenda of getting rid of Saddam Hussein, destroying his chemicals, destroying all the rest of it. It is going to be all out.'[27] Elizabeth Drew reported a similar assessment of this view:

> 'It was clear from very early on that some officials saw sanctions and diplomacy as the necessary political precursors of war – that each would be, as one official put it,' a box to check.' In the early days, an official said to me that by the time we went to war the President would be able to say that he had tried sanctions and tried diplomacy.'[28]

During the Senate hearings, Senator Biden referred to the 'real objective' for some decision-makers as the elimination of Saddam Hussein and his military machine. He argued that some of his colleagues and possibly President Bush perceived American goals in this way:

> 'Getting (Iraq) out of Kuwait is important but that is not even close (to enough) . . . So the real objective can only be accomplished through war. There is no other way to accomplish that objective. Therefore there is the need to make the assertions early on and quickly that a) the original policy is not working, b) the coalition cannot hold and is frayed, and, c) thus you are required to move very rapidly.'[29]

Biden presumed that the US Administration was deliberately moving in the direction of wider goals against Iraq: 'I am beginning to come to the conclusion that I do not know why else there was a change in policy (by the Bush Administration).'[30]

Bush Administration officials described any partial Iraqi withdrawal from Kuwait, i.e. if Iraq retained Warbah and Bubiyan or the Rumailan oil field, as 'the nightmare scenario.'[31] If the Kuwaitis would have found this hypothetical territorial outcome unacceptable then presumably the international blockade of Iraq could have continued. For the Bush Administration it seemed that the 'nightmare' was that Saddam Hussein would remain well armed and in power, regardless of Kuwait. Drew reports that as the January 15th deadline for the use of force neared,' some officials spoke with obvious anxiety about the possibility that Hussein would make enough of a move toward withdrawal that it would become politically impossible for us to go to war.' Once the war began, a senior official reflected, 'all along we worried about the implications of a diplomatic success.'[32]

These statements and journalistic reports do not represent definitive evidence that the Bush Administration actually preferred the destruction of Iraqi military capabilities to other, especially non-war, scenarios. It is more that they create such a cumulative impression. The combination of 500,000 American troops deployed, the seeming unwillingness to pursue a political settlement, and the pervasive suggestion that the greatest danger is future Iraqi aggression, to some extent indicts the policy of the Bush Administration. This impression is given more substance by the conduct of American military operations against Iraq once the war began.

The Offensive War

The American-led offensive against Iraq was, from the very outset until the cease-fire, designed to deny Iraq its future military power. When President Bush formally proclaimed the beginning of war, launched on schedule on January 16, 1990, he stated objectives which were not part of the United Nations' mandate: 'We are determined to knock out Saddam Hussein's nuclear bomb potential. We will also destroy his chemical weapons facilities.' Within days, the Pentagon was explicit in its commitment to eliminate Iraq's power projection capabilities. Secretary Cheney announced: 'Our objective is to get Saddam Hussein out of Kuwait and to destroy that military capability that he's used to invade Kuwait and to threaten the other nations in the Middle East.'[33]

Once the war was under way, there was even more candid and widespread reference to the unstated but acknowledged attitude of the Bush Administration. 'Before the war began, it would have been difficult for American officials to say in public that the US wanted to eliminate the Iraqi Army's ability to project power abroad, since that would have made war the only logical outcome.' The *New York Times* analysis went on to suggest 'that through a combination of expediency and design, the war has allowed the United States to articulate and undertake objectives that were left unstated, or stated only indirectly.'[34]

There was a pervasive sense from Washington reporters that the key decision-makers were committed to the disarming offensive which did not fit the justifications as presented.' Although they never admit it publicly, Administration officials acknowledge in private that American interests will be served if Kuwait is not only liberated but Iraq's armed forces are sharply cut down in size, its ability to produce weapons of mass destruction is eliminated and Mr. Hussein is removed from power . . . (T)he bombing of Iraq can accomplish the administration's stated objectives while also accomplishing its unstated objectives.'[35]

Technically, coercive and disarming military strategies can be concurrent or parallel. The massive aerial bombing of Iraq could possibly have been directed towards compelling Iraq to back down and retreat from Kuwait. At the same time the thousands of daily sorties, accuracy in targeting, and sheer amount of firepower which was used *on* Iraq left little doubt that the aggressor state was being disarmed. Three weeks into the offensive campaign, the US commander of gulf operations, General Schwartzkopf, described the continuation of the military campaign as indefinite because targets in Iraq were 'infinite', which implies targets beyond relevance to the Kuwait theatre of operations. Furthermore, it is commonly believed that Saddam Hussein himself was targeted in US operations. This decapitation strategy goes beyond enforcing the UN demands for the eviction of Iraq from Kuwait.

The transition between the air war and ground offensive against Iraq also betrays the American eagerness to proceed with its broader agenda. This is reflected in Bush's response to the Soviet peace plan just before the United States began the ground war. On February 22, 1990, after a meeting between the Iraqi and Soviet Foreign Ministers, President Gorbachev announced a proposal composed of six elements; Iraq would carry out Security Council R-660 and withdraw their forces to the positions they occupied 1 Aug, 1990, the Iraqi troop withdrawal would start the day after a cease-fire and the end of all military operations, and be completed within 21 days with troops evacuated from Kuwait City during the first four days. The compliance with R-660 would then remove the validity of the remaining Security Council resolutions since they followed from the premise of occupation. The other two aspects of the plan called for all prisoners of war to be freed and repatriated within three days after a cease-fire and, finally, that the control and monitoring of the cease-fire and withdrawal of the Iraqi troops would be carried out by observers or peacekeeping forces as determined by the Security Council. The same day, President Bush announced that he would not accept the proposal because it contained conditions and 'any conditions would be unacceptable' to the coalition and would not comply with the Security Council Resolution 660.

In Bush's rejection of the peace plan, he presented an ultimatum to Iraq: Iraq had until noon of the next day, February 23nd, to begin immediate and unconditional withdrawal 'if a ground war is to be avoided.' The Administration's criteria for withdrawal did not differ dramatically from that within the Soviet plan. Instead of allowing Iraq one day to begin, Bush's demanded that withdrawal 'commence immediately.' Under Bush's terms, one week, instead of three, was allotted Iraq to get back to its August 1st positions and two days rather than four to leave Kuwait City. If these differences in conditions were militarily relevant, it was not argued as such. However if so, these criteria could presumably have been a subject for further diplomatic effort, even a 'back-channel' approach. The issue of one day hence or the immediate beginning of the Iraqi withdrawal in compliance with the UN does not justify the catapult into the ground war which the US launched the day after its ultimatum. The five preceding weeks of the massive and punishing bombing of Iraq had surely demonstrated the seriousness of the American commitment. However there was no US effort to reach a settlement or to allow a wider window in which to have the American terms accepted by Iraq. The rapid American escalation at a juncture where peace proposals were in the offing impugns the political choices made by the US Administration. We have no evidence that the US sought a path to avoid further warfare to resolve the conflict. However, if the American goal was limited to coercion, then the political decision to reject peace terms out-of-hand does not make sense. At that point it appears the incentive existed to maintain the pressure on the Iraqi forces to the full extent possible.

Just as the war to liberate Kuwait began with promising the destruction of Iraqi military strength, so did it end. Announcing the suspension of the American-led offensive, President Bush put the achievements side-by-side: 'Kuwait is liberated, Iraq's Army is defeated.'

Cease-Fire and Post-war American Policy

Another level of evidence about American objectives *vis à vis* Iraq concerns the Bush Administration's response to the Iraqi withdrawal from Kuwait. On February 25, 1991 Baghdad announced that Iraq had ordered its forces home. The White House pressed onward with 'undiminished intensity' and announced the war against Iraq 'goes on.' Though Iraq was complying with the UN demands, the US was explicitly going after the Iraqi force. The day before Iraq's decision to withdraw, 'senior officials acknowledged publicly that American political goals exceed the simple military objective of liberating Kuwait.'[36] The press reported a 'general sense in the Administration and in Congress that the White House . . . wanted to finish off the Iraqi Army as a fighting threat.'[37] The Administration was prosecuting the elimination of the Iraqi threat. Members of Congress also noted this interpretation of Administration goals. After meeting with Bush at the White House on February 26th, Republican and Democratic leaders of Congress said Bush gave them the clear impression that he was trying to damage Saddam Hussein as much as possible to make sure that if he did stay in power, he could not be a military threat in the future.[38]

This American objective was reflected in the decision to target retreating Iraqi soldiers if they retained their weapons – their ability to fight in the future. Withdrawing from Kuwait and heading home was not sufficient to end attacks on the Iraqi troops. The White House announced 'if they retreat with their equipment they'll be pursued just as they were in the heat of any battle.'[39] The President said that Iraqi troops 'must lay down their arms, rather than simply retreat toward their homeland, in order to avoid attack.' The *New York Times* remarked that this policy 'pushed into the open the unstated goal of American policy: to go beyond evicting Iraq from Kuwait and smash Mr. Hussein's military while the opportunity is at hand.'[40]

Before the ground war began, however, the Bush Administration said, 'The US and its coalition partners reiterated that their forces will not attack retreating Iraqi forces, and further will exercise restraint so long as withdrawal proceeds in accordance with total capitulation and UN resolutions.'[41] One senior Administration official said on February 25th, 'We're not going to shoot people walking backwards but we do want to continue the campaign until they're all gone.'[42] During the final stages of the war, the US forces did essentially shoot Iraqi soldiers in the back. One now notorious incident is the 'highway of death'. American-led forces attacked a seven mile-long corridor of retreating soldiers as they were caught in a bottleneck of vehicular traffic heading out on the main road back to Baghdad.

Significance

The US attitude toward Iraq had profound bearing on the outcome of the conflict. The American determination that Iraqi regional military power could no longer be tolerated led to a massive international military effort to destroy Iraq's fighting force. The definition of the problem shifted from reversing and punishing Iraq's invasion of its neighbour to eliminating Iraq's ability to repeat its aggression. We are interested in the implications of this for future conceptions of collective security as well as for the American role in the Middle East.

President Bush coined his phrase the 'new world order' during the conflict with Iraq. Its laudable aspiration of cooperative security, the peaceful resolution of conflicts, and rules of respect between countries had a popular rallying effect. However, while drawing on the support for these principles in the abstract, the consequence of the argument here is that Bush was systematically undermining this 'new vision' of collective security with unofficial American offensive goals and the conduct of the war against Iraq.

This offensive form of international response to aggression has considerable significance for the capabilities of the international community *qua* community. It goes to the heart of the operative conception of collective security. The coalition forces dismantled Iraqi military force and that exceeded the UN resolutions – it did not uphold international law as it is written. The US-led forces enacted a version of collective security that can substantially violate sovereignty in order to preempt aggression. This form means striking against *potential* threats. It is quite different to stop a crime in progress rather than to preempt an identified 'bully' in the neighbourhood because he retains a military force which could be used disadvantageously to the outside.

While some may advocate this preemptive approach as the operative principle of the 'new world order', it must be explicitly recognised as such. In the Iraqi conflict the record suggests that American leaders who pursued this type of goal against Iraq were unwilling to admit this conception. The US tenaciously called for the enforcement of the Security Council resolutions while knowingly overstepping this internationally approved posture towards Iraq.

If the US is seen as using this crisis as an opportunity to engineer a more palatable American role or presence in the Middle East then the notion of a consolidation of international support to redress aggression could be rendered a fig-leaf or a ruse. This undermines the potential for a legitimate 'collective security' response to the next crisis. The Security Council at least allowed itself to be used in a legitimating role as the US pursued goals outside its international purview.

While the offensive campaign against Iraq served to undermine the credibility of the United Nations conflict resolution capabilities in the future, there are further reasons why this crisis is not likely to provide the prototype for post Cold War conflict resolution. The combination of widespread high levels of US and international salience, enormous resource demand, local states who could pay their own defence costs – or in fact hire an outside coalition, the parallel security interests of Israel and US Gulf allies, and an unambiguous aggression by a 'made-to-order' central villain present in this case is nearly unique in international politics. Even in a United Nations freed from the bonds of superpower competition, it is improbable that it can produce another wide consensus on the use of force. Therefore, it was even more important to use the unprecedented international commitment engendered in the Iraqi crisis as a precedent for the success and sustenance of collective *diplomacy*. The seeming preference for a military campaign against Iraq did not allow the fuller workings of cooperative diplomatic incentives.

A potential US approach in the Gulf is finally to establish a relatively permanent and substantial military presence in the Gulf region. American military entrenchment would allow the US to pursue a narrow track – a unilateral, unidimensional protection of American oil and trade interest, or a broader set of influence relationships through direct regional hegemony. Close, visible American military ties with Gulf régimes are basically unpopular in the region. The durability of an American presence would depend on several factors, i.e., the Gulf states' (régimes' and citizens') perceived level of external threat, the US willingness to satisfy the Gulf régimes' appetite for increasingly sophisticated weaponry, the American response toward political changes evolving in the Middle East, and the ability of the US to sustain some peace-making process.

The most positive approach is for the US seriously to accept and confront the challenges of regional conflict resolution. This would mean literally assuming what President Bush described as 'the responsibilities imposed by our success.' The US could sustain rigorous substantive efforts in the Arab-Israeli-Palestinian peace process (which several Arab leaders regard as a promise that Bush has already extended). Other pressing regional issues would need to be addressed – demands for increased political participation and for economic redistribution. The US could not effectively handle these larger problems on its own. An authentic multilateral process would be required.

This direction could foster a new international dynamic with the Middle East as a genuine test case. The US could make credible its emphasis on a new world order and an international community by promoting a meaningful role for the UN in such wider and ambitious endeavours. If world politics moves in the direction of seriously engaging in regional conflict resolution then the community will have gained something which transcends the Iraqi conflict.

Notes

1. I am grateful to Doug Blum, Ted Hopf, and David Weitz for their useful comments on an earlier draft.
2. A thorough and definitive decision-making record unfortunately does not yet exist and this relegates some of our analysis to inference based on reported statements. It also limits our inquiry: some pertinent questions about diplomatic communications, as well as operational warfare, remain unaddressed due to the incomplete information available at the time of writing.
3. Don Oberdorfer, 'Missed Signals in the Middle East,' *Washington Post Magazine*, March 17, 1991, p. 21.
4. March 11, 1991, p. A-3.
5. *Ibid.*, Reporting on records from House of Representatives *Government Operations Subcommittee on Commerce, Consumer and Monetary Affairs*. The US Commerce, Defense, Energy and State Departments are reported to have fully concurred as did the interagency committee on nuclear export controls.
6. Oberdorfer, p. 20.
7. US Senate Committee on Foreign Relations, Hearing, 'US Policy Toward Iraq: Human Rights, Weapons Proliferation, and International Law.' 101st Cong., 2nd sess., June 15, 1990 p. 92.
8. *Ibid.*, p. 92 and p. 93.
9. There is a substantial legislative record on sanctions against Iraq rejected by the White House. In 1988 Chairman of the Senate Foreign Relations Committee, Pell proposed the 'Prevention of Genocide Act' and the 'Iraq International Law Compliance Act' would have required the US to cut off credits to Iraq for noncompliance with the Geneva Protocol on Chemical Weapons and the Nuclear Non-Proliferation Treaty. The Bush administration defeated the legislation July 17, 1990 – six days before the Iraqi invasion of Kuwait. If the President had ever determined that Iraq's conduct constituted 'a consistent pattern of gross violations of internationally recognized human rights' he would have been required by law to cease relations with Iraq. Senate hearings, op. cit., June 15, 1990, p. 22.
10. *New York Times*, July 13, 1990, p. A 1, A 4.
11. There are continuing investigations by both houses of Congress into whether there was an intelligence failure preceding the Iraqi invasion of Kuwait.
12. This August resolution (665) required an energetic American diplomatic effort, particularly *vis à vis* the Soviet vote, and was seen as an important success for the US crisis strategy.
13. See, for example, Bush's speech of 15 August, 1990 printed by the Department of State's *Current Policy* No. 1293.
14. US Senate Committee on Armed Services, Hearings, 'Crisis in the PG

Region: US Policy Options and Implications,' 101st Cong. 2nd sess. September 11, 1990.

15. Lecture 12/21/90, published in *The Aspin Papers: Sanctions, Diplomacy, and War in the PG.* Center for Strategic and International Studies, 1991, p. 12.

16. *New York Times* 12/6/90, p. A 16.

17. Les Aspin lecture 12/21/90, op cit., p. 20.

18. *Los Angeles Times* 10/30/90.

19. Eventually there were approximately half a million American forces deployed.

20. US Senate Committee on Foreign Relations, Hearings, 'US Policy in the Persian Gulf,' 101st Cong., 2nd sess. testimony, December 12, 1990, p. 133.

21. Senate Foreign Relations Committee, Testimony, op cit. December 6, 1990, p. 21.

22. Ibid, p. 23.

23. Senate Foreign Relations Committee, Testimony, December 5, 1990.

24. For example, detailed information about the US target-set in Iraq, or the exact structure of the operational American force, may provide evidence by which to deduce the nature of the US mission. Even when that type of information becomes available, however, the evidence may well remain ambiguous. For example, if we find that the majority of Iraqi forces not in the Kuwaiti theatre were housed near Baghdad, the intent of American-led bombing sorties there remains consistent with both the drive to 'pin down' Iraqi assets so that they do not participate in the theatre warfare as well as the motive to disarm Iraq's future power projection capability.

25. Senate Armed Services Committee, Hearings, 'Crisis in the Persian Gulf Region: US Policy Options and Implications,' September 11, 1990.

26. See for example, Senate Foreign Relations Committee hearings above, December 13, 1990, p. 211 and 229.

27. *Ibid.*, December 12, 1990, p. 177.

28. 'Washington Prepares for War,' *New Yorker*, Feb 4, 1991, reprinted in Sifry and Cerf, *The Gulf War Reader* p. 181.

29. Senate Foreign Relations Committee, Hearings above, December 12, 1990, p. 129.

30. *Ibid.*, p. 134.

31. For example, Drew, p. 185.

32. *New York Times*, January 22, 1991.

33. NBC News interview report. *Ibid.*

34. Andrew Rosenthal, January 22, 1991.

35. Thomas Friedman, *New York Times*, February 11, 1991, p. A 13.

36. *New York Times*, February 25, 1991.

37. *New York Times*, February 26, 1991, p. A 1.

38. *New York Times*, February 27, 1991, p. A20.

39. *New York Times*, February 26, 1991, p. A 12.

40. *Ibid.* February 27, 1991 p. A 1.

41. *Ibid.* February 26, 1991, p. A 12.

42. *Ibid.*

3

The Arab States and the Middle East Balance of Power

Anoushiravan Ehteshami

That the Iraqi invasion of Kuwait exacerbated the factional tendencies of the Arab system is beyond doubt; that it opened new wounds without healing the old is equally unquestionable. It both challenged the existing rules and set new precedents in inter-Arab relations. This was the second time in ten years that the Ba'thist regime in Iraq, under the leadership of Saddam Hussein, had pushed the fragile Arab system to its very limits, forcing uncomfortable and unpalatable choices on Arab and non-Arab regimes alike. As a direct consequence of this Gulf crisis, the pervasive centrifugal pressures in the world of Arab states reached breaking point, threatening the very symbol of unity of the 21 Arab states and the epitome of the Arab order, the Arab League.

The Gulf crisis offered both challenges and opportunities to the non-Arab actors in the Middle East. How each actor responded to an essentially Arab generated and inter-Arab crisis and what they aimed to achieve from their respective postures was tempered by their abilities, modes of interaction with the Arab world and relations with the relevant non-regional actors. While some had the relative power to capitalise on the crisis, it was not at all clear that any actor, Arab or non-Arab, could decisively tilt the balance of regional power to its own advantage. The crisis forced the hands of every one concerned.

In order fully to understand the impact of the Iraqi invasion of Kuwait and of the subsequent military campaign against Iraq on the region, some attention must be paid to the structure of power in the Middle East sub-system and particularly to the balance of power amongst the Arab states themselves leading up to that fateful day in August 1990.

The Radical Arab Camp and Regional Balance of Power in the 1980s

The thread can be picked up from the 1978–80 period, when President Sadat of Egypt signed a peace treaty with Israel, the Western-supported Imperial regime in Iran was overthrown and replaced by a militantly (Shi'i) Islamic one, and the Iraqi invasion of Iran led to the eight-year long Iran-Iraq war (1980–88). Of these, Egypt's unilateral peace with Israel and the Iran-Iraq war are particularly relevant to this chapter, for it will be argued that the former event facilitated the emergence of a potentially powerful radical Arab camp at the end of the 1970s, and that the latter development led to the evaporation of the same and gave birth to new Arab alliances which survived the turbulent years of the Iran-Iraq war.[1]

The peace treaty removed Egypt from the centre stage of Arab affairs and marginalised its influence on Arab issues. Secondly, the imposed isolation of Egypt, culminating in the withdrawal of Arab ambassadors from Egypt, suspension of Egypt's membership of the Arab League and the transfer of the League headquarters to Tunis, meant that the stage was cleared for new aspirants to claim the title of 'leader of the Arab world'. The treaty with Israel, furthermore, imposed uncomfortable decisions on the moderate camp who had rallied around the Sadat presidency since 1973. They could not support Egypt's action, nor could they readily succumb to the powerful radical camp that had emerged from the November 1978 Baghdad Arab heads of state summit and the Extraordinary Meeting of the Arab Foreign and Finance Ministers, held the following March. Opposition to Egypt's unilateral peace process led to the fusion of the hitherto disparate radical Arab entities and the concentration of their efforts in the rejectionist Steadfastness Front, comprising Algeria, Iraq, Libya, the PLO, PDRY and Syria. The Front involved the integration of a geographically disparate group of Arab states and movements, rather adding to its overall influence.

The start of the Iran-Iraq war, however, fractured the short-lived rejectionist front of the late 1970s and led to the atomisation of the radical camp. While many of the moderate states rallied around radical Iraq's war effort, the radical states tended to support the overtly Islamic non-Arab Iran. In addition to Ba'thist Syria and Marxist Yemen (the only country of the Arabian Peninsula to do so), Libya and Algeria also tacitly supported the Islamic Republic. Syria's orientation was particularly significant because it provided credibility for Iran and helped blunt Iraqi criticism that Tehran was waging an anti-Arab war.

The Iraqis, on the other hand, enjoyed the military and financial support of the larger conservative-moderate Arab regimes. The traditionalist Gulf Arab monarchies did not hesitate for long in aiding their old Gulf rival, but the fact that the PLO was prepared to support Arab Iraq unconditionally against non-Arab Iran provided Baghdad with much needed pan-Arab legitimacy for its action. More material and diplomatic support was forthcoming from a number of other Arab countries including Egypt, Jordan, Morocco, North Yemen and Tunisia. Egypt's support for Baghdad was crucial as it culminated in a close military relationship between the two (part of which included the exchange of military technology and personnel, as in the Condor II or Badr 2000 project). An extension of the same equation was Iraq's insistence, vigorously promoted by 1983, on reintegrating Egypt into the Arab system as soon as possible.

In so far as the war acted as a moderating influence on Iraq, it was not too difficult for it to become the champion of the moderate cause. Egypt, under President Mubarak, could climb the same war ladder to try and restore some of its former regional glory and influence. Thus, even Egypt's gradual readmission into the Arab system was done under Iraqi auspices and not at the expense of Iraq's influence. Egypt was not to become an immediate counterweight (or threat) to Iraq's regional position, but rather the necessary reinforcer of the latter's status vis-a-vis Syria. The accommodation, in short, was designed to bolster Iraq. The advantage for Egypt was that it was to regain access to the Arab world without compromising its 'independent' stance on Israel, or its close alliance with Washington. These sets of mutually reinforcing objectives were not only to survive the Iran-Iraq war. Soon after that war ended, in 1988, Iraq was able to cement its relations with a number of its moderate Arab supporters.

The Arab Cooperation Council, which comprised Iraq, Jordan, Egypt and North Yemen (created in 1989) epitomised this trend.

From the Syrian perspective, Iran's inability to destroy the rival Ba'thist regime, indeed that President Hussein had emerged boldly strengthened, was alarming. Arab conventional wisdom at the time alleged that Syria had made a strategic mistake by supporting Iran in the war and was now going to pay for it. The creation of the ACC on its doorstep and increased Iraqi interference in Lebanon on the side of the anti-Syrian Christian forces after the 1988 cease-fire was given as tangible evidence for Syrian isolation. Syria was increasingly being regarded as the declining regional power, financially dependent on the traditional monarchies of the Gulf and in danger of losing even its coveted superpower cover.

As far as implications for Arab alignments went, the Iran-Iraq war had four important consequences for the Arab order. First, it marked the end of the collective pursuit of the radical agenda and its landmark, the Steadfastness Front. Secondly, their unambiguous support for the Iraqi war effort facilitated the transformation of the conservative-moderate states into the Arab nationalist pretenders. Thirdly, with the convergence of superpower views (on the Iraqi side) the ties with the 'client' states were relaxed to such an extent that Arab actors were able to pursue their objectives without overriding external considerations. And lastly, the conduct and outcome of the war enabled Iraq to emerge as the champion of the Palestinian cause and the main ally of the PLO. This, by extension, gave Saddam Hussein *de facto* 'leadership' of the Arab world. It was left to the Iraqi president to translate this honour into material rewards after the 1988 cease-fire.

The 1988 Iran-Iraq War Cease-fire and Its Aftermath

The joint acceptance of the UN-administered August cease-fire was perceived by many as the beginning of a new era in the region's life. In Arab circles, Iran's unconditional acceptance of SCR 598 was interpreted as an Iraqi victory. Certainly Iraq had succeeded in the sense that Iran had not achieved its war aims, foremost amongst which was the Ba'thist regime's overthrow (moderated to 'removal' of only Saddam Hussein in the post-1986 period). Whether Iraq had achieved any of its own war aims sufficiently to warrant a victory call was a moot point. Saddam Hussein was an Arab hero. The jubilations surrounding the end to hostilities overshadowed the discussion of a number of serious outstanding problems regarding the virtues of the campaign in the first place, its cost to Iraq and the multitude of difficulties its war had in fact created for the Arab world in general.[2]

Shortly after the cease-fire, Iraq was seeking to emphasise the war's importance to the new Arab order and the solidity of its new alliances. In a clear reference to Egypt, for instance, the Iraqi president declared: 'An Arab country, although this country does not have a direct geographical border with us, used to send a brigade of fighters every two months throughout the war years. The number of the brigade personnel ranged from 300 to 400 fighters. They used to come a long distance by plane'.[3] On the other hand, he was publicly rebuking those who had not helped his cause in similar fashion, and was skilfully taunting his regional opponents.

One direct result of the war and the Arab military alliance against Iran in the 1980s was the birth of two purely Arab regional groupings.[4] The first, born in 1981, was an exclusivist club of the conservative Gulf Arab countries. The Gulf Cooperation Council pointedly refused entry to the Arab republics of the Gulf, Iraq and, at first the two Yemens. Its overall function was to coordinate the economic, political and military policies of these six states, and in reality served to put a distance between these states' strategic interests and those of Iraq's. It soon began to represent the views of the six in Arab forums and in many of their relations with the world at large. The GCC's assertiveness established a new pattern in inter-Arab relations. Unlike many of its predecessors in the Arab world, the GCC was not created to bring about Arab unity. This entity did not pay homage to Arabism as a political being and pointedly did not envisage itself as a servant of Arab nationalist aspirations.

The GCC, however, had another, more problematic, side to it. It unashamedly stood to represent the interests of the rich Gulf Arab petroleum exporters. The rich and poor division in the Arab world was, thus, formalised by the creation of the GCC.

For the best part of the 1980s, the GCC remained the only effective subregional Arab body. In addition to enabling the unhindered birth of the GCC, the Iran-Iraq war also served as a catalyst for the creation of the Arab Cooperation Council (ACC). The ACC fused Ba'thist Iraq with three of its staunchest moderate supporters. Unlike the GCC, which reflected the sheikhdom/traditionalist membership preferences of its members, the ACC was characterised by the political diversity of its membership. The Hashemite kingdom of Jordan, for instance, provided the territorial bond between Ba'thist Iraq and pluralist Egypt. The geographical and political diversity of the ACC served as a strengthening feature of the organisation. Territorial diversity meant that the collective influence of the body could stretch well beyond the immediate neighbouring areas. It gave the Arab eastern members of the group, for instance, legitimate and easy access to the furthest reaches of the Arabian Peninsula.

Syria remained outside these groupings, isolated and on the fringes of the Arab mainstream which had now come to endorse the PLO's 1988 formal acceptance of the two-state solution to the Arab-Israeli conflict. Damascus had become the last bastion of Arab radicalism, but this was no longer enough to retain in its own domain even the main feature of Arab nationalism, 'the Palestinian revolution'.

Notwithstanding these setbacks, Syria struggled hard to re-enter the new Arab system. Its bilateral Arab relations continued to strengthen in this period, inspite of its continuing alliance with Iran. The high point of these efforts was the restoration of diplomatic ties with Iraq's close war-time ally, Egypt, in December 1989. The Egyptian president's visit to Syria in May 1990 was the icing on the cake of Asad's diplomatic offensive in the Arab world. The last such visit had taken place in 1977 by President Sadat, shortly before his trip to Jerusalem. President Mubarak's high-level visit to Syria took place amid PLO efforts to hold an emergency Arab summit in Baghdad to discuss the impact of the Soviet Jewish immigration into Israel on the Arab-Israeli conflict. The significance of this trip and the call for a Baghdad summit were not lost on seasoned observers of the Middle East. The last Baghdad summit (1978) had put Iraq at the apex of the Arab world and at the centre of its activities. It was obvious that this time round neither Damascus nor Cairo wanted a repeat of the same. Syria's participation, it was anticipated, would undoubtedly steal some of the thunder from Saddam Hussein. It would also have strengthened the moderates' position by providing a counterweight to Iraq and to the Iraqi president's increasingly visible regional ambitions. Mubarak's trip to Damascus was significant in this context, because it highlighted the reality that any constructive discussion of the Arab-Israeli conflict could not take place without Syrian participation or approval.

The return trip of President Asad to Egypt in July 1990 (the first of its kind in 14 years) was equally significant, because it put to an end the vestiges of open hostilities between the two powerful Arab actors and filled the cleavage that Saddam Hussein had skilfully exploited during the Iran-Iraq war. In essence, the fluidity of inter-Arab relations in the post-1988 period and the very dynamism which facilitated Egypt's re-entry into the Arab system in 1987 and its readmission into the Arab League in 1988 (both measures supported by Iraq and opposed by Syria) had weakened Iraq's relative superiority in Arab circles. The Baghdad summit was intended, in part, to address this problem and to breathe new life into Iraq's hegemonic ambitions.

The Iran-Iraq war had conditioned the behaviour of all the major regional actors. In the absence of Egyptian hegemony, the war accelerated the scramble for new alliances in the Arab world. By virtue of not having lost his mantle, the Iraqi leader had come to dominate the emerging Arab order. But the end to the war had changed the rubric of intra-Arab and inter-Arab state relations. With hegemony no longer guaranteed, Iraq sought to impose its own will on the shifting Middle East landscape. The Iraqi army's battle-hardened 99 brigades and 1,080,000 able-bodied soldiers were viewed as providing the right configuration in this struggle. The flux in the Arab system in 1990 coincided with a number of challenges to the Arab world, to which neither President Hussein nor his regional opponents had any easy answers. In view of the sub-system's instability, the new challenges helped create new divisions.

1990: Countdown to War

The optimism of the post-cease-fire era in the Middle East had given way to a period of unfulfilled promises and new anxieties on the eve of the new decade. The region's internal problems were compounded by the remarkable political transformations in Eastern Europe in 1989 and the rapid erosion of the world 'progressive camp' upon which radical and nationalist Third World régimes had become so reliant. Although the liberalisation of the Warsaw Pact countries directly affected the fortunes of only a handful of Arab states, their collective impact, and the continuing traumas associated with Moscow's 'balance of interests' doctrine, was great. The removal of pro-Moscow régimes in Eastern Europe had dramatic consequences for the foreign relations of these countries *vis-a-vis* the Middle East. At the same time as re-examining their close ties with the radical Arab states, they began to improve their relations with Israel, effectively still the enemy of all but one of the Arab states. Improvements in Israel's bilateral relations with Moscow's former European allies followed the same pattern already established between the Jewish state and the Soviet Union. Technical exchanges accelerated Jewish emigration to Israel. In regional terms, the restoration of diplomatic relations between Moscow's former allies and Israel began to tip the demographic and political balance in favour of Israel. As the radical Arab states were losing important foreign backers, Israel was improving its position in absolute terms: it was gaining new friends at the expense of the Arab states, it was increasing the flow of European Jews to Israel, and it was doing so without disturbing its strategic alliance with the United States. On the other hand, in the absence of an all-powerful Soviet bloc, Israel's Arab adversaries were unable to find alternative influential foreign friends without compromising their pan-Arab policies and reforming their foreign policies to make them more palatable to Western appetites. For the first time in many years Israel had both the strategic as well as the political edge on its Arab competitors.

Accelerated Jewish immigration into Israel (and the Occupied Territories) and the 'changing international environment' afforded the Iraqi president the right atmosphere in which to launch his most pronounced bid yet for Arab supremacy. However, this was tempered by a number of structural weaknesses. The first among these was Iraq's inability to bring Egypt under its own hegemony. While the two states cooperated extensively in both economic and military fields, differences over Israel (Iraq was emerging as militantly anti-Israeli, Egypt had diplomatic relations with Israel), Egyptian–PLO tensions, Egypt's *rapprochement* with Syria and the entrenched Cairo–Washington alliance remained points of contention. Egypt's inability to alleviate Iraq's chronic economic difficulties and its unwillingness to use its influence with the rich Gulf Arab states to encourage them to invest in Iraq (or forgive part or all of Iraq's outstanding loans) merely added to the existing tensions. An appreciable element of rivalry between the two main pillars of the ACC, Egypt and Iraq, had crept in and Baghdad was unable to resolve this to its own advantage. Furthermore, Iraq's inability to break the Iranian–Syrian alliance or limit Syria's sphere of influence added to its geopolitical constraints. The Iraqi leadership's failure to establish the country as the dominant force lent itself to Saddam Hussein's search for a realistic way of imposing his will on the Arab system. Iraq skilfully reduced the tensions on its eastern border (through initiating direct contacts with Iranian leaders) as a means towards bolstering its Arab standing. By this act, it also inadvertently offered Iran a foothold in Arab affairs.

During 1990, Saddam sought to dominate Middle East politics in two forums: the ACC and OPEC. Within the ACC, he exploited both rising anxieties in the Arab world about Israel's immigration policy and sympathies concerning the West's 'aggressive' campaign against his country.[5] In a major policy speech in April, he put Iraq in the front-line of the Arab-Israeli conflict, declaring that his country's missiles were deployed 'in the direction of Israel'.[6] PLO leader Yasser Arafat, responding to Iraq's anti-Israel policy, shuttled from one Arab capital to another in order to convene an extraordinary Arab summit. However, Iraq's bid for pre-eminence also aggravated Arab tensions; Iraqi-Syrian relations worsened – thus ensuring Israel of a fragmented eastern front, in spite of the degree of radicalisation in the Arab world.[7]

In the wake of both the Arab League Council's emergency meeting in support of Iraq in late March against 'Western intimidation' and many of the Arab states'· call for a coordinated Arab response in support of Iraq,[8] the Extraordinary Arab summit which opened in Baghdad on 28 May, 1990 was expected to give Iraq unconditional support in its confrontation with the West. Iraq had also expected endorsement of its position *vis-a-vis* the new crisis in the Arab-Israeli stand-off.[9] The summit was significant for what it achieved, but also for the things that it did not achieve. It failed, for instance, to present a united Arab front. Syria's refusal to participate in the summit dented Saddam Hussein's prestige and devalued his claim to represent the Arab world in the face of challenges to it. Syria did not oppose the holding of an Arab summit *per se*. Its objections were two-fold; it would not participate if the summit was held in Baghdad and, secondly, if the agenda remained confined to the two topics advanced by Iraq (Soviet Jewish emigration to Israel and the Occupied Territories, and the 'current hostile campaign against Iraq'). Syria was in no mood to accept Iraqi hegemony. As the rest of the Arab world was inextricably moving towards hero worship of the Iraqi leader, Syria was belittling Iraq's 'spiteful rulers' and the way they had 'squandered its energies' and diverted Arab attention 'to trivialities'.[10] Paradoxically it was Syria which was acting rationally, in order to avert the escalation of tensions at this critical juncture and not its moderate counterparts, many of whom were spellbound by Saddam Hussein's projections.

The summit also produced differences amongst those who partici-pated. Two competing trends emerged, both of which were rep-resented by members of the ACC. In sharp contrast to the GCC's coordinated response, the two powerful pillars of the ACC stood in opposite camps. Egypt's pro-American line (opposing any calls for a summit resolution condemning the US) advocated patience behind the scenes diplomacy as the constructive way forward; Iraq's more confrontational stance recommended a hard line to be taken against Israel and its main ally, the US. The adoption of the hard line, needless to say, depended on Arab strength as represented by Iraq. In general terms, Iraq's line proved more popular. While Jordan and the PLO (those most directly affected by Jewish migration) supported the Iraqi position, Saudi Arabia and some of its smaller Gulf allies tended towards Egypt's line. Other Arab states not directly affected by the implications of the summit's resolutions were happy to go along with the general mood. Crucially, the participants fully supported Iraq's right to self-defence and 'to reply to aggression with all the means [Iraq deemed] fit to guarantee [its] security and sovereignty'.[11] The coming to power in June of the right-wing Likud coalition in Israel bolstered Saddam's tough line.

Of particular concern to Saudi Arabia was Yemen's pro-Iraqi stance.[12] A new Arab force had emerged in the Arabian Peninsula to challenge the hegemony of Saudi Arabia. To add to Riyadh's worries, Yemen was not only in a formal alliance with Iraq (the ACC), but was gravitating towards Iraq's orbit. The Saudis faced the problem of having two neighbours belonging to a different Arab camp, and the prospects of an alliance that could threaten Saudi Arabia's own security.

The multiplication of power centres, in short, had made alliance building precarious. For any régime, like Ba'thist Iraq's, seeking hegemony in this new environment, the same opportunities could become frustrating obstacles to the satisfactory fulfilment of their wishes. In the end, any victory could prove to be, at best, only half a victory.

There was, however, another struggle going on in the Middle East, its boundaries less marked. Competition for the control of OPEC was not new, nor was it confined to the Middle East. The power struggle within OPEC ran along a different axis from that of the political crisis in the Middle East. Its net result was the introduction of some tension amongst the Gulf states. The end to the Iran-Iraq war enabled both Iran and Iraq to play a more active role in OPEC, largely at the expense of Saudi influence. Unlike the 1980s, Saudi Arabia could no longer take advantage of the war to dominate the oil industry.

Competition for the control of OPEC surfaced in earnest in 1989 when Iraq announced its willingness and preparedness to act as an OPEC '*swing*' producer.[13] With this declaration Iraq entered into direct competition with the traditional swing producer, Saudi Arabia. The capacity to be able to produce oil in sufficient quantities to affect the price of oil is the essence of this role. Iraq's bid had two dimensions: a demand for a higher Iraqi oil quota within OPEC's annual production structures and an attempt to put an end to Saudi Arabia's undisputed power to influence the price of oil unilaterally. Iran wholeheartedly supported the Iraqi move to dethrone Saudi Arabia, and began publicising quota violations by some of its Arab neighbours. By early July 1990, Iran and Iraq had reached agreement on the outlines of a plan to raise the price of oil to $25 per barrel. To add credibility to their plan, both parties openly accused Saudi Arabia, Kuwait and the UAE of overproduction. An Iraqi Oil Ministry official stated: 'The big powers . . . have benefited from the disunity that was created by Kuwait and the UAE'.[14] On July 17, Iraq accused Kuwait and the UAE of deliberately harming Iraq through their higher-than-allowed oil production. Having already charted the path for Arab responses to Israel, the Iraqi régime was intent on dominating OPEC, more specifically its Gulf Arab component, as the means towards realising its regional ambitions. It could either do this indirectly, through the organisation's structures, or directly, by intimidating the smaller Gulf states. Although, with Iran's support, Iraq did manage to raise the OPEC benchmark price of oil to $21 per barrel at the organisation's meeting on 26–27 July 1990, it was in no position to impose the new price structure on its OPEC partners, nor able to dominate the cartel's production system. With hindsight, we can say that the countdown to war probably began at this time.

Thus the focus of attention shifted away once more from the Arab-Israeli arena and towards the new tensions in the Gulf. The threat of war still seemed to hang over the Arab-Israeli theatre, but the momentum of the crisis had moved to the Gulf. This was hardly surprising as Iraq, the Arab force of the moment, had already been active in both theatres. No regional (or external) actor, however, was prepared for what followed.

Iraq's Invasion of Kuwait and the Regional Balance of Power

Iraq's invasion of Kuwait set in motion a new Gulf crisis and, in its pre-war stages at least, eclipsed the Arab-Israeli conflict and the regional problems associated with rising Jewish immigration. The invasion of one Arab country by another had a profound impact on Arab alignments and severe implications for Arab unity – in both substance and form. The inability of the Arab states to present a united front in the face of the new crisis was not surprising. That this self-inflicted wound badly shocked the Arab system is beyond doubt. The divided Arab League's response to this crisis epitomised the paralysis of the organisation as a forum of Arab opinion and a vehicle for its actions. More fundamentally, it illustrated the deep divisions within the Arab order as a whole. Although the Arab League's Ministerial Council issued a strongly worded statement on 3 August condemning the invasion, only 14 of the League's 21 members had voted in favour. As the crisis deepened, it transpired that elements from those opposing or abstaining from the vote would form the nucleus of the pro-Iraqi camp, and many of those who voted in favour of Iraqi withdrawal became the core of the anti-Iraqi front. In neither case was the radical/moderate Arab distinction a determinant factor in the formulation of policy. As much for Iraq as for its Arab opponents, national interest and not supranational Arab ideals, helped shape regional policy.

The emergency Arab summit in Cairo, held a week later, highlighted the composition of the new Arab alignments.[15] A majority of those attending supported the measures to be taken against Iraq. This in itself was not surprising. A similar summit in 1978 had imposed sanctions on Egypt for violating Arab principles. There were some differences: the 1990 summit was held in Cairo (with the full support of Syria even before the official return of the Arab League HQ to the Egyptian capital); it was unable to return a unanimous verdict on the Iraqi action and the clear violation of its own charter; it advocated the use of Arab force against one of its members. The emphasis by all sides was still on finding an 'Arab solution' to the crisis, but the serious divisions within the Arab world and the League belied its effectiveness to function as one structure. A week into the crisis, the United Nations' interest in the matter, coupled with the arrival of Western forces to bolster the GCC's Desert Shield operation, had begun to overshadow Arab efforts at mediation.

Whereas it had taken seven years for Iraq's strategy of internationalising the Iran-Iraq war to work, the Kuwait crisis was internationalised virtually overnight. In consequence, its control slipped through Iraq's fingers with each passing day. This reality increased the pressures on the other Arab actors to fall into line. In addition to the principle of opposing aggression, members of the anti-Iraq Arab coalition, thanks to their resolution, found ways of actually advancing their national interests as well. Syria regained much of its lost glory and international respectability, and Egypt saw its national debt reduced by one-half in the course of the crisis.

Israel could afford to sit on the sidelines – to a point – and still profit from events. With regard to Israel's interests in the Arab balance of power, the Kuwait crisis provided further fragmentation in the Arab world and the prospect of the largest Arab force in modern history being drastically reduced. Israel expressed concern about the Iraqi-Jordanian-PLO alliance that emerged in the course of the crisis, but, in the end, considered this axis ineffective. It capitalised on the Kuwait crisis by striking a blow against the *intifadah*; it was also content to watch the PLO shoot itself in the foot. On the other hand, that Israel was a potential liability to the Western alliance was graphically illustrated by the popularity of Saddam's 'linkage' strategy. If the Cold War was finally over and regional conflicts, such as this one in the Middle East, were to preoccupy NATO, what value was the US-Israeli alliance, if the US had to devote its energies to shielding its ally and defending it diplomatically, instead of being able to draw upon its resources?

Despite the sympathy for Israel after Iraqi missile attacks, it was clear that Israel's embroilment would have hampered rather than helped the Allies' efforts. Israeli retaliation might well have resulted in shifting the battlefield to the detriment of the Alliance. On the other hand, the non-retaliatory response and the fact that, for the first time in its history, American forces had to be stationed on Israeli soil to protect the Jewish state from Arab attack, will have far-reaching consequences for the future of the Arab-Israeli balance of power. The breaching of Israel's elaborate defences by weapons fired from the territory of a non-front-line Arab state challenged Israel's strategic depth doctrine and the continued occupation of the West Bank as an important buffer zone. The political implications for both Israel and the Arab states of the military realities arising out of the Gulf war are far-reaching.

Within the Arab world itself, the crisis caused a number of major changes. It enabled Syria and Egypt to consolidate their bilateral relations and co-operate militarily for the first time since the October war of 1973. Their responses to the crisis also endeared them both to the hearts of rich Gulf states, so much so that their participation in restoring Gulf security redounded significantly to the advantage of their economic viability. Syria used the Kuwait crisis to come in from the cold. Egypt utilised the crisis to play centre-stage, diplomatically and militarily: its 35,000 troops commitment to Operation Desert Shield was the largest single non-Gulf Arab or Islamic country deployment.

Implications of the War for the Regional Balance of Power

The Kuwait crisis had a direct impact on the sub-regional balance of forces. In the Persian Gulf region, although Iraq's military power was considerably reduced, its armed forces remained one of the largest in the Middle East. The biggest blow to Iraq's regional standing was political. The fact that Saddam Hussein failed to translate his military defeat into a diplomatic victory (*à la* Nasser in 1956) cost him a significant regional role during a crucial phase of reshaping in the Middle East. This inability to transform relations with his regional supporters into an alliance added to Iraq's isolation as former sympathisers proceeded to mend relations with many members of the anti-Iraq camp. In the Gulf itself, the crisis did not reduce the ongoing competition between Iraq, Iran and Saudi Arabia. But in absolute terms, Iraq was weakened (albeit temporarily) to the benefit of the other two.

The Kuwait crisis brought into sharp focus several issues relating to the Arab order. For many Arab régimes and for most of the Arab masses, Iraq's invasion of another Arab country was an inter-Arab matter. The fact that Iraq had wiped out a member of the UN system was irrelevant. Indeed, some prominent Arabs maintained that if the Iraqi action was to initiate the movement towards the unification of other Arab lands all the better! The notion of inviolability of international law and principles was deemed, by many Arabs, to be as relevant to the Kuwait crisis as the role that the international community had played in implementing its other wishes in the Middle East and elsewhere. Yet the desire to keep the dispute in the Arab family was undermined by the inability to act collectively and, most of all, consistently at regional or international level.

This was well illustrated by Arab Yemen's positions at the heart of the international system; the Security Council. As the only Arab member of the SC when the crisis broke, Yemen was placed in an unenviable position. Should it follow the mood of the Council, should it pursue its own interests, or should it try and represent the Arab line? The majority of the Arab League membership had condemned Iraq's invasion, but a substantial minority had not. In the end, it seems not to have followed any of these options in a consistent fashion. Of the twelve UNSC resolutions on the crisis before the outbreak of war, Yemen opposed two (SCRs 666 and 678), abstained from voting on four (SCRs 660, 661, 665 and 674), and voted in favour of six (SCRs 662, 664, 667, 669, 670 and 677). Hardly a consistent Arab response.

The problems associated with the place of an Arab order in, or alongside, the international system of sovereign actors was compounded by historical antagonisms created by the role Western powers had played at the turn of the century in dividing the Arab lands into independent states. Historical legacies added to accumulating tensions. Colonel Qaddafi put the riddle succinctly:

> The presence of Iraq in Kuwait is illegal and it is unacceptable. The presence of US troops in Saudi Arabia is legal in terms of international law, because an independent country has asked another independent

country for troops to defend it. However, it is unacceptable in pan-Arab terms and in terms of the region's security.[16]

The fact that the UN machinery took charge of the crisis resolved the practical problem of an appropriate response, but the fact that this had to come from a body outside the Arab world created conceptual problems which could turn into concrete problems in the future.

Intra-Arab differences multiplied as a result of the Kuwait crisis. Above all, Kuwait and Saudi Arabia displayed total mistrust of those Arabs who supported Iraq after August 2 1990. In a clear rejection of pan-Arabist principles, both took steps to limit the influence of nationals from the pro-Iraqi Arab states in their economies. Previously, commitment to pan-Arabism had become synonymous with support for Iraq, even for the usually cautious Saudis. Before Iraq's invasion of Kuwait, Saudi opinion was clear:

> Israel will not stop at swallowing the West Bank and Gaza but it hopes to swallow other lands from other Arab states. We must link this new fact (Israel's territorial ambitions fuelled by new Jewish immigration) to the unjust propaganda campaign being waged against our beloved Iraq. There is no doubt that world Zionism is behind these virulent campaigns.[17]

None of these anxieties appeared important or relevant to the reality of intra-Arab relations after Iraq's invasion. The total lack of trust which came to characterise intra-Arab relations could not disappear overnight.[18] The fact that the Iraqi president sent Id al-Fitr greetings in 1991 only to those Arab leaders (Algeria, Jordan, Libya, Sudan, Tunisia and Yemen) who stood by his side during the crisis indicated that even Iraq was not ready to bury its differences with members of the pro-Kuwait coalition. The net result was prolongation of the agony and a further deepening of wounds. This hostile environment served as an ideal breeding ground for Sunni Muslim fundamentalists to preach the virtues of pan-Islamic unity. The inability of Arab nationalists to deal with the real issues of the day meant that their uncompromising message might find many sympathetic listeners. The paralysis of the Arab order swung the pendulum towards their agenda.

On a different level, the Shi'i *intifadah* in southern Iraq and Saddam Hussein's brutal suppression of it may have reopened the deep wounds between the two prominent sects of Islam, within both the Arab world and across the Islamic community. Whereas Iranian efforts to stir the Arab Shi'i of the Gulf in the 1980s failed, in March 1991 the Shi'i's movement in Iraq flourished with very little direct Iranian agitation. The armed uprising in Iraq was the first of its kind amongst the Arab Shi'i of the Gulf. Its memories would linger on and its lessons be learnt by the Shi'i of other Gulf Arab countries.

The crisis revealed intra-Arab differences in regional alliances – the ACC and the GCC. Although two of the ACC's members took Iraq's side, Egypt's anti-Iraq stance ensured its ineffectiveness. It became unlikely that it could recover its former position. Nonetheless, accession of Syria to a revamped ACC could not be ruled out. The GCC's performance as the other sub-regional Arab organisation directly affected by the Kuwait crisis was not impressive. It remained intact and it did formulate a military response; but it singularly failed to deter aggression without outside assistance. The fact that it was not able even to warn of the imminence of hostilities undermined its credibility.

Iraq's swift defeat in the ground war put an end to the vestiges of the pro-Iraq Arab camp. Through the tried and tested call for Arab unity, Jordan, Yemen, the PLO, Tunisia and Sudan sought to reach a new 'understanding' with the victorious Arab allies. Their argument that the crisis was water under the bridge now was not well received by the Gulf states. Far from attempting to mend bridges with Saddam Hussein's regional allies, the Gulf states took important steps to formulate new security structures to cater specifically for their own needs, not the Arab peoples in general. Thus, the anti-Saddam Arab alliance found a new form in the substance of the immediate post-war period.

The 'Damascus Declaration' of 6 March 1991 signified the emergence of a new loose Arab grouping to meet the need for viable security structures (initially at least) in the Persian Gulf region. The '6 plus 2' configuration (the GCC countries plus Egypt and Syria) built around the new Cairo-Damascus-Riyadh axis was expected to provide the most durable Arab-based security structure. Although it was hoped that its jurisdiction would be extended to the rest of the Arab world, the mechanisms by which this would happen and the likely role of the security pact outside the Gulf context remained a mystery.

The '6 plus 2' group did not signal the birth of yet another Arab organisation, but, although a loose coalition, it did result in the emergence of an entity that encompassed both sub-regions of the Middle East. The exclusion of Iraq, Iran and other Arab countries in these deliberations gave the strong impression that the priority for the group was to provide a deterrent force for the conservative Gulf Arab states. The dissident Arab actor, Iraq, was pointedly disregarded. Its Arab allies, who had attempted to turn the focus of the crisis from Iraq's invasion of Kuwait to that of opposition to an US-led war against Iraq were by-passed. Inclusion of Iran at a future date was regarded as desirable, but its participation at the preliminary planning stages was clearly discouraged.

One product of the Kuwait crisis was the emergence of a loosely-knit group of nascent popular Arab democracies (Algeria, Jordan, Tunisia) and neutralists (Libya, Sudan and Yemen). The fact that these governments adopted an ambivalent position on the crisis can be explained by the growth of pluralist institutions in their countries in the year preceding the Iraqi invasion and the impact of popular opinion.

It was not beyond the realms of possibility that the most significant element in determining future developments in the Middle East balance of power might prove to be the role of democratic institutions and popular opinion in both the Arab and non-Arab states of the region. Whether this is an inherently positive development or a precursor to other crises in the Middle East remains to be seen. It should be clear to all régimes in the region, however, that possession of obtaining a popular mandate ought not be seen to serve as a justification for violation of the rights of others.

The fact that both pluralist Egypt and authoritarian Syria had chosen to join the anti-Iraq alliance while the pluralist Arab states mentioned above remained sympathetic to dictatorial Iraq may fog the issue at this stage. But stranger things have happened in the Middle East, stemming from events whose humble origins were much less significant than the concerted emergence of democracy in the Arab world as a new political force.

At the state level, if Iraq was the net loser of the crisis in the Gulf, then Israel was the overall beneficiary. It used the crisis to improve further its military power. It did not feel compelled to make compromises on the Palestinian issue, and any concessions made in the context of the Arab-Israeli conflict could not result in real losses for Israel, as the Arab side was expected to sacrifice much more than merely 'an extra mile' for the few inches that Tel Aviv was prepared to travel. Israel's relative position in the Levant, therefore, was not adversely affected by the crisis. Indeed as the crisis unfolded, it transpired that the Syrian-US *rapprochement* would not have a negative bearing on Israel's status. The Syrian-Egyptian alliance (even in the context of the Gulf crisis and the anti-Iraq Arab coalition) compounded the isolation of Jordan as a front-line state, and increased Israel's leverage over the Occupied Territories.

This was significant for Israel's regional interests. The war considerably weakened the most powerful (and increasingly) belligerent Arab regime. The challenge to Israel's military superiority was removed. In terms of the regional balance of power, Arab divisions enhanced Israel's position. Paradoxically, Iraq's rapid military collapse in the war helped to cement Israeli-US relations, an unexpected development, given the coolness between the two countries in the pre-Kuwait crisis period. The '6 plus 2' configuration was likely to moderate the Syrian position on the Arab-Israeli conflict and there was a possibility that Arab peer pressure could also help to deradicalise Syria's regional policies. However, such an outcome might engender a *rapprochement* between Syria and the PLO. The engineering of such a *rapprochement* would not be in Israel's long-term interests, but was possible in view of the PLO's isolation and its need to find new Arab friends in the post-war Middle East.

The Arab states bordering Israel remained divided. In the final analysis, therefore, the dynamics of the Kuwait crisis did not cause a reverse in the Levant balance of power – Israel maintained its military superiority. The Iraqi-led Arab charge of 1990 had all but disappeared in 1991. In the end, the attempted redrawing of the landscape to the advantage of Israel's militant Arab opponents led to their own eclipse in both regional and international terms.

The demise of the ACC on the one hand, and the ineffectuality of the GCC on the other created grounds for a rationalisation of competing regional bodies. Certainly these two bodies' poor performance (relative to their stated goals) opened up new opportunities for forming new Arab groupings. However, despite the emergence of the '6 plus 2' group, there was little prospect of new alignments emerging from the ashes of the war which would decisively tip the Arab balance of power in their own favour. The Arab world was set to remain fragmented and the Middle East region multipolar in character. This was to Israel's advantage.

Notes

1. For a detailed analysis of these developments see Anoushiravan Ehteshami, 'Wheels within wheels: Iranian foreign policy towards the Arab world', in Amirahmadi and Entesar (eds), *Reconstruction and Regional Diplomacy in the Persian Gulf* (Routledge, 1992).
2. For a more in-depth analysis of the 1980s and post-1988 period in the Gulf region see A Ehteshami and G Nonneman, *War and Peace in the Gulf: Domestic Politics and Regional Relations into the 1990s* (Ithaca Press, 1991).
3. BBC Summary of World Broadcasts (SWB), ME/0321 A/6, 29/11/1988. Ostensibly, as a message of reconciliation, he warned in the same speech: 'We must not equally criticise those who could have given more but did not and those who betrayed the principles and the cause by siding with Iran'. Not many others in the Arab world, besides the Iraqi authorities themselves, were in fact criticising anybody at the time!
4. The Arab Maghreb Union was also born in 1989 but an analysis of that grouping is beyond the scope of this paper.
5. The significance of Jewish immigration to the stability of the region and

its impact on Arab attitudes was articulated well by former Egyptian Foreign Minister Mahmoud Riad; 'Now we are living in the same stage, the same story, the same act as 1947–48'. Quoted by Hugh Carnegy and Tony Walker, 'The war that nobody wants', *Financial Times*, 26/5/1990.

6. SWB, ME/0744 A/1, 21/4/1990. Iran had announced that Iraq had constructed a new missile base near its western border with Syria in early April, but they interpreted this as an aggressive gesture against Syria and not Israel. As if to underscore the Iraqi-Jordanian alliance, it also transpired that Jordanian officials had prior knowledge of the existence of the new missile facilities.

7. Syrian distaste for Iraq's efforts to win favour in the Arab world was summed up in the following way by General Mustafa Talas (Deputy C-in-C and Defence Minister): '. . . the army of Hafiz al-Asad, not the Iraqi or the Jordanian army, is the one who prevented Israel from occupying the sources of oil. Everybody knows that when the issue concerns Israel the Iraqi army would say: "we have no orders". However, when the issue is massacring Muslims the Iraqi army has orders'. SWB, ME/0708 A/6, 9/3/1990.

8. Kuwait, for instance, advocated a collective Arab response in support of Arab Iraq against the West; 'Whether the attack on Iraq remains confined to smear campaigns or takes the form of military action, Arab countries must come up with a common stance in support of Iraq and agree on specific reactions'. SWB, ME/0729 i, 3/4/1990. Similar calls were made by the PLO, Jordan, Egypt and Saudi Arabia amongst others.

9. It is important to note that in fact Iraq's Israel policy was no longer 'radical' in the sense of being in the leftist/nationalist Arab camp. To begin with, it accepted the 'two states solution', recognised the new 'state of Palestine' and regarded the PLO under Chairman Arafat to be representative of the Palestinians, and even (albeit implicitly) accepted Egypt's peace with Israel. These positions are not too dissimilar to say Jordan's or even Saudi Arabia's.

10. SWB, ME/0765 A/2, 16/5/1990.

11. SWB, ME/0778 i, 31/5/1990.

12. The two Yemens united on 22nd May, 1990. With a population of 12 million, Yemen became the Arabian Peninsula's most populated country. Its geopolitical significance also increased as the country with the longest coastline around the strategic Bab al-Mandab checkpoint. In the 1980s, the Yemens ended up supporting each of Saudi Arabia's northern Gulf neighbours. As a consequence of unification, Saudi Arabia expected Yemen to play a much more influential role in Arab forums. It was unfortunate from Saudi Arabia's perspective that when the Kuwait crisis broke, it was Yemen which had a seat in the Security Council.

13. 'Swing producer': a state whose oil production is great enough to enable it to exercise a decisive influence on oil prices. Iraqi Finance Minister, Hikmat Al-Hadithi, stated that his country's aim was to stabilise the oil price. In a direct challenge to Saudi Arabia, he stated at

the World Economic Forum's 1989 meeting that; 'We have the capacity and willingness to be a swing producer . . . We are going to play a bigger role in OPEC now'. *OPEC Bulletin*, February 1989, p. 48. Iraq's official quota at the time was 2.64 mb/d, but with its oil reserves standing second only to Saudi Arabia's it projected a potential export capacity of over 8.50 mb/d.

14. SWB, ME/0815 A/4, 13/7/1990.
15. The 10/8/1990 meeting was urged by Syria on the day of the invasion itself. Its seven point resolution was supported by 12 countries: the six GCC countries, Djibouti, Egypt, Lebanon, Morocco, Somalia and Syria. Iraq and Libya voted against. Algeria and Yemen abstained, and Jordan (also abstaining), Sudan and Mauritania had 'expressed reservations'. The PLO apparently abstained as well, even though it was suggested that it had voted against. Tunisia did not attend the summit. Egypt, Morocco and Syria agreed to join the 'Arab force'. A day later Egyptian military forces were arriving in the Gulf region.
16. Interview with Cable News Network, 13/8/1990.
17. Statment of Crown Prince Abd al-Aziz. SWB, ME/0749 A/1, 27/4/1990.
18. As one Kuwaiti diplomat put it; 'We must stop embracing and kissing each other when our hearts harbour something different'. SWB, ME/1050 A/4, 19/4/1991.

4

Reactions in North Africa

George Joffe

For most of the states of North Africa – Egypt, Libya, Tunisia, Algeria, Morocco and Mauritania – events in the Gulf have, in recent years, been of secondary importance to their relations with Europe and their concerns in Africa. Egypt, as a result of its past role as the leader of the Arab world, particularly during the Arab nationalist régime instituted by President Jamil 'Abd al-Nasser (1954–1970), had a far greater concern over Gulf issues because of its ideological involvement with Middle Eastern affairs. Yet, even here, al-Nasser's vision of the inter-penetrating 'Three Circles' of Arab nationalism – covering the Arab world, Islam and Africa[1] – meat that, generally, Gulf affairs were not a dominant concern in Cairo.

The same disinterest in the affairs of the Gulf and of its leading states, such as Iran and Iraq, has been even more marked among the Sahel states, from the Horn of Africa – Sudan, Djibouti, Somalia and Ethiopia – across to the Atlantic coast – Chad, Niger, Mali and Mauritania. Even though four of the states concerned – Sudan, Djibouti, Somalia and Mauritania – are members of the League of Arab States[2] – their foreign policy interests have always been dominated by African affairs. Although the Arabian peninsula has often influenced their affairs, as with Saudi and Yemeni concerns over developments in Ethiopia or with support from Saudi Arabia and some of the Arab Gulf states for the Islamic régime created by Jacafar Nimayri in Sudan after 1983, in general it has been African issues that have conditioned their diplomatic concerns.

During the past decade, however, this picture has been slowly changing. Indeed, as early as 1973, the tripling of international oil prices by OPEC as a result of pressure from the Gulf oil producers together with Libya and Algeria, the two major North African producers, had forced North African and Sahelian states to place greater emphasis on their relations with the Gulf for economic reasons. This concern was repeated in 1979, in the aftermath of the Islamic revolution in Iran, which led to a further doubling in international oil prices.

The economies of the non-oil producing states in the region suffered severely as a result of these developments, which contributed – to a greater or lesser extent – to their growing foreign debt burdens during the 1980s. As a result, they increasingly turned to the oil rich states of the Gulf region for economic development aid and for favourable terms for oil purchase. The Gulf states, in turn, began to look on certain of the states in the region – particularly Tunisia and Morocco – as suitable locations for investment and aid.

Iraq, however, played little part in these developments. During the latter part of the 1970s, it shared, it is true, a common interest with Algeria and Libya as Rejectionist Front states, actively opposing Egypt's participation in the Camp David Accords in 1979 and the peace treaty between Egypt and Israel in 1979. However, apart from this common interest and Iraq's general radical stance inside regional organisations such as the Arab League and OPEC (which was shared, *inter alia* by Libya and Algeria), Iraqi foreign policy interests were directed towards the traditional objective of the Fertile Crescent[3]. After British withdrawal from the Gulf in 1971 and Iran's consequent assumption of the regional security mantle there, Iraqi attention was drawn towards the need to counter growing Iranian hegemony over the Gulf region[4].

Iraq's Influence Before the Conflict

In one respect, however, this general and mutual disinterest did not typify relations between Iraq and Northern Africa. The development of independent states in North Africa was paralleled by a growing popular awareness of the region's links with the Middle East and with the ideologies which generated its political dialogue – in which Iraq, particularly after 1968, occupied a central role. This area of common interest reflected the ideological implications and geographical influence of Ba'athism amongst the populations of the region.

Iraq's Relations with Egypt

Indeed, even before the Ba'athist revolution of 1968, the Arab nationalist sympathies of Iraqi regimes during the intervening decade after the 1958 revolution had stimulated a growing interest and sympathy in Baghdad over the leading role of Egypt inside the Middle East. The antagonism expressed by the Nuri Said government towards Egypt in the 1950s was replaced by sympathetic interest from the Qassim régime and its successors as they found common cause with Jamil 'Abd al-Nasser over the principle of Arab unity and over the Arab-Israeli conflict and the Palestinian issue. The arrival of a Ba'athist régime to power in Baghdad in July 1968 intensified these links yet, conversely, also set Egypt and Iraq on a collision course when, after the death of Jamil 'Abd al-Nasser, his successor, Anwar Sadat, began openly to court Western political and economic support.

After Egypt's peace treaty with Israel in 1980, Iraqi hostility towards the Sadat régime became explict and codified through the Rejectionist Front movement. In part, this reflected a long-felt desire by Ba'athist Baghdad to supplant Egyptian leadership inside the Middle East as Egypt abandoned the ideological paraphernalia of Nasserism. However, it also reflected the genuine determination in Iraq to avoid compromise over the Palestinian issue and the Arab-Israeli conflict. Two events, however, were to alter this position during the 1980s. The first was the assassination of Egypt's leader, Anwar Sadat, in 1981, for, in the Middle East, the peace treaty with Israel was seen as his personal achievement and his removal auto-matically removed one of the major bones of contention between the two states.

The second was the outbreak of the Iran-Iraq war in September 1980. Under President Sadat's successor, Hosni Mubarak, Egypt gradually moved towards support for Iraq in the conflict, largely as a means of re-establishing Egyptian diplomatic pre-eminence within the Middle East. Egyptian support was soon of considerable material significance to the Iraqi war effort and political relations grew ever closer as a result. By 1988, when the Arab League's Amman summit authorised Arab states individually to renew formal diplomatic re-lations with Egypt, Iraq was the first state to take advantage of this opportunity. In February 1989, Egypt and Iraq collaborated in creat-ing an embryonic integrated economic market – along with Jordan and Yemen – through the *Arab Cooperation Council*. It is hardly surprising, in this context, that President Mubarak suffered from the illusion that he was privy to Iraqi intentions and able to control Iraqi actions towards Kuwait right up to the actual invasion on August 2, 1990.

Iraqi Influence in North Africa

The ideology of Ba'athism itself also had a relevance to North Africa, in that it excited, as had Nasserism, a popular response. Up to 1967 and the massive and unexpected defeat of Arab armies by Israel, most politically aware people in North Africa accepted that a secular political dispensation was the appropriate model for socio-political development[5]. It was a view buttressed by the examples of the new political structures in independent Algeria and Tunisia[6] and, after 1969, appeared to receive[7] further reinforcement from the revolution in Libya as well. For most people, too, this secular dispensation was intimately associated with Arab nationalism in its Nasserist, Ba'athist or, later, Libyan varieties[8]. Official views, however, while supporting a formalistic ideological, cultural and diplomatic identity with the Middle East, were antagonistic to Arab nationalism as such. As a result, professed Nasserists and Ba'athists (who, during the 1970s became associated in the official mind with violent political change) have always been in a minority in North Africa and have often been persecuted.

In Libya, for example, after the Great September Revolution in 1969, Ba'athists had been distrusted and persecuted by the Qadhafi regime. They, in turn, played a significant role within the various exile opposition movements, particularly inside the *Libyan National Front* (not to be confused with the better-know *Inqath* – Libyan National Salvation Front – which has a strong Islamic component in its ideological make-up). Ba'athists also played an important role inside a shadowy terrorist group, the *April 7 Group*, which organised attacks on economic targets in the early 1980s. Iraq apparently provided logistical and financial support to this organisation.

Baghdad had specific interest in such groups for reasons quite apart from ideological conviction. After 1990, Libya had enjoyed a formal unity treaty with Syria, Iraq's ideological arch-enemy[9], and Tripoli provided material aid and moral support to Iran during the Iran-Iraq war. Libyan support only began to wane after February 1986, when there seemed to be a real possibility that Iran would conquer and hold Iraqi territory. Baghdad noted Libya's diplomatic choices, which only confirmed the Saddam Hussein Regime in its determination to undermine its ideological rival in North Africa. Indeed, Colonel Qadhafi's warnings to Tehran that Libya could not tolerate any infringement of the territorial integrity of Iraq merely earned him contemptuous criticism in Iran and did not lessen Iraqi hostility at all.

Ba'athism in Algeria also played a significant, if minor, role within political development. The links went back to the anti-imperialist tradition that developed after the Iraqi revolution in 1958 and the moral support offered by the revolutionary authorities in Baghdad to Algeria's national liberation movement, the FLN. Some FLN servers, who normally operated outside Algeria, accepted self-imposed exile in Baghdad during the War of Independence and maintained personal and ideological links with the Ba'athism movement thereafter. Inside the FLN, Ba'athism was a significant current as part of President Huwari Bu Madian's (Houari Boumédienne) '*Revolution socialiste*' of the 1970s, similar to that of the '*Pagsistes*'– members of the banned Algerian communist party (*Parti de l'Avant-Garde Socialiste*). Indeed, after 1978, when the post-Boumédienne era began, the increasing tensions in Algerian political life stimulated interest in Ba'athism in both Syria and Iraq as examples of political effectiveness, order and ruthlessness[10]. This became particularly strong in the mid-1980s, as social discontent mounted.

In the end, however, the Algerian government opted for the more messy solution of greater democratisation in the aftermath of the massive riots of October 1988, despite its confrontation with the major Islamic fundamentalist movement, the FIS (*Front Islamique de Salut*). This choice probably also coincided with a faint distaste in official Algerian government circles for Iraq ever since Algeria had attempted to mediate between Iran and Iraq during the Iran-Iraq war. Algerian mediation attempts ended abruptly after the mysterious death of the then Algerian foreign minister, Muhammad Ibn Yahya (Mohamed Bin Yahya), in an air crash in 1982 during shuttle diplomacy between the two countries. Although Algiers suspected Tehran to have been responsible, Algerian officials also noted that Baghdad was equally as intransigeant and abandoned further attempts at mediation. Iraq, for its part, had always been suspicious of Algerian interests in mediation since it had considered Algeria as basically pro-Iranian at the start of the conflict and had not been completely convinced of Algerian good faith later on.

Nonetheless, the Ba'athist current – inside the FLN, at least – did not disappear. Instead it blended into formal political life as some of its better-known supporters were given official and semi-official posts – apparently to satisfy their supporters inside the movement that, although their policy preferences have not been adopted, government has not rejected the individuals concerned. At the same time, at a popular level, Ba'athism became associated with demands for stronger official reaction to threat to public order and political orthodoxy. Those inside the government and the FLN – mainly from Eastern Nigeria – who were identified with pro-Arabist educational policies, secularism, opposition to Islamic fundamentalism and demands for military intervention during popular unrest between 1980 and 1988 were frequently termed the *Baathistes* in the media and in daily conversation.

They included personalities such as Muhammad Salah Yahyawi (Mohamed Salah Yahyaoui), an influential former government minister and FLN leader during the Bu Madian era and Ahmad Massadia (Ahmed Messadia), the former secretary-general of the FLU. Ironically enough, Mr Massadia's successor, Abdulhamid Mahri, actually was a known Ba'athist sympathiser and, because of his appointment, was used by the Shadli Ibn Jadid (Chadli ben Jedid) régime to re-assure Ba'athist sympathisers within the FLN that they had not been excluded from modern Algerian political life. Another and equally striking figure is Bashir Bumaza (Bachir Boumaza), who became an influential political commentator, explaining to the Algerian public, through the columns of the Algerian press, Iraqi policy objectives during the conflict in the Gulf.

Mr Bumaza was originally a member of the forerunner to the FLN, the MTLD of Massali Hajj (Messali Hadj) and, despite his origins as a Berber from *Petit Kabylie*, demonstrated his support for Arab nationalism during an attempted take-over of the MTLD by Berber nationalists in the early 1950s. During the Algerian War of Independence, Mr Bumaza was part of the French section of the FLN and became minister for the economy in the Ahmad Ibn Balla (Ahmed Ben Bella) government just after 1962. Eventually he went into exile in 1967, after profound disagreement with Huwari Bu Madian, who had taken power in 1964. At that point, Mr Bumaza made contact with the Ba'athist movement in Iraq, then about to seize power. He maintained close contacts with Baghdad thereafter and enjoyed a personal link with Saddam Hussein. As a venerable Algerian nationalist and Ba'athist sympathiser, he was been ideally placed to explain Iraq to the Algerian public and, in this, he enjoyed government approval, since he acted as a secular counterweight to Islamist propaganda over the recent conflict.

Iraq's role in the Sahel

The influence of Ba'athists in Tunisia and Morocco was far more marginal. In fact, they did not play a cohesive political role in either country. In Mauritania, however, this was not the case. For the past two decades the junior officer corps of the Mauritanian armed forces – which has also dominated the government and which is, itself, dominated by baydan (northern Moorish) tribal elements – has also been traditionally pro-Ba'athist. Ba'athist influence, of course, waxed and waned during recent years as the factions within the armed forces involved in Ba'athism saw their hold on government power strenghten and weaken. However, after April 1989, both Ba'athist and Iraqi influence in Mauritania strengthened significantly.

In part this arose from Mauritania's crisis with its southern neighbour, Senegal, over the border area between the two countries along the Senegal River. In the wake of the crisis, on the orders of President Maaouiya Ould Sid'Ahmed Taya, a virtual pogrom was apparently waged against Mauritania's black Peuhl-speaking Hal-Pulaar population by militias recruited from haratin (former slaves) groups and trained by Iraqi military advisers[11]. This policy derived from the Mauritanian government's decision in April 1989 to abandon attempts at national reconciliation between the many ethnic groups within the population and to move, instead, towards accelerated Arabisation. The change of policy was accompanied by the rehabilitation of large numbers of Ba'athists who had been purged from the armed forces and the police service in July and August 1988[12], together with the appointment of Ba'athist ministers.

The reason for these moves appeared to have been the president's realisation that he could not resist popular Ba'athist pressure, despite his own personal tribal support base in the Atar region. This was primarily because of the continuing social tensions between the baydan and the rest of the population which had undermined the policy of national reconciliation. However, the role played by Iraq in supporting Mauritania's small but politically vital armed forces was also significant, since the armed forces were the ultimate guarantor of presidential power and were also dominated by the baydan. Iraq certainly exploited its position in Mauritania. There were rumours that it intended to create missile testing ranges there.

Iraq also treated the country as a base for arms supplies to the Hissan Habre régime in the neighbouring state of Chad. Indeed, Baghdad provided much of the military and logistical support for the government's campaign against Libya during the 1987 campaigns which expelled the Qadhafi régime from the Uzu (Aozou) Strip. It also provided arms and air transport to Habre's army in its ultimately unsuccessful campaign against its Zaghawa opponents, led by Idriss Deby, during 1989. Iraq had also brokered the return to the Chadian capital, N'Jamena, of the important pro-Libyan factional leader, Acheikhu Ibn Omar – the event which triggered the Zaghawa revolt against the Hissan Habre regime, an event which encompassed its downfall in early 1990[13].

Iraq and the Horn of Africa

Iraqi influence had also developed during the 1980s throughout the Horn of Africa. In part, this was predicated on Baghdad's desire to counter Libyan influence in the region and in part it was designed to expand Arab nationalist influence at the expense of states such as Egypt, Saudi Arabia and the USA which considered the region to be crucial to Red Sea security. Indeed, the Red Sea, because of the weight of tanker traffic through it to the Suez Canal, had been designated by the Pentagon as a Strategic Line of Communication (SLOC) and its security was of material interest to Washington. Not surprisingly, therefore, the extension of Iraqi influence in this region caused considerable anxiety in the Middle East and in the West, particularly after the Iran-Iraq war and the Cold War had been ended. However, compared with its potential role in the Sahel, Iraq's influence in the Horn was, in reality, limited.

Iraq's links with Sudan stemmed from a reconciliation with the Nimayri régime in the late 1970s and from Sudanese support for Iraq during its conflict with Iran. Despite an eclipse in the wake of the collapse of the Nimayri regime in 1985, when the Al-Mahdi government appeared to incline towards Iran, Iraqi influence was restored after the military-backed Bashir régime came to power in 1989. In the months before the Iraqi invasion of Kuwait, Baghdad had become the second largest arms supplier to Khartoum after Tripoli and there were rumours that these supplies had included chemical weapons to be used against the Sudanese People's Liberation Army's rebellion in the southern part of the country, which has bedevilled Sudanese political life ever since September 1983[14].

In Somalia and Djibouti, Baghdad found itself in competition with the Arab states of the Gulf for influence. In Mogadishu, for example, Iraqi influence, which was strong during the 1970s when arms were supplied to the Sayid Barre régime in its struggle with Ethiopia for control of the Ogaden, was replaced by Kuwait, Abu Dhabi and Saudi Arabia. In Djibouti, Baghdad exercised a degree of influence because of gifts of arms and aircraft, but, given France's predominant role there, never really obtained an effective foothold. Baghdad also had an intermittent interest in supporting the Eritrean People's Liberation Front, largely to counter Saudi influence there.

Initial Reactions to the Conflict[15]

The actual Iraqi invasion of Kuwait on 2 August 1990 seemed to have taken everyone – both governments and populations – completely by surprise. In the immediate aftermath of the invasion, most governments in the region reacted predictably, with both Egypt and Morocco roundly condemning the Iraqi action. Egypt, indeed, enthusiastically espoused Washington's views of the need to confront Iraq militarily and championed Arab participation in the proposed Multinational Force to be stationed in Saudi Arabia. Algeria also condemned the invasion, although in more measured tones than Egypt and Morocco. Libya, however, did not take the same position, particularly once it became clear that the USA was prepared to intervene militarily to protect Saudi Arabia. Tunisia, surprisingly in view of its traditional pro-Western stance and its moderate position within the Arab political world, also hesitated to condemn the Iraqi invasion of Kuwait outright.

Over the next eight days – until the fateful Arab League meeting in Cairo 10 August which called on Arab states to participate in the military forces being organised to counter Iraq's aggression – these positions hardened. At the Arab League summit, Egypt steamrollered through the decision on a majority vote (the first time that the League had taken a substantive decision without a unanimous vote of its members) with Syrian, Gulf and Moroccan support. Algeria, however, although it condemned Iraq's action, abstained from the vote in protest and the Tunisian government avoided having to take sides by refusing to attend the meeting. Later, the Tunisian leader, President Zin Abidin Ibn Ali (Zine Abidine Ben Ali) condemned the majority decision as being based on 'imaginary legitimacy', while the Algerian foreign minister described international measures to freeze Iraqi assets abroad as 'the holdup of the millennium', Libya actually voted against the Cairo decision and Colonel Qadhafi was so incensed by it that he threatened to walk out of the organisation.

One important reason for Tunisian and Libyan irritation with the decision was that both governments favoured mediation to bring the crisis to a close and believed that the Arab League's action would make any such initiative less likely to succeed. Tunisia, for example, supported Jordanian efforts in this respect, while Libya had participated in a joint initiative with the PLO before the Cairo meeting and joined Jordan, Sudan and the PLO in another abortive attempt to resolve the crisis peacefully just after it. There was also some doubt initially whether Libya and Tunisia would observe United Nations sanctions against Iraq, particularly over the matter of humanitarian aid. Algeria, for its part, preserved a chilly reserve towards the crisis in the early weeks, not offering its mediation although Algerian governments have habitually taken a mediatory position in most regional conflicts. Morocco, on the other hand, by mid-August had begun to back away from its earlier position of whole-hearted support for the US-led military intervention.

The reason for this caution – which was signalled by an interview with King Hassan II in the influential French daily, *Le Monde*, on 16 August in which he was surprisingly critical of the Gulf states and Kuwait and insisted that Moroccan troops there (1,300 in Saudi Arabia and 5,000 in the UAE) were merely a symbolic contribution to the Multinational Force – was the realisation in official circles in Rabat that popular attitudes over the Iraqi invasion of Kuwait were quite different from those taken by the government. Indeed, the Moroccan public's reaction to the crisis was typical of that throughout North Africa, except for Egypt; one of condemnation of Iraq's invasion, tempered by profound dislike for the Gulf states and angry condemnation of the hostile Western reaction and intervention against Iraq in the light of years of Western indulgence towards Israel. In Egypt, these sentiments were profoundly modified by intense popular hostility towards Iraq because of the treatment of Egyptian workers there in the wake of the Iran-Iraq war, when demobilised Iraqi soldiers were held responsible for widespread attacks on Egyptians which had resulted in hundreds of deaths.

There were widespread and massive demonstrations of popular anger at international hostility shown towards Iraq throughout North Africa during the autumn of 1990. In Tunis, a major opposition demonstration was officially permitted for the first time. Hundreds of thousands of persons repeatedly demonstrated in the Algerian capital and a massive demonstration, officially estimated at 300,000 but unofficially put at 800,000 took place in Rabat. Even in Libya, widespread unofficial demonstrations took place in Tripoli, resulting in two deaths in fighting outside the Saudi embassy after Friday prayers and an even bigger demonstration the following day under official auspices which was estimated to have involved 700,000 persons – about one quarter of the total population of the country. There were also a series of pro-Iraqi and pro-Ba'athist demonstrations in the Mauritanian capital, Nouakchott.

It was striking that in Tunisia, Algeria and Morocco, the Islamic fundamentalist movements took a leading part in these demonstrations alongside secular parties. Indeed, in Algeria, leaders of the FIS actually visited Baghdad to express support in the face of Western threats, although they also condemned the actual invasion of Kuwait. Even in Egypt, Islamic fundamentalist groups, including the *Ikhwan Muslimin*, initially opposed the government's participation in the Multinational force, despite the fact that they depend heavily on Saudi financial backing. In the end, however, the threat of Saudi disapproval forced them to mute their hostility.

There was also a profoundly hostile reaction to Western threats of military action to force Iraq out of Kuwait from North Africa's intellectuals. Many of their comments surfaced in the French press, which is habitually used by Francophone North African writers when they wish to address a European audience. Figures, such as the Moroccan poet, Abd al-Latif La'abi (Abdellatif Laabi), highlighted the contrast between the speed of Western reaction to Iraq's invasion of Kuwait and the disinterest shown towards Israel's continued rebuffs to the United Nations over its activities in the Occupied Territories. His comments, made in late August, were echoed some weeks later, in an article in *Le Monde*, by Morocco's most famous political prisoner, Abraham Serfaty, imprisoned in Kenitra Civil Prison in perpetuity. The issue was widened by a Tunisian lawyer, Jilani Jaddi, who pointed to the irony that the widespread public support in the USA for Washington's invasions of Grenada and Panama should have been paralleled by an equally widespread US support for Iraq's invasion of Kuwait, '. . . for international law is indivisible'. He also attacked Western criticism of popular Arab hostility towards the US-led mobilisation of international opinion against Iraq, pointing out that the Arab world was really expressing its opposition to what it perceived as a Western attempt to establish a new military hegemony in the aftermath of the end of the Cold War and its dislike of the obscurantism and selfishness of the governments in the Gulf.

The Consequences for Regional Policy

The degree of popular unanimity over the issue of Iraq's invasion of Kuwait had significant consequences for government policy in the region, particularly in the run-up to the actual conflict between January 16 and February 28, 1991. It was modified only by US pressure on certain governments during September 1990. This particularly affected Tunisia, whose leaders took care to make it clear to Washington that they would abide by United Nations' resolutions on sanctions because of the threat of loss of vital aid. It also affected Libya, where Colonel Qadhafi was privately warned by Egypt's President Mubarak in September that US hostility would be directed towards Libya if Tripoli persisted in supporting Iraq. The warning was repeated by the Egyptian leader during a visit to Libya in November. Baghdad indirectly helped to persuade Libya to adopt a cautious pro-Western stance by rejecting Libyan offers of humanitarian aid unless they were accompanied by overt political support for Iraq.

Although Egypt continued to support the Western-led United Nations military initiative in the Gulf, sending 30,000 troops to join the force, despite the adverse economic effects of its participation (estimated in November by Egyptian sources to have been equivalent to $9bn), other North African states sought to establish a common diplomatic position. This was articulated through the UMA (*Union Maghreb Arabe*), a regional unity organisation created in February 1989, where the emergency heads-of-state meeting called by Algeria on September 3 rejected the use of force to resolve the Iraqi-Kuwaiti dispute and the use of sanctions to starve Iraq into submission or to undermine the Iraqi economy. The five governments involved – Libya, Tunisia, Algeria, Morocco and Mauritania – also began a series of peace initiatives that were to last up to the outbreak of hostilities on 16, January, 1991.

On 19 September an UMA mediation initiative designed to provide Arab supervision of an Iraqi withdrawal from Kuwait and to organise an international peace conference over the Palestinian issue – thus satisfying Iraq's demands for 'linkage' despite its insistence on withdrawal – was brusquely rejected by Iraq, which appeared only to be interested in face-to-face negotiations with the USA. Further peace initiatives were delayed by two other events which also provided the UMA members with opportunities to show mutual solidarity. The first was united UMA condemnation of Israel's actions in the killing of thirteen Palestinians at the *haram al-sharif* in Jerusalem on 13

October at an emergency Arab League summit in Tunis – which put Morocco at odds with its colleagues in the Multinational Force. The second was a similar unified protest at the surreptitious transfer of the Arab League headquarters from Tunis to Cairo at the end of October. The UMA was joined in its protest by the PLO and Iraq, so that the issue came to symbolise the profound split inside the Arab League that had developed as a result of the Iraqi invasion of Kuwait and the Western military response.

On 11 November, however, Morocco made an independent bid to broker a peace agreement between the Gulf states and Iraq. The proposal foundered, however, on combined Iraqi, Egyptian and Gulf hostility to it. King Hassan had also omitted to obtain prior UMA support and, in the end, only had positive support from the PLO and Jordan, Morocco's initiative was picked up by Algeria in mid-November, when President Shadli Ibn Jadid undertook a lengthy tour of the Middle East to establish whether or not a basis existed for a peaceful solution to the crisis. Algeria's initiative was supported by France and, in late December, hints emerged that a new plan was to be put to Washington for approval. In the event, the plan never materialised because of the meeting between US Secretary of State James Baker and Iraqi Foreign Minister Tariq Aziz in Geneva on 9 January 1991. Despite the failure of that encounter, Algeria continued to push for a peaceful settlement through French and European good offices right up to the outbreak of hostilities. The other governments of North Africa had, however, come to accept that military confrontation was inevitable.

The War and its Aftermath

The actual conflict in the Gulf produced little direct reaction in North Africa, once the realisation of the overwhelming military superiority of the Multinational Force was complete. Iraq's passive response evoked considerable disenchantment with the claims of the Saddam Hussein regime towards leadership of the Arab world. There was also a growing realisation that the other problems of the region – particularly the Arab-Israeli conflict and the Palestinian issue which has always struck a deeply sympathetic chord throughout the region, especially in Morocco would be adversely affected by what had happened. North African governments, in consequence, maintained a cautious distance from the Middle East.

They could not, however, avoid the economic consequences of the Gulf crisis, as oil prices rose. Tunisia was the most adversely affected, with losses of $1,071 bn in terms of export sales and aid inflows expected. Morocco had to face increased oil import costs and the destruction of its tourist trade, although these losses were offset by additional Saudi Arabian aid of $700 m donated during the autumn of 1990. Algeria and Libya benefited from increased oil prices and the removal of OPEC quotas to make up for the shortfall in Kuwaiti and Iraqi oil exports as a result of United Nations sanctions. Algeria enjoyed a $2.5 bn windfall, which relieved the expected $600 m arrears in import payments that had been expected in 1990. Libya enjoyed an even bigger windfall profit from increased oil sales.[16] Egypt was, perhaps, the one state that could point to real benefits, as its foreign debt was reduced by more than half and it finally came to terms with the IMF over standby support and economic restructuring.[17]

The real changes, however, occurred at a popular level. Quite apart from the severe rioting in the Moroccan city of Fez in mid-December – occasioned by worsening economic conditions there, although popular perceptions that the Laraki government covertly supported the US-led action in the Gulf intensified popular anger – North African governments have become aware of growing popular anger and of the effect it could have on their survival. In Tunisia, governmental claims of fundamentalist activity designed to destabilise the regime and to replace it by an Islamic system culminated in mass arrests in June 1991. Similar tensions in Algeria, where the FIS forced a change of government but were unable to force a change of government policy through a programme of strikes in early June 1991 culminated at the end of the month in mass arrests which decapitated the movement. In both cases, popular support for the Islamist movements had been amplified by anger at the West because of the war, while the apparent inability of governments to influence international events tended to discredit them in the popular mind. Support for the beleaguered Saddam Hussein regime also began to rise again, once hostilities were ended, because of the failure of the international community, through the United Nations, to attend to the basic problems of the Middle East.

There were also more basic changes, for the conflict in the Gulf spawned a mass of spontaneous reactions, quite outside the control of government, particularly in Morocco and Algeria. Public outrage at conditions in Iraq after the Coalition bombing campaign resulted in hundreds of medical personnel volunteering to serve there under the auspices of the Algerian Red Crescent. In early March 1991, popular feeling was canalised into a highly successful twenty-four hour 'telethon' which raised large sums of aid for Iraq – and, incidentally, castigated the Algerian authorities for not doing more to help Iraq.

In Morocco, popular feeling was heightened just after the end of hostilities by rumours of clashes between US military personnel and Moroccan units in the Saudi capital, Riyadh. The political opposition also tried to maintain the momentum it had built up during public protests before the conflict began. All major opposition parties and their trade union organisations had collaborated in organising the protests and, after the riots in Fez in mid-December 1990, they were quick to seize on the popular mood once again. Both the government and the Royal Palace felt weakened by these displays of opposition solidarity and had to moderate their traditionally pro-Western policies as a result. King Hassan was quick to sense the popular mood and to exploit it. He summed up his position by saying, 'My heart is with Iraq, but my head is with the Gulf.' There was little doubt where Moroccan hearts were. In the immediate aftermath of the conflict the Moroccan Red Crescent sponsored an appeal for aid through a support committee called, '*Musamadat al-Sha'ab al-'Iraq Shaqiq*'. Vast amounts of aid were flown to Iraq via Iran in a spontaneous demonstration of popular support and disgust for what had occurred.

At the time of writing, in mid-1991, there was little doubt that governments in North Africa would continue to feel the chill wind of popular anger over the conflict in the Gulf and the associated popular suspicion of their own actions during the crisis. It seemed likely that they would be forced to concede additional democratic reforms to mitigate this growing crisis of confidence. If they did not, as Tunisia and Algeria demonstrated, there was always the Islamic alternative. Even in Egypt, where disillusion over the expected benefits from President Mubarak's participation in the Multinational Force began to spread, there was increasing anxiety over the political and diplomatic stagnation that faced a Middle East divided between those who supported Washington and those who did not. Once again, the opposition was likely to exploit this sense of disappointment by pushing for greater democratic reforms. Perhaps the most significant development, however, was not at the formal level of political organisation. Instead, the growth of non-governmental organisations, created specifically to channel popular anger over the conflict, was expected to intensify the growth of civil society in North Africa and thereby create the institutions that would make democratic change a permanent reality.

Notes

1. Mortimer E, *Faith and Power: the politics of Islam*, Faber & Faber (London), 1982; 282.
2. Daume D (ed.), *Britannica Book of the Year 1990*, Encyclopaedia Britannica (Chicago, USA), 1990; 756–61.
3. Under the monarchy, foreign policy was dominated by potential rivalry with Saudi Arabia and, after the rise of Nasserism, by anxieties over Egypt and communism – hence the Baghdad Pact arrangements which eventually destroyed the Hashemite monarchy in 1958. Ghareeb E 'Iraq

in the Gulf', Axelgard F W (ed), *Iraq in transition: a political, economic and strategic perspective*, Mansell (London) 1986; 61.

4. In fact, apart from the on-going quarrel with Kuwait which led to abortive invasion threats in 1961 and 1970, Iraq's attention was first drawn towards the Gulf in 1964, as a result of an Arab League initiative designed to persuade Gulf states to end their dependence on British protection. Niblock T, 'Iraqi policies towards the Arab states of the Gulf 1958–1981', Niblock T (ed), *Iraq, the contemporary state*, Croom Helm (London) 1982; 139.

5. Fouad Ajami has well described the cathartic and catalytic effect of the 1967 war on Arab political thought and on the discrediting of the Arab nationalist ideal. See Ajami F, *The Arab predicament: Arab political thought and practice since 1967*, Cambridge University Press (Cambridge), 1981.

6. In fact, in both Tunisia and Algeria, Islam played an important role in the formulation of the ideologies of the neoDestour and the FLN. See Boulby M, 'The Islamic challenge: Tunisia since independence', *Third World Quarterly, 10*, 2 (April 1983); 590–601, and Roberts H, 'Radical Islamism and the dilemma of Algerian nationalism', *Third World Quarterly, 10*, 2 (April 1988); 562–574.

7. In fact, the Libyan revolution has a profound Islamic basis to its ideology, even if it is considered heterodox by most Muslims. See Joffe EGH, 'The role of islam', Lemarchand R (ed), *The green and the black: Qadafi's policies in Africa*, University of Indiana Press (Bloomington – USA), 1988; 40–50.

8. There were, of course, large numbers of Berbers who rejected the assumption that secularist politics automatically meant Arab nationalism, particularly in Algeria. However, amongst urban communities, changing educational patterns and the continuing modernisation of social structures tended to reinforce this ideological identity.

9. For a discussion of this issue, see Kienle E, *Ba'th v Ba'th: the conflict between Syria and Iraq 1968–1989*, I.B. Tauris (London), 1990.

10. Roberts H, *op. cit.*; 87–8.

11. *Africa Confidential, 31*, 13.

12. *Africa Confidential, 29*, 20.

13. *Africa Confidential, 30*, Nos. 9, 22 and 25.

14. *Africa Confidential, 30*, 24.

15. This account is based on news reports in *Le Monde, Middle East Economic Digest, Middle East Economic Survey*, on Joffe EGH, 'North African responses to the Gulf crisis' in Anon, *North Africa: economic structure and analysis*, EIU, London, 1991; 5–14 and on interviews in the region during May 1991.

16. Ghiles F, 'The impact of the Gulf war on the Maghreb economies', *Middle East International*, May 3, 1991.

17. *Middle East Economic Digest*, June 7, 1991; 24–25. Debt has been reduced from $46.6 bn in July 1990 to $21.1 bn a year later, largely because of a 50 per cent reduction in Paris Club debt ($10.1 bn), the forgiveness of US military debt ($7 bn) and the annulment of debt to Gulf states ($6 bn).

5

Europeans, the EC and the Gulf

Trevor C Salmon

Although co-operation among the member-states of the European Community in the areas of foreign security and defence policy was not mentioned in the Treaty of Rome of 1957, it was always a fundamental objective of the member states to bring about both political integration and union, and a collective European voice in the world. Whilst there were several false starts in trying to give effect to these aspirations, the Hague summit in 1969 led to what became European Political Co-operation(EPC), a system involving an organisational system outside the actual framework of the Treaty and based upon intergovernmental cooperation. In the 1970s and 1980s, various efforts were made to make these loose, informal arrangements rather more formal, structured and coherent. These efforts appeared to culminate in the Single European Act, (SEA), of 1986, which contained the basic organisational structure and operational parameters of EPC which were operative during the Gulf crisis of 1990–91.[1]

The SEA reasserted the distinctive juridical bases of EPC and the EC *per se*, although it did state that the external policies of the EC and the policies agreed in EPC should be consistent. Title III of the SEA is replete with exhortations 'to inform and consult' one another about foreign policy, and to 'endeavour' to harmonise positions, but it contains no legally binding commitment to undertake common action. EPC was to remain intergovernmental and consequently subject to individual vetoes. The SEA also made clear that EPC covered the 'political and economic aspects of security', and hence by implication, *not* the military aspects.[2]

One of the successes of EPC to which the states often pointed was the formulation of a common, distinctive European position on the

Middle East in the Venice Declaration of May 1980. Despite coming from different original positions, the member-states managed to agree a common position, revolving around 'the right to existence and to security of all the states in the region, including Israel, and justice for all the peoples, which implies the recognition of the legitimate rights of the Palestinian people.' It recognized the PLO would have to be associated with the negotiations, that the status of Jerusalem should not be changed unilaterally, that the continued occupation of the 'occupied territories' was unacceptable, and that the renunciation of violence by all was crucial to peace.[3]

This and other successes stemmed from the habit or reflex of consultation built up over the years, but the overall record of EPC was at best mixed, since solidarity was not complete and a number of states continued to maintain their freedom of manoeuvre. That divisions occur is not surprising, given that the states in the Community are far from agreement on many aspects of their internal arrangements, face one another in direct commercial competition, have differing historical and geographical perpectives, and have very different domestic pressures upon them.[4] To some extent, these tensions are submerged, given the highly declaratory nature of EPC and the fact that it consists largely of statements and has few other instruments. This has been coupled with a tendency to unite 'behind a common position sufficiently loosely defined to allow each to add his own interpretation, so producing some forward movement without confronting the major obstacles ahead.'[5] This makes assessment of the record of EPC prior to August 1990 difficult, and partly explains the problems the member-states faced in trying to co-ordinate their positions subsequent to 2 August.

A further factor exacerbating these problems was that in 1990 the Twelve were gearing themselves up to focus on their future institutional development. Various, widely differing, proposals were being put forward, in an attempt to reach common positions on foreign policy, security and defence, perhaps even by majority vote. All of these were contentious to one or other of the participants, and the Twelve were by no means ready to agree upon them in the summer of 1990.

A Community of Domestic Considerations

At the level of individual states, domestic politics played an important part in determining reactions to the Gulf. In Italy, for example, there was a coalition government and there were divisions between the Prime Minister, Andreotti, a Christian Democrat, and the Foreign Minister De Michelis, a Socialist. These divisions were embarrassing as Italy had held the Presidency of the EC since the beginning of July 1990, and they contributed to a number of complaints from some of

Italy's allies. The complaints concerned lack of leadership; the inadequacy of some of Italy's own decisions as a state, especially over what was perceived as a limited initial response to the crisis, both in terms of sending only two frigates and a support ship and of the lack of any sense of urgency over EC meetings. Furthermore, the ambiguity of Andreotti's earlier statements gave cause for concern, although, by late September, there were signs of a firmer and more united Italian reaction. In January, the Italian Parliament did agree to participate in an 'international policing operation', that wording being used because the Italian constitution forbids recourse to war to settle disputes. Some of the Italian military believed war could have been avoided and resigned. The position of Andreotti himself was seen to reflect domestic political exigencies, and public support for war was approximately 61 per cent in mid-February. One way Italy tried to overcome these problems was by emphasising its EC responsibilities and by making clear that Italy would only contribute initially to the naval embargo if it was covered by the WEU umbrella. Italy ultimately sent 3 frigates and 10 Tornado planes, and suffered one death.

Another state with internal difficulties was the Federal Republic of Germany. It was preoccupied with unification – its costs and the need to give support to the Soviet Union for pulling its forces out of the former DDR. The real issue, however was the Basic Law. The relevant articles appear to be *24, 26, and 87a. Article 24*, paragraph *(2)* states 'For the maintenance of peace, the Federation may enter a system of mutual collective security; in doing so it will consent to such limitations upon its sovereignty as will bring about and secure a peaceful and lasting order in Europe and among the nations of the world.' *Article 26*, paragraph one refers to Acts tending to, and undertaken with the intent to disturb the peaceful relations between nations, especially to prepare for aggressive war, shall be unconstitutional. They shall be made a punishable offence.' *Article 87a(1)*, states that 'The Federation shall build up Armed Forces for defence purposes. . . .' and *(2)* 'Apart from defence, the Armed Forces may only be used to the extent explicitly permitted by this Basic Law. . . .'[6]

Not unnaturally there has been debate in the Federal Republic and elsewhere as to what these articles taken together mean. The initial reaction of Chancellor Kohl was that the FRG would take part in any action 'within the framework of its legal and practical means', particularly if there were coordinated WEU action.[7] A narrower view was held by his coalition partners, the FPD, and by the opposition SPD. They argued that the paragraph *87a(2)*, implied that the use of German force anywhere outside the NATO area was prohibited. Kohl was more impressed by the argument that there was a need to repay the US for its support over unity, and that a Germany coming of age needed to show a willingness to undertake responsibilities. However, by mid-September Kohl reluctantly bowed to domestic pressure and decided that military action was impossible, and instead pledged financial and economic support. He pledged himself to seek a constitutional amendment that would release the apparent restrictions on 'offensive' German military activity abroad.[8] This row has lingered on as Kohl promised his military leaders that the matter will be resolved by the end of 1991, although that date was later in doubt.[9] The coalition FPD supports a wider role but only under strict UN control, and missions such as those in the Gulf would still not qualify as permissible. The SPD wishes any change to limit action outside NATO to UN peacekeeping. Kohl needs the support of other parties because constitutional change requires a two-thirds majority. A poll in early January 1991 showed that 75 per cent of Germans felt that Germany should keep out of international crises. Other responses suggest that the Germans may be becoming rather more inward looking.

Germany did send some forces abroad. NATO had announced in August 1990 that it would honour its treaty commitments to Turkey. In January 1991 Germany sent Alpha fighter aircraft and some 300 air personnel to help defend Turkey, this representing the first deployment of German forces outside German territory since 1945. It was later to send Patriots to Israel, and, at the end of the war, it sent a flotilla of minesweepers to the Gulf to help the Allies mop up. There was, however, a certain *angst* in Germany over these actions, especially in relation to Turkey. This *angst* caused some to observe that NATO had protected FRG for forty years, but now the Germans were hesitant in doing their duty to Turkey. The Germans also allowed the US to use its bases in Germany for transport and similar purposes. More importantly, it was assiduous in its financial and economic support of the coalition and provided support for Turkey, Egypt, Jordan, and Syria. With some reluctance, it agreed to provide financial support in terms of technical aid to US troops in Saudi Arabia and to contribute to American and British costs. Subsequently, however, it refused to sell arms to the Saudis, in line with its apparent policy of not exporting arms to areas of tension, although this provoked a certain reaction, given the alleged involvement of German firms in exporting certain chemicals earlier on to Iraq.

In France there were divisions within the government and society. Governmental division centred around Jean-Pierre Chevenement, Minister of Defence, who sought to distance himself from a more combative French position. He was concerned with the conflict spilling over into other areas of the Middle East and was impressed by the likely number of casualties. He also became entangled in a row as to whether French forces would confine their activity to targets in Kuwait, Chevenement claiming on 17 January 1991 that French forces would only fight in Kuwait but not in Iraq. However, on 20 January, President Mitterrand denied there was any geographical limitation. And on 24 January, France started bombing Iraq. The French also faced criticism from Jean-Marie le Pen on the Right and from the radical Left. The government was concerned about the size of the Arab community in France and had difficulties because of its previous enthusiasm for the Iraqi régime, and its general support for the Arab cause.

A further difficulty was how to maintain and assert traditional French independence in a collaborative endeavour clearly led by the United States. In the earlier phase it sought to maintain a discreet distance from American and British military plans, and in August it launched a major diplomatic offensive to try to explain its position. France gradually evolved its role towards a less independent position, especially after the Iraqi incursion into the French, Belgian and Canadian diplomatic compounds in Kuwait. Nonetheless, they continued to insist that French forces would remain under French control, that France would keep its 'autonomy of decision and autonomy of action', that any decision would be Mitterrand's.[10] On the other hand, on the eve of conflict, the French Premier, Rocard, announced that French forces would be placed under US military command 'for a strictly defined time and missions.'[11] France also broke with Gaullist precedent when it allowed American combat aircraft to be based temporarily on French soil in the context of refuelling B-52s. French policy in the Gulf in January/February 1991 achieved 70–78 per cent popular support.

The real issue over France was the continuing suspicion on the part of its friends that the French were trying to arrange separate deals in their own interests. These fears emerged, for example, as a result of Mitterrand's speech to the UN General Assembly in October. Having said that no compromise was possible until Iraq withdrew from Kuwait and complied with UN resolutions, Mitterrand tempered his remarks with the promise that, if Iraq withdrew its troops and freed its hostages, 'everything is possible', and appeared to open the door to an international conference and a Kuwaiti referendum.[12] Some of France's neighbours, especially Belgium, noted that Mitterrand's speech did not tally with repeated French calls for a joint EC foreign policy.[13] This ambivalence became a real issue in January 1991 when the French appear to have maintained contact with Iraq through an 'unofficial' envoy, Michel Vauzelle. At an EPC meeting on 4 January, the French Foreign Minister, Dumas argued for EC talks with Aziz, the Iraqi Foreign Minister, and again floated the idea of 'linkage' between an Iraqi withdrawal and a peace conference on the Middle East. The disagreement within the EC was overcome by the Iraqi attitude on other matters which made it moot. But the French persisted with their basic position and attracted criticism of 'free-lance diplomacy'.

Criticism was substantially increased when on 14 January the French made new proposals to the UN Security Council, calling for an Iraqi withdrawal but also stating that a peace conference would be held on the Middle East at some appropriate time. Not only was there displeasure at the nature of the French proposal, but more particularly that France had not informed its Community partners, even though there had been a Foreign Ministers' meeting on the morning of the French proposal. Indeed, the ministers had agreed that the conditions for a new European initiative did not exist at that moment. At lunch time on that day the British Premier John Major had met President Mitterrand and again had been told nothing. The British played down suggestions of irritation but were unhappy not to have received any hint of a French proposal. The French argued that they had mentioned the idea of an initiative but had not gone into detail because the text was still being worked on. Dumas, apparently did phone, British Foreign Secretary Douglas Hurd after it had been drafted. The Germans and Italians appeared ready to support the French initiative. However, in the absence of any Iraqi response, it all came to nothing.

In Britain there was little real internal debate. From the outset the UK was an enthusiastic supporter of action. In Parliament in two votes in January only 50 and 30 MPs voted against the bipartisan policy. In January, that policy had 61 per cent popular support and this increased to 78 per cent in February. Only fringe parties and politicians objected to government policy on substantive points. The United Kingdom took a tough stance against Iraq from the beginning, with unreserved condemnation of the invasion. It argued the UN should assert its new authority. In general, this met with cross-party support and, except for aberrations, the only real divide was on the issue of whether further military action, initially to enforce the embargo and later to engage in military action over Kuwait and possibly Iraq itself, required further UN resolutions and approval. The Foreign and Communication Office was clear that Britain was prepared to go to war with Iraq over Kuwait without further UN sanction.

A feature of the British response was a certain readiness to criticize the EC response. At the end of August, Mrs Thatcher called the European response 'patchy and disappointing'. In her view, Europe's faltering response gave the lie to the rhetorical commitment to a common security policy as part of a move towards political union in the EC.[14] John Major, her successor, made the same point on 22 January.[15] Douglas Hurd made clear that the United Kingdom would find any question of majority voting on such matters intolerable. He was clear that it was not absence of machinery that had caused the problem but differences in view on questions of substance. He was clear that NATO already dealt with defence, and that WEU should become 'an effective bridge between the 12 and NATO. It is not feasible to consider a mutual defence commitment among the 12'[16]. Neil Kinnock, Leader of the Opposition, broadly concurred.

The crisis highlighted his dichotomy between the European and Atlantic tendencies within British policy in recent years. It provided an opportunity for Mrs Thatcher to reinforce the 'special relationship' between London and Washington. There was not the same insistence in Britain, as in France, on keeping autonomy of control, decision, and action. General Schwarzkopf had *de facto* command of the British contingents, and took the Operational command decisions on the conduct of the war. Nonetheless, the Saudi-based commander of the British forces in the Gulf had power of veto over Schwarzkopf's orders as they affected British activity, after prior consultation with the Prime Minister.

Other member states of the EC similarly exhibited a variety of nuances and emphases in their response. The Dutch, for example, agreed to a military response because of the 'vital importance for Europe of the stability, territorial integrity and sovereignty of the Gulf States.' They were also concerned to bolster 'international solidarity' and discourage aggression.[17] For them, the despatch of two frigates to the Gulf had the advantage of providing a highly flexible presence during the naval blockade. These were put under US command on 11 January. The Dutch also sent Patriots and some personnel to Turkey. This reflected their general desire to be near to the United States.

Both the Dutch and the Belgians showed a preference for a WEU umbrella for operations. The Belgians, for example, delayed sending two minesweepers and a logistics vessel, pending a WEU meeting. Only after the WEU meeting on 21 August, did they confirm that they would send vessels to enforce the UN embargo on Iraq. In January the minesweepers were declared as hospital/refugee ships, and a few aircraft were placed at British and French disposal.

A discordant note was struck at the end of 1990 by the Belgian refusal to sell ammunition to the British. Fortunately, the Dutch and Germans responded favourably to the British request. In January, the Belgians met a similar request from the Americans even though, earlier in the month, Mr Martens, the Prime Minister, had spoken of his country having chosen 'not to become embroiled in a military conflict'. Belgian polls suggested that some 80 per cent of the population was opposed to the war. Denmark praised the American response to the Iraqi invasion and stressed the importance of international organisations.

After some hesitation, the Greeks sent a frigate to join the blockade, but there were protests from both socialists and communists. The Greeks became concerned about the aid being directed towards Turkey as events progressed. Portugal supported international action, contributed to the Western fleet, and made commitments of cargo ships and airliners to aid the deployment of US forces. It allowed the United States to use the air base in the Azores as a staging post. Spain had rather more problems, there being considerable agitation over the decision to use conscripts to help crew three warships on their way to the Gulf. This reflected a fear that the intervention could prove a watershed in Spain's traditional policy of seeking a placatory relationship with the Arab Middle East and Muslim North Africa. It was something of a right/left divide, but Premier Gonzalez insisted that Spanish membership of the EC demanded that Spain should play a role. He was also firm that Spain would only contribute to the naval operation to enforce the embargo if it was covered by the WEU umbrella. When the war came, Spain did not become involved in the fighting, and the three combat ships were removed from the combat zone. Spain did allow the use of bases for B-52s but was particularly outspoken after the bombing of the Baghdad building in which hundreds reportedly died, calling for a halt to aerial attacks against cities. Some Spanish demonstrations during the war gathered the support of up to 100,000 people, and some polls suggested only 30 per cent supported the war.

The Irish had a number of problems, given their policy of rhetorical neutrality. Ireland is not in NATO or the WEU, but has claimed to be a loyal member of the UN and the EC. In the Gulf crisis, of course, the UN did not order its members to take military action in January. The issue thus became whether the Republic would provide facilities for those states cooperating in the liberation of Kuwait, it being clear that Ireland would not be involved in any direct military action. The Dail agreed to provide facilities, although, ingenious as ever, Mr Haughey sought to distinguish this from participation in war, arguing that 'It would place an extraordinary strain on ordinary language if the mere granting of peripheral facilities could be interpreted as making Ireland a participant in the war.' Minority parties thought that it did. Interestingly, the Gulf has apparently convinced a majority of Irish people that the EC should have a common European military intervention force, although a majority also wanted to preserve Irish 'neutrality'.[19]

*   *   *

Given the foregoing it is not surprising that the EC and EPC should have found certain difficulties in seeking to arrive at a common European position on the Gulf. Hardly any two positions within the Twelve were identical. It is also obvious that domestic political considerations were very important. It is difficult to gainsay the argument that if unity is impossible on such a clear-cut issue, then it will be incredibly difficult to reach a common position on a whole range of matters.

The European Institutional Response

European officials were initially apparently pleased with the speed and nature of the European response to the crisis and the invasion, particularly the speed (48 hours) with which the Twelve members of the EC implemented the UN resolution on sanctions. The Twelve determined to impose economic sanctions on Iraq before the UN embargo was agreed. What, however, became clear very quickly were the inhibitions felt about the relationship of the EC to military aspects of the crisis, the embargo, security, and later the war, despite the fact that early in September the Italian Foreign Minister, De Michelis, was claiming that the most important aspect of the EC's response was that the defence and security issues had been discussed within an EC framework, without any problems.

As early as the second week of August, it became clear that the general expectation in Europe was that the WEU would be the pivotal European organisation dealing with the military aspects of the question. It would be the substitute for the defence arm that the EC lacked, reconciling British and French positions, providing an umbrella under whose coverages states would contribute and coordinating the activities of NATO's European members.[20] WEU was also regarded as a source of legitimation for European responses and enabled hesitant governments to commit forces to the Allied military effort in a way that they would not have been prepared to do unilaterally. (Table 1 shows the contributions made by the EC nations to the Coalition effort). France was especially keen to see a WEU role and, coincidentally, was the WEU President at the time and had obvious interests in promoting a WEU involvement given its long-standing attitudes to various other institutional arrangements and its non-membership of a range of others. WEU also appeared to offer a way in which French troops could operate in the Gulf without appearing to follow American orders. In the earlier phase of the crisis, France sought 'symbolically' . . . to . . . 'stress the continuity' of WEU and EC processes.[21] It did this, for example, by inviting all 12 members of the EC to attend a WEU meeting on 21 August, even though only nine of them were WEU members. Denmark and Greece

TABLE 1   EUROPEAN CONTRIBUTIONS TO THE COALITION EFFORT IN THE GULF

Involvement	Belgium	Denmark	France	Germany	Greece	Italy	Luxembourg	Netherlands	Portugal	Spain	UK
Offensive Air Ops in Iraq and Kuwait			*			*					*
Offensive Land Ops			*								*
Offensive Naval Ops			*			*			*		*
Naval Embargo Ops	*		*		*	*		*		*	*
Mine-clearing	*		*			*		*			*
Defence of Key Areas in Saudi Arabia			*								*
Deployed Medical Unit	*	*	*	*		*		*			*
Practical or Financial Assistance to the Coalition	*	*	*	*		*	*	*	*	*	*
Defensive Ops in the NATO Area	*			*	*	*		*	*	*	*

Note: Ireland allowed re-fuelling of United States aircraft at Shannon Airport
(Source: Based upon the *Statement on the Defence Estimates: Britain's Defence for the 90s* (HMSO London 1991))

agreed to send their ambassadors as observers, whilst Ireland declined the invitation. The links between the WEU and the EC were also shown by the number of occasions foreign ministers went immediately from meetings in one forum to meetings in the other. At the initial stage, there seems to have been some hesitation over a number of responses and some moments of tension. For example, at the WEU meeting on 21 August, Germany disappointed some of its allies by stressing its economic commitment to help Jordan, Turkey and others, but not offering anything significant in the military field. Whilst apparently supporting the WEU's basic position on the need for Europe to act together militarily in the crisis, it seemed to others as if it was a question of merely sounding positive.

More concretely, the WEU meeting on 21 August produced a communiqué outlining the principles of European coordination, saying it would cover 'overall operational concepts and specific guidelines for coordination between forces in the region, including areas of operation, sharing of tasks, logistical support and exchange of intelligence.'[22] Translating these principles into operational practice was complicated by Anglo-French disagreements with some other members who wanted further UN endorsement for further use of force. The WEU agreement opened the way for a meeting of European and American military commanders to tighten their cooperation. It was held under the joint chairmanship of the US and France.

The issues of coordination and command, both intra-European and European-US remained difficult, especially in the light of a European preference (the UK excepted) to stake out a distinct role for Western Europe in the Gulf. Exacerbating the issue was the desire on the part of many European states for explicit UN backing if military action was to be undertaken to force Iraq out, although not all took that position. The WEU did play a role during the naval embargo, and then continued to do so throughout the war, but when it came to fighting the war, those contributing forces made their own arrangements with the United States.

And what of the EC's response to the crisis? In the economic domain it was immediate. During the weekend following the Iraqi invasion of Kuwait, the Commission decided to place an embargo on oil imports from both countries and to adopt economic sanctions. Before the UN Security Council had responded to the situation, the EC had agreed to call for UN sanctions and, condemning the Iraqi action, froze all Iraqi assets and military sales, and suspended cooperation on military, scientific and technical matters. The EC was also first to send relief aid to Jordan, and moved to draw up a new energy policy to deal with the oil price rise, as well as beginning to think about a revived Mediterranean and Middle East policy to deal with the underlying political problems of the area. By mid-August, the EC sent a 'troika' mission to Jordan, Saudi Arabia, and Egypt. The troika included Irish, Italian and to Luxembourg ministers, as well as Abel Matutes of the Commission. The last was somewhat unusual but reflected the need for any action jointly to involve EPC and the EC, a matter raised in Title III of SEA, but was also a matter of urgent necessity in the Gulf case. The troika looked at ways of mobilising the EC-Jordan cooperation agreement so as to provide and demonstrate practical support for Jordan as an incentive to Jordan to enforce the UN sanctions. Part of the mission's rationale was to demonstrate that the conflict over Kuwait should not be seen as a conflict between Arabs and the West. This reflected a view that in the 1980s the EC demonstrated a more even-handed approach to the Middle East than had the United States, and that this might allow it a special role in the current crisis.

In the diplomatic field the EC states had to face the issue of the Iraqi demand for their embassies in Kuwait to close down and move to Baghdad. This demand was rejected. Whilst initially impressive, the EC states failed to maintain a consensus on this issue in practice if not in principle. A month later, there was renewed consensus in response to the Iraqi incursions into diplomatic missions in Kuwait, however, although the moves were coordinated, they were not identical, given the differing levels and nature of Iraqi representation in the different member states.

In September Jacques Delors, President of the EC Commission, expressed his satisfaction with the unity shown by the Twelve since the crisis broke in August, adding that fears of a split had proved groundless, the Community as a whole agreeing to uphold international law and to apply UN resolutions. Delors spoke of the EC's special role in the Middle East, because of historical links, and emphasized that it was not a North/South conflict, and that the Europeans had to act on the blatant inequalities that existed in the region. He warned of the need to avoid the errors of 1973–4, the steps to set up oil reserves which could be called upon and the regular pooling of information. He called for action to curb speculation in the oil market. He stressed, however, that the Community did not possess adequate institutional means to respond rapidly to the invasion and expressed sympathy with those that would have liked to have seen an EC task force sent to the region. Perhaps one lesson to be learnt, he thought, was the need to improve political cooperation and so to enable the Community to make that leap forward and take on a new role in the future.[23]

In March 1991 Delors' basic analysis was unaltered. The EC had taken some steps well, but 'once it became obvious that the situation would have to be resolved by armed combat, the Community had neither the institutional machinery nor the military force which would have allowed it to act as a community.' He reaffirmed his view that the 'only option compatible with the complete vision of European union [was] . . . to insert a common security policy. Not that transitional arrangements should be ruled out. . . . However, we must make it clear that what we are proposing is a single community as a logical extension of the ambitions of European union heralded by the Single European Act.' Furthermore, a 'common defence policy will be meaningless unless it reflects two types of solidarity: unity of analysis and action in foreign policy; and a reciprocal commitment to come to the aid of any member state whose integrity is threatened.' He wanted the commitment of Article V of the WEU treaty to be incorporated into the Union, namely that they would agree that 'any of the member states [becoming] the object of an armed attack in Europe [would lead to the other members] affording the party so attacked all the military and other aid and assistance in their power.' Delors hoped that '[L]ittle by little, a framework for decision-making and action would be set up between the Community and the WEU'. The war had shown the 'limitations of the European Community'.[24]

Initially, the analysis from EC officials had been rather upbeat. De Michelis insisted that EC states had acted 'effectively and with clarity of intentions and decisions' to the Gulf crisis.[25] He saw the crisis and the EC's response as greatly enhancing the possibility of the Twelve making significant steps towards political union. He felt their reaction had been 'light years ahead of any of its previous actions to major international crises both in speech and in content.' Whilst in July it had been an open question whether defence and security questions could be built into deeper foreign policy collaboration, by early September 'in a certain sense the problem is solved and we will now have to discuss the legal aspects, institutions and powers.'[26] Not everyone agreed then (or indeed agrees now) with this assessment of the response or the upbeat view of the future.

Sceptics rather than looking at the rhetoric, saw the resurfacing of old national positions and divergences of interests and views. They pointed to the limitations in the Community's response, and particularly the clear divergence between those who were reluctant to back any policy with force, especially the Italians and Greeks, with the more resolute British attitude. The rejoinder to this argument was that the EC could not have done more with its current legal, indeed quasi-constitutional framework. It is sometimes overlooked that the EC is a very Treaty-based organization and that, notwithstanding EPC, the starting point of any discussion is always what treaty article is the legal basis of any action.

Although EPC procedures are not so treaty-bound, the member states are then faced with the question of what instruments to apply to implement their foreign policy decisions. These are either fundamentally national measures, and, therefore a matter for each individual state, or are EC based. If the latter, the states are again driven back to the treaty issue. It is this issue which provoked the perception of Delors, De Michelis and others that the framework needs to be changed in the direction of closer and swifter political integration and the frustration felt by Sir Leon Brittan, who argued for a new 'European Security Community' to pool the defence and military strategies of the twelve member states of the present Community.[27]

More Difficulties

As the crisis unfolded, the Community faced a number of difficulties. One such was over the much vaunted EC humanitarian aid for refugees and financial support for the states most affected by the UN embargo. On 7 September, the Foreign Ministers met in Rome to discuss the Commission's proposals for this and agreed in principle to offer £1 billion to the three Arab states hardest hit. It was clear that, following this aid, the EC would not accept arguments for any of the three trying to break the UN embargo.

Embarrassingly for the EC, and epitomising both its internal decision-making problems and the member states' divergent interests, the EC Finance Ministers meeting one day later put off a decision, although not challenging the principle that aid should be provided. As a result of British and Dutch pressure, they insisted on more details of the three states' needs and a study of the competing demands for EC emergency aid. The British also took the view that financial aid must take into account the military costs of those EC states that had sent forces to the Gulf. Hence, it was only at the beginning of October that the EC Foreign Ministers finally reached agreement on aid totalling £1.04 billion to Jordan, Egypt, and Turkey. Later, a further issue became a Greek bid to require interest on the loan to Turkey, an attempt that was voted down. Even in January 1991, the Commission was still trying to speed up the delivery of the EC aid. At that time, only one-third of the aid pledged by individual EC member states had reached the putative recipients. The Commission was given responsibility for sharing out the EC aid.

In the first week of September 1990, the Foreign Ministers decided not to contribute directly to the cost of the US's deployment of troops in the Gulf. This decision caused some internal tension. There was general sympathy for the American call for burden-sharing, but De Michelis made the point that 'we want to contribute autonomously and directly, and not to the national expenses of a single country, even if that country is an ally.' The US also had to appreciate that the EC economic aid package to the front-line states would 'relieve' the

US of a burden it would otherwise have had to meet.[28]

A further problem in the financial area was the question of aid to Syria. The British government had blocked EC–Syrian talks since 1986 when it broke off diplomatic relations with Syria. By the middle of September 1990, Hurd gave consent for the Commission to open talks with Syria on grants and loans expected to be worth at least £105m over five years. Despite this change of view, a few weeks later, at the request of the United Kingdom, some diplomatic sanctions remained against Syria. On 28 November, Britain announced it would resume diplomatic relations with Syria.

As problematical was the attempt to relaunch the Euro–Arab dialogue. Following the issue of a declaration by EC Foreign Ministers which reaffirmed their 'determination to consolidate and reinforce the historic ties of friendship which bind them to the whole of the Arab world',[29] it had been hoped that the Euro- Arab dialogue, which had had some success in the 1970s, might be revived. However, because of a profound rupture among the Arab League members, this proved difficult. A complicating factor for the EC itself in its Middle East policy was whether or not there should be any 'linkage' between the Gulf crisis and the Palestinian issue.

Even more problematical became the hostage crisis. In mid-August it was thought that some 7,000 EC nationals were involved, and it was also felt to be crucial that EC solidarity was maintained over their plight, given the EC declaration that 'any attempt to harm or jeopardize the safety of any EC citizen will be considered as a most grave offence directed against the Community and all its member states and will provoke a united response from the entire Community',[30] a step which de Michelis saw as the introduction of a common EC citizenship. The EC condemned both the detention of foreigners, and their positioning in or near military targets. It warned that individual Iraqi citizens would be held responsible for any illegal actions affecting the security of EC and other foreign nationals.

By the end of September there was growing concern that Iraq's selective release policy might erode EC unity over the Gulf crisis, particularly given the decisions to free all of the more than 300 French hostages and to allow 33 Britons to fly home after the visit of Mr Heath. The French tried to insist that the release was a unilateral action by Baghdad. President Mitterrand said France had had 'no contact with Iraq, no delegates, no emissary,'[31] although some entertained doubts, when Baghdad claimed that there had been contact with Claude Cheysson (former French Foreign Minister and EC Commissioner) shortly before the hostages were put on the plane.

It was concern over such initiatives by former statesmen, including Brandt, and Heath, that prompted a clear declaration by the EC Heads of State and/or Government at the European Council meeting in Rome in October 1990. The Twelve expressed concern at Iraq's persistent violation of international law, the continuing occupation of Kuwait, the holding of hostages and the repeated violations of conventions relating to diplomatic relations. They reaffirmed the importance of the resolution of the crisis on the basis of UN Security Council resolutions and noted especially 'their determination not to negotiate with Iraq the release of foreign hostages and to discourage others from doing so.'[32] Within hours a problem arose over the proposed visit of Willy Brandt to Baghdad. This caused outrage in a number of European capitals, partly because it came so soon after the Rome Declaration, and partly because it was a fairly devastating example of national interest and concern that undermined the goal of united action.

The Germans tried to put a brave face on it, as well as belatedly seeking to surround the visit with an EC and UN mantle, although, despite some apparent official Italian support for the former, this was not successful. In Germany Foreign Minister, Genscher, claimed that the visit was purely humanitarian. Brandt somewhat undermined this approach when he argued 'It's obvious what humanitarian means. It means political efforts to find out if there is still an alternative to war.'[33] The Federal Republic claimed the visit was not out of line with the Rome Declaration, that it was still against individual action, but that 'a mission of leading European personalities acting on its own responsibility [was] the most suitable way in the current situation to put the case by international society to the Iraqi leadership for the release of the hostages.'[34] More pertinently, what appears to have been decisive for Bonn was not EC solidarity, but concern at opposing an apparently humanitarian visit by a respected elder statesman with an election only weeks away. A caustic British comment was that it was a 'bad example of governments deciding on a policy in conclave and then one of them deciding to do something else and trying to persuade other European governments to copy its bad example.'[35] The Belgians and Dutch called for an emergency EC Foreign Ministers meeting, and this led to another declaration, including reaffirmation of the Rome Declaration not to bargain with Baghdad. Ultimately this paled into insignificance besides the problems posed by the last minute French initiative, although that too was soon overtaken by events – the fact of war.

The Europeans and the European Community did not cover themselves with glory during the Gulf crisis, showing notable examples of breaking rank and following their own perceived interests when it suited them. This experience has clouded the IGC on political union, and has raised profound questions as to the relationship between rhetoric and common action.

Notes

1. See William Nicoll and Trevor C. Salmon, *Understanding the European Communities*, (London, Philip Allan, 1990) Chapter Four for an outline of EPC development, and P. Ifestos, *Contemporary European Diplomacy: National or Supranational? The EEC's European Political Cooperation* (Aldershot, Gower, 1987).
2. Single European Act, *Bulletin of the European Communities Supplement 2/86.*
3. Declaration on the Middle East issued by Venice meeting of Heads of State and/or Government 12–13 June 1980, *EC Bulletin 6/1980* pp10–11. See also David Allan and Alfred Pijpers, (eds), *European Policy-Making and the Arab-Israeli Conflict.* (The Hague, Martinus Nijhoff, 1984).
4. Roger Morgan, *High Politics, Low Politics: Towards a Foreign Policy for Western Europe*, (Sage Publications, 1973) pp21–25.
5. W. Wallace, 'Cooperation and convergence in European Foreign Policy', in C. Hill(ed.), *National Foreign Policies and European Political Cooperation* (London, Allan and Unwin, 1983) p10.
6. The Basic Law (FRG Press and Information).
7. As quoted by De Michelis, *International Herald Tribune*, 15 August 1990. According to *The Financial Times*, 16 August, Kohl claimed he has been misquoted.
8. *International Herald Tribune*, 17 September 1990.
9. *International Herald Tribune*, 14 March 1991.
10. Chevenement, *Times*, 21 September 1990.
11. *Keesing's Record of World Events for January, 1991* p37941.
12. *Financial Times*, 25 September 1990.
13. *Scotsman* and *Times*, 2 October 1990.
14. *Times*, 31 August 1990.
15. *Financial Times*, 23 January 1991.
16. *International Herald Tribune*, 11 December 1990.
17. *Times*, 14 August 1990.
18. *Independent*, 28 January 1991.
19. See Trevor C. Salmon, 'Call a spade a spade', *Fortnight*, No.292.
20. See, for example, interview with Willem van Eekelen, Secretary-General of WEU, *International Herald Tribune*, 20 August 1990 and Willem van Eekelen, 'The WEU and the Gulf Crisis' *Survival*, Vol.XXXII, No6 (Nov./Dec.1990).
21. *Financial Times*, 21 August 1990.
22. *Financial Times*, 22 August 1990 and 5 September 1990.
23. *The Week in Parliament*, PE 144.551, 10–14 September 1990.
24. Delors'speech to IISS, 7 March 1991, reprinted in *Survival* Vol.XXXIII, No.2(March/April 1991).
25. *International Herald Tribune*, 1–2 September 1990.
26. *Financial Times*, September 1990.
27. *Times*, 12 September 1990, and *The Week in Europe*, WE/31/90 EC Commission.
28. *International Herald Tribune*, 8–9 September 1990.

29. *Financial Times*, 3 October 1990.
30. *The Week in Europe*, WE/30/90.
31. *International Herald Tribune*, 29 October 1990.
32. Conclusions of the Presidency: European Council, Rome, 27–8 October 1990(SN 304/90rev.2).
33. *International Herald Tribune*, 6 November 1990.
34. *Times*, 2 November 1990.
35. *International Herald Tribune*, 6 November 1990.

6

An Iranian Perspective

Elahe Mohtasham

The invasion of Kuwait by the Iraqi military forces on 2 August 1990 sent shock waves through Iranian politics as the grave implications and consequences of such an invasion became immediately clear. The most significant of these were Iraq's improved strategic position by gaining control of Kuwait's coastline, which extends 499 kilometres on the Persian Gulf, and increased foreign military involvement in the area. The irony of the situation regarding the ousting of the Kuwaiti rulers, who had given the most open financial and political support to Iraq during the eight years of the Iran–Iraq war, did not pass unnoticed by the Iranians.[1] Despite this, the Iranian government adopted a policy of neutrality during the crisis.[2] Nonetheless, it condemned Iraq's invasion and formally adopted United Nations (UN) resolutions, 660 demanding Iraq's immediate withdrawal from Kuwait, and 661 imposing economic sanctions on Iraq and Kuwait.[3]

However, probably the most ironic of all the subsequent events for the Iranians was when the Iraqi air force decided to take refuge from the allied air attacks in Iran, a country which, for eight years, its mission had been bombardment.[4] Consequently, Iran, which was viewed largely in the West as a belligerent and an international law breaker, emerged from the Gulf conflict as a peacemaker and mediator.

The official Iranian stance during the crisis raised the hope that Iran was on the path of return to the international system and respect for its law and order. How far such an assessment was correct depended on how far Iran's view of world order issues, such as the invasion of Kuwait, coincided with that predominant in the West.

Although the area of the conflict between the Allied forces and Iraq during the crisis did not extend beyond the north-western part of the Gulf, it is significant that Iranian officials and mass media, along with their Western counterparts, adopted and used a similar vocabulary when describing events affecting the whole region. That is, they spoke of a crisis in the Persian Gulf, rather than merely referring to it as 'Iraq's invasion of Kuwait', or 'the US – Iraq war'. Whereas the vocabulary adopted was the same, this was not the case regarding perspective, which will be discussed here.

Study of Iran's perspective on the conflict provides an insight into the strategic thinking of the Iranian authorities, their security preoccupations, and the way they would be most likely to react in similar circumstances. In addition, although the strategic and economic importance of Iran has been written about widely, the relationship between these, the ideological developments which have taken place in Iran since the 1979 Revolution, the government's decision-making process, and the roles both of personalities and influential non-governmental institutions need to be analysed.

Finally, as the experience and successes of East-West security and arms control dealings in the 1980s illustrated, measures to improve confidence-building between states are vital in preventing war. This has been especially so between countries whose security interests have been perceived in many respects to be irreconcilable. Examples include the West and the Soviet Union before the advent of *perestroika*, or between an increasingly concerned liberal West and some Islamic nations. A better understanding of strategic thinking in these states is only one of the methods for improved confidence-building measures. An analysis of Iran's perspective on the Gulf conflict is a contribution towards that end.

An Overview of Iranian Beliefs and Responses to the Conflict

Iran's response to the Gulf conflict can best be understood within the context of its overall foreign policy prior to the event, and political developments within Iran following it. On the eve of Iraq's attack on Kuwait, Iran's position in the international system was unclear. Although it was slowly improving its relations with West European governments, there were still no diplomatic relations between Iran and the United Kingdom.

Amongst the Arab countries of the Middle East, there were no diplomatic relations with Jordan or Egypt, although the Iranian Foreign Ministry was using Syria to act as a mediator to pursue the possibility of establishing relations with Egypt.[5] Iran's relations with Saudi Arabia had been tense since the 1987 Hajj incident, when a group of about 400 Iranians were killed during a political rally and others injured, among them the wife of Imam Khomeini, Batool Khomeini. However, Iran's relations with Oman and the United Arab Emirates had remained close, even during the Iran–Iraq war. Its links with the other littoral states of the Gulf were improving rapidly.

Prior to the Iraqi invasion, Iran's foreign minister, Ali Akbar Velayati, had just paid an official visit to Kuwait for the first time since the start of the Iran–Iraq war.

Internally, President Rafsanjani, who had been elected on 17 August 1989, was successful in consolidating his power as head of the executive, at the expense of the religious extremists who held a majority in the *Majles* (Parliament). Economically, Iran was busily engaged in a reconstruction programme when, on 21 June 1990, a devastating earthquake struck its north-western province of Gilan and Zanjan. As a result of humanitarian gestures by Western governments towards the victims of that earthquake, and despite the controversy surrounding it, there were clear prospects for improved relations with the West, including the United States.[6]

At the time of Kuwait's annexation, a cease-fire had been in force between Iran and Iraq since 20 August 1988, but there was still no substantive progress on UN resolution 598 by which it had been achieved or on the terms of a peace treaty. Surprisingly, almost exactly one month before Iraq's invasion of Kuwait, on 3 July 1990, foreign ministers of Iran and Iraq agreed to meet in Geneva for direct peace talks for the first time.

Whilst peace negotiations were improving rapidly, the two countries' policies in OPEC were also becoming identical. Iran's oil minister, Gholamreza Aqazadeh, criticised Kuwait, the United Arab Emirates and Saudi Arabia for over-production and blamed these countries for the fall in oil prices. He told Reuters that 'Iran lost a billion dollars for every dollar the spot crude price fell.'[7] These developments formed the basis of much speculative analysis later in the press of the exiled Iranian opposition that Iran was involved in, or at least was informed of, the invasion of Kuwait by Saddam Hussein.[8] Some went as far as to suggest that a military alliance between the two countries was in existence.[9] However, this remained speculation and did not materialise.

The immediate Iranian reaction to news of the invasion was mocking. On one hand, the Iranians were somewhat jubilant over the demise of the ruling Kuwaiti régime, which was principally blamed for the direct introduction of foreign military forces in the region in Iraq's favour during the latter stages of the Iran–Iraq war. On the other, however, as the humanitarian and strategic implications of the invasion became clear, an intense internal debate unfolded, involving various personalities, the government and non-governmental institutions. Two distinct perspectives could be identified, which for convenience can be labelled as 'religious extremist' and 'religious moderate'. Although there were other perspectives in the complexities of Iranian politics, these two were the ones controlling legislative and governmental institutions. The term 'religious' is used to distinguish them from other extreme or moderate, nationalist, liberal and more secular views.

The relationship between these two religious groups is complex.[10] They were able to co-exist alongside one another, despite each pursuing different foreign policy objectives, mainly because they agreed on certain Islamic principles with regard to internal Iranian politics. Both groups agreed on the principle of *Velayate Faqih* (the Guardianship of Jurisprudence)[11] and the Islamic *Shari'a* (religious law). However, it is the religious extremists who have mainly been identified with the general violation of human rights in Iran and measures such as the stoning to death of convicted women and men. The religious moderates, whilst not publicly condemning these measures, have generally tended to adopt policies in line with Iran's international treaties and obligations, especially in the realm of foreign affairs.

The period between 2 August 1990 and 17 January 1991 can be characterised as a period of intense debate – on the nature of the conflict, on the question of whether there would be a war or not, and on the appropriate policy. As the crisis progressed, however, convergent opinions did not emerge and both groups continued their parallel existence from 17 January to 28 February. If Iran's response to the Gulf war can be summarised as a mixture of extreme rhetorical pronouncements, uttered by the religious extremists, and practical foreign policy, adopted by the religious moderates, then the United States was the prime victim of the rhetoric, whilst the Soviet Union, and France were the main beneficiaries of Iranian '*Realpolitik*'.

Iranian Response to the Foreign Military Intervention

There was a clear distinction between Iran's response to the military presence of the United States and Britain, on one hand, and other members of the alliance, on the other. The Islamic régime's antagonism towards the United States was neither for strategic-security reasons, nor because Iran had historically felt threatened by that country. On the contrary, the United States was traditionally viewed as a 'natural' strategic ally of Iran, a position which it continued to hold in the minds of many Iranians. The nature of Iranian antagonism was 'ideological'.

Extreme religious groups in Iran had long been in favour of establishing 'linkage' between disputes in the Middle East and Iranian politics. The proponents of such a 'linkage' policy (Mohtashami, for example) spent some of their lives in Lebanon and in Palestinian military camps, prior to the Revolution.[12] Their condemnation of the US stemmed not from its policies towards Iran but from its association with Israel. From their perspective, there was, and continued to be, a close link between the interests of the United States and Israel in the region, a link in which other Western powers were also directly or indirectly involved.

Such groups perceived the international system through Palestinian eyes.[13] Their aim was to establish an Islamic state throughout the Middle East and the whole world if possible; they were prepared to employ any means, violent or otherwise, to achieve that end. They wanted 'to serve Islam by means of Iran' rather than 'to serve Iran by means of Islam'.[14] They were so devoted to their ideological beliefs that they viewed Iranian interests only within the context of an overall Islamic interest.

However, the exact nature and definition of such interests was not always clear. This led them to adopt such contradictory policies that, at the start of the   Gulf conflict, they were demanding support for Saddam Hussein, whom they had been condemning for nearly a decade.[15] At the end of the crisis, however, they were faced with no option but to condemn him again, following his massacre of the Shi'as and Kurdish population, and especially because of Ayatollah Koh'i's arrest.[16]

Religious moderates and nationalist elements in Iran did not share the same values and perspective as these extreme religious groups. They preferred to separate Iranian politics from developments in the Middle East. Anti-Israeli, anti-Zionist slogans, much repeated in the press and by politicians, were largely alien to them and to most of the Iranian public. Even at the popular, non-governmental level, the Iranian people, many of whom had lost relatives in the Iran–Iraq war, hoped that the United States would destroy Saddam's military machine which had killed so many young Iranians during eight years of war.[17]

Iran viewed Britain's role in the region with great suspicion. This view   was based on psychological rather than politico-military factors. Iran was neither threatened by Britain's military presence in itself, nor was it afraid of that country's political links with the littoral states of the Gulf. Iran's largely psychological fear related to historical incidents, such as the British and Russian Empires' division of Iran into two major spheres of influence in 1907, or the Allied forces' invasion of Iran in 1945 to join ranks with the Soviet military to defeat Nazi Germany.[18]

In post-revolutionary Iran, the nature of Britain's threat to Iran was viewed within the context of its substantial political influence on the superpowers' policies in the region. It was significant that such a perspective on Britain's role was shared by both religious extremists and by moderates. This may partly explain the slower rate of progress in UK-Iranian relations *vis à vis* those with France, Germany or the Soviet Union. On 27 September 1990, Iran and the UK agreed to restore diplomatic relations, however, the formal exchange of ambassadors had yet to take place nine months later.

Iran's ties with France, Germany and other members of the European community remained close throughout the crisis. President Mitterrand phoned President Rafsanjani to discuss the Gulf crisis;[19] Iranian foreign minister Ali Akbar Velayati made official visits to Paris and Bonn.[20] Iran's friendly relations with France went back to the time when the first generation of Iranian students were sent to French universities to become acquainted with the skills of modern life. In the 19th and the early 20th Century, France and Germany were seen as 'neutral' countries, and in 'balance of power' terms, potential allies to help Iran combat Russian and British influence in the area. As a result, Iran allowed itself to be influenced by French culture, history and way of thought, and adopted some aspects of that country's civil law, and constitution, both in its 1908 and 1979 Revolutions.[21]

Similar strategic needs led Iran to maintain close contacts with Germany, even during the First and the Second World Wars, despite remaining officially neutral in both.[22] Iran's business connections with Germany also remained substantial, both during the Shah's reign and after the 1979 Revolution. These historical experiences created a positive, 'trustful' attitude towards these countries – to such an extent that it even overshadowed France's and Germany's substantial military assistance to Iraq during the eight years of the Iran–Iraq war. As Italy and the smaller members of the European Community had not been seen in recent history as a major threat to Iran, their presence in the Gulf was not regarded as significant.

Iran's cordial relations with the Soviet Union during the conflict were based on two sets of principles: the assertion of Iran's neutrality and bringing the conflict to a quick end in order to restrain the involvement of outside powers in the region. Iran's 'peace ideas' and its efforts to persuade Iraqi envoys travelling to Tehran and Moscow, via Iran, to withdraw from Kuwait, were to achieve these twin aims. The aims happened to be shared also by the Soviet Union. President Gorbachev phoned President Rafsanjani on 23 February to discuss them.[23] The Gulf conflict brought the two countries closer together, but that was not surprising. The nature of the relationship during the crisis was the logical continuation of Iran's foreign policy towards the Soviet Union prior to the conflict.

The Soviet Union, which inherited the Russian Empire, had traditionally been seen as the main potential threat to Iran's security, because of its geographical proximity, its military status as a superpower and, historically, its expansionist ambitions.[24] However, following its withdrawal from Afghanistan in February 1989 and the implementation of the policies of *glasnost* and *perestroika* in its

Moslem republics, Iran neither felt threatened by Soviet Marxist ideology nor by Soviet military might. Iran's cordial relations with the Soviet Union in recent years owed as much to the Soviet Union's preoccupation with its internal political, social and economic problems, as it did to the Islamic government's confidence in itself and its Islamic ideology .

Iran's response to the involvement of the neighbouring state of Turkey was interesting. Turkey's involvement was largely excused and understood to be inevitable for a member of NATO. President Rafsanjani, in reply to a question on Turkey's Persian Gulf policy, said that 'Turkey has not caused trouble in the Persian Gulf issue and in view of its membership of NATO the present situation is not unexpected.'[25]

The Iranian mass media did not criticize Turkey's contribution to the war and the use of its air bases by NATO members of the alliance, some minor and brief rhetorical pronouncements notwithstanding.[26] President Turgut Ozal of Turkey exchanged views with President Rafsanjani over the crisis on 4 August 1990. He came to Iran on 11 November 1990 and was in close contact with President Rafsanjani by telephone and via regular diplomatic channels throughout the conflict.[27]

On the subject of Iran's view of the Arab countries' involvement in the crisis, there was a distinction between the littoral states of the Gulf, the members of the Gulf Cooperation Council (GCC), and other Arab states. There was also a distinction between Syria and the rest. The presence of Egypt in the Gulf was generally viewed with great scepticism in the light of that country's manpower and military support to Iraq during the Iran–Iraq war.[28]

The contribution of the other countries in the Middle East was not seen as very significant with the exception of Syria's involvement. This was accepted and even welcomed by moderate elements in the Iranian government. It was expected that Syrian involvement would have a moderating influence on the United States' activities in the region. Such a positive attitude to Syria was largely due to that country's close support for Iran during the Iran–Iraq war. President Asad visited Tehran for talks with the Iranian leaders on 22 September 1990 and was in close contact with President Rafsanjani throughout the crisis.[29]

The involvement of the GCC states was seen as significant only in their potential use as a launch pad for an attack against Iran by extra-regional forces. Such a feeling of threat and insecurity was especially apparent in the earlier stages of the crisis when Iran was alarmed by some largely speculative analysis that the United States' presence in the Persian Gulf was to combat the Islamic Revolution of Iran, and that there was a plan to attack Iran after defeating Iraq. The Joint

Chief of Staff of the Pakistani Armed Forces, General Aslam Beig, warned Iran on 6 December 1990 that 'if the United States attacks Iraq, their next target will probably be Iran,'. He proposed the formation of a defence pact between Iran, Pakistan and Afghanistan.[30] Ali Akbar Mohtashami, a religious extremist, in a speech in the *Majles* said 'the U.S. and the other Western soldiers have come to the region in order to destroy the Iraqi war machine, and then is the turn of the Islamic Revolution of Iran and all liberation movements in the region.'[31]

The criticism levelled at Saudi Arabia during the crisis was consistent with Iran's belief and long-standing policy that Gulf security could be achieved only through the establishment of a regional security pact which embraced all the littoral states and was free from foreign military involvement. However, there were intense debates in Iranian newspapers over the nature and feasibility of such a pact, given the ideological differences amongst these states.[32]

Despite the controversy surrounding this topic, the Iranian Foreign Ministry actively pursued closer and friendlier relations with the GCC states. Even the Iranian Foreign Minister, Velayati, in a meeting with the Omani Foreign Minister in Tehran, expressed publicly the possibility of extending existing political and economic cooperation into the realm of security and defence.[33] After the end of the conflict, Iran's relations with all the GCC states, including Saudi Arabia, improved substantially. At a meeting on 5 May 1991, the GCC Ministerial Council recognised the importance of Iran's role in any future security arrangement in the Persian Gulf.[34]

The underlying theme in Iran's internal debate on the crisis illustrates a deep psychological concern about 19th Century-style Western imperialism in the Persian Gulf. In Iranian strategic thinking, a crude conspiratorial analogy is often used to explain regional and international events. This was the case regarding Iraq's occupation of Kuwait which was simply viewed as an excuse by the United States to establish its long-term presence in the area.

However, as far as foreign policy overall was concerned, Iran's response to the allied intervention in the Gulf was neither based on a simplistic condemnation of all Western forces in the region nor was it based on criticising all Arab states on racial grounds. Iran's response was a mixture of rhetorical pronouncements to satisfy internal and outside 'revolutionary' commitments, and a pragmatic foreign policy, determined by a set of strategic, historical and ideological considerations.

Implications for Regional and International Security

Iran's moderate posture and its neutral stance during the conflict was neither easy nor inevitable. The option of joining forces with Iraq was left open, especially in the event of an Israeli retaliatory attack on Iraq.[35] On a rare occasion, at a conference about the Palestinians held in Tehran, the Iranian Foreign Minister, Velayati, a religious moderate, said 'Over the past few weeks Israel has once again spoken of creating a "greater Israel", stretching from the Nile to the Euphrates.' On that basis he identified 'the Palestinian issue as one of Iran's strategic goals.'[36]

However, France and the Soviet Union's close relations with Iran during the crisis were very important to the maintenance of Iran's neutrality, as were those of Syria and Turkey. They provided a line of communication between a relatively isolated, nervous and concerned Iran and the Allies, especially in the earlier stages of the conflict between 2 August and 17 January.

France and the Soviet Union were successful in reassuring the moderates in the Iranian Foreign Office and President Rafsanjani that the Allied aim was confined to forcing Iraq out of Kuwait, and contrary to widespread rumour, there was no plan to attack Iran. In the absence of such a reassurance, there had been the possibility of Iran joining forces with Iraq under pressure from the religious extremists in the Majles.

Vladimir Petrovski, the Soviet Deputy Foreign Minister, during a visit to Iran on 28 November 1990, met President Rafsanjani and reassured him that 'The U.S. has said that it does not intend to remain in the region permanently . . .'[37] The establishment of relations with the United Kingdom in September also helped to relax attitudes towards the military presence of Western forces in the Persian Gulf. Consequently, the religious moderates could implement their policies, despite opposition from the extremists.

The difference between the religious extremists and the religious moderates, and their parallel existence in Iran, had significant ramifications for the future of regional and international security. As the former group could not base its hostility towards the United States and Israel on territorial, or historical grounds, it argued that there was an inherent and uncompromising conflict of interest between an Islamic Iran and a 'Zionist' United States. Hojatoleslam Kho'iniha, the head of the Centre for Strategic Studies, in a two-day conference on the Gulf crisis on 3 December 1990 said, 'There is a conflict of interest in principle between the Islamic Republic and US imperialism.' He said the US victory in the Gulf 'costs Iran more than Iraq's occupation of Kuwait.'[38] This makes the nature of the conflict ideological, dogmatic and, in comparison with other territorially-based security conflicts in the Middle East, less tangible, and consequently more difficult to resolve.

It was this kind of perceived ideological linkage that Saddam Hussein tried to exploit, by first accepting Iran's terms for a peace treaty on 15 August 1990, and then sending his top envoys, Tariq Aziz and Izzat Ibrahim, to Iran for further negotiations, in the hope of obtaining military or economic assistance.[39] However, the religious moderates proved that they were both able and willing to negotiate with the Western world and at the same time remain neutral in a regional conflict. Although the process of moderation in Iranian politics began well before the crisis, probably when Ayatollah Khomeini under a set of economic and political pressures, symbolically 'drank the poison' by accepting an end to the Iran–Iraq war in July 1988, the process was accelerated during the Gulf conflict. This was so especially after reassurances had been given that Iran was not an Allied target. It was significant that, about two weeks before the start of the ground war, according to the Tehran Times (7 February 1991), President Bush sent a letter to the Iranian authorities pledging that the US forces would be withdrawn from the region once the war with Iraq was over.[40]

Conclusion

As long as the religious moderates remained in control of Iran's Executive and the Foreign Ministry, they could be expected to continue to keep Iran away from any regional or superpower rivalry. However, it was unlikely that they would either give up their Islamic Revolutionary ideals or their covert support for the various revolutionary groups demanding political reform in the Gulf or other Middle Eastern countries. Nonetheless, at the same time, they could exert a moderating influence on some of the extreme religious groups in the Middle East.

The idea of a 'New World Order' was not generally welcomed by the Iranian authorities. References to it were sporadic; the concept was widely condemned as an American plot to usurp the world's resources. Although academic studies on the subject acknowledged the end of the Cold War era, they stated that an established set of rules of behaviour had yet to emerge. They understood the international system to be at a 'transitional juncture', linking the Cold War to the post-Cold War era. In relation to the Gulf conflict, they argued that the 'fluidity' of the rules and regulations during this period 'played a critical role in bolstering the misperception of the Iraqi leaders.'[41] Moreover, it was believed that the differences between the United States, the European countries and the Soviet Union would make any 'New World Order' unworkable and thus irrelevant.[42] However, the religious moderates responded favourably to the idea of a regional arms control process under the auspices of the United Nations. In a political commentary about Security Council Resolution 687 which dealt with the destruction of chemical, nuclear and biological weapons and (or) missiles with a range of over 150 km, applicable to all countries in the region, Iranian radio judged that it might be 'the last resolution concerning the current Persian Gulf crisis but it could be a prelude to addressing other problems of the Middle East region.'[43]

With regard to the future shape of regional and international security, it is probably easier to point to those aspects which were seen by Iran to increase insecurity rather than those which could promote security. First, there was a belief that any security pact based on purely Arab-nationalist aspirations and which therefore excluded others who were also willing to contribute, sowed the seeds of insecurity. Iranian radio in a commentary argued that the Damascus Declaration was 'not broadly based' and, so 'could be detrimental'.[44] Secondly, any concept of security which did not take into account popular demands for political, social and economic reform could also be expected to fail. Iran was very conscious of this aspect of security, which partly explained why leading religious personalities in their speeches addressed the people of the region rather than their rulers.[45]

However, what the Iranian government had not yet acknowledged was that an 'Islamic notion of security' which could increase feelings of insecurity among liberal, secular Western governments and the Soviet Union was also bound to fail. Although the concept of security had been broadened from its narrow military definition to include political, social and economic spheres, it had not yet been extended to 'human rights' issues. The absence of respect for human life in itself, in a region which had been witness to so much bloodshed, could undermine all other efforts to achieve security both at regional and international level.

Notes

1. Kuwait's foreign minister has estimated his country's financial contribution to Iraq during the Iran-Iraq war as being $14 billion; *Kayhan Hava'i*, 27 August, 1990.

2. On 3 August 1990, Ayatollah Mohammad Emami Kashani, a leading cleric and a member of the Council of Guardians, addressing the Friday prayer congregation at Tehran University said 'the fact that Kuwait supplied Baghdad with massive aid during the Iraqi-imposed war on Iran and supported Iraq in its aggression against Iran, does not stop us from condemning the Iraqi wrong action', *Kayhan Hava'i*, August 1990.

3. Regarding the imposition of the economic sanctions, President Rafsanjani admitted on 12 April 1991, at a Friday prayer speech, that during the conflict Iraq was importing foodstuffs from Iran to such an extent that the food prices in Iran increased unexpectedly. He added that although we were aware of this, we preferred to turn a blind eye to it; *Kayhan Hava'i*, 17 April 1991.

4. On 27 January 1991, Iran announced that 12 Iraqi aircraft had sought refuge in Iran. President Rafsanjani has denied any prior knowledge of them coming to Iran; *Kayhan Hava'i*, 13 February 1991. Any explanation on why they chose to go to Iran, and why Iran accepted them is still largely speculative. The number of these aircraft has been announced by Iran to be 22. Iranian Foreign Ministry Statement, 14 April 1991; BBC/SWB/ME, 16 April 1991 (A/3). However, Iraq has said there are 148 civil and military aircraft. Iraq's Foreign Minister, 12 April 1991; BBC/SWB/ME, 15 April 1991.

5. However, such moves were criticised by some in the media who saw no radical change in Egypt's position regarding the Palestinians, and the recognition of the state of Israel since the Camp David Treaty. *Kayhan Hava'i*, 25 July 1990.

6. For a brief summary of the comments by the various Iranian newspapers on the foreign relief assistance to the victims of the earthquake, see *Kayhan Hava'i*, 4 July 1990.

7. *Kayhan Hava'i*, 11 July 1990.

8. *Kayhan* (London), 9 August 1990.

9. *Nimrooz* (London), 20 July 1990.

10. The nature of the relationship has been described as 'kaleidoscopic' by R K Ramazani, 'Iran's Foreign Policy, Contending Orientations', in R K Ramazani (ed.), *Iran's Revolution, the Search for Consensus*, (Indiana University Press, Bloomington Indiana, 1990, p. 59).

11. For the first time in the *Shi'a* history, the principle of *Velayat-e Faqih* was introduced to the Constitution of a state at the beginning of December 1979, in order to ensure the presence of a supreme religious authority (either a person or an elected council), in the Iranian politics at all times.

12. See *Who's Who in Iran*, (Iran Research Group, MB Publishing Co Ltd., West Germany, 1990).

13. For example, Mohtashami spent part of his life in Najaf, famous for its theological schools in Iraq, studying under Ayatollah Khomeini's supervision in 1960s. He was also a member of the central council of the Militant Clergy abroad, and underwent military training in Palestinian camps. see *ibid.*, p. 201.

14. See Mohandes Mehdi Bazargan, *Engelab-e Iran dar Dow Harekat*, (Naraqi, Tehran, 1363 (1984/85), p. 111).

15. Ali Akbar Mohtashami, whilst criticising the US policies in the Persian Gulf, in a speech in the *Majles* said 'regional Muslims, and particularly Iranians, have a divine obligation to rise up and fight the apostate forces of the US, NATO and Zionists.' *Kayhan Hava'i*, 30 January 1990.

16. *Majles* deputies condemn 'massacre of Iraqi people,' Iranian Radio, 19 March 1991; BBC/SWB/ME, 20 March 1991.

17. Most Iranians were not convinced that the US would go to war with Iraq over Kuwait. Some newspapers argued that 'the West will not topple Saddam, unless a replacement is provided.' They predicted only a limited attack on Iraq. *Jumhoori Islami*, 24 November 1990. When the war started, the Anti-American demonstrations organised by some of the members of the Majles, were not popular. *Kayhan* (London), 24 January 1991.

18. For a historical analysis of Iran's foreign policy see, R Ramazani, *Iran's Foreign Policy 1941–1973: A Study of Foreign Policy in Modernizing Nations*, (University Press of Virginia, US 1975).

19. *Kayhan Hava'i*, 13 February 1991.

20. *Kayhan Hava'i*, 27 February 1991.

21. For the English translation of the text of the Constitution of 1906–1907 see *Iran Almanac*, 7, 1968. For the English translation of the text of the Constitution of the Islamic Republic of Iran see *Middle East Journal*, Vol. 34, No. 2, Washington 1980.

22. R Ramazani, *op. cit.,*.

23. Tehran radio, 23 February 1991; BBC/*SWB*/*ME*, 25 February 1991.

24. For an historical examination of the Soviet Union see, G Lenczowski, *Russia and the West in Iran 1918–1948: A Study in Big Power Rivalry*, (Greenwood Press, US, 1968).

25. *Kayhan Hava'i*, 13 February 1991.

26. Ayatollah Meshkini, *Qom* Friday prayer, denounces Turkey; Iran Radio, 18 January 1991; BBC/*SWB*/*ME*, 22 January 1991.

27. *Kayhan Hava'i*, 27 Febraury 1991.

28. *Ibid.*

29. *Ibid.*

30. *Kayhan Hava'i*, 12 December 1990.

31. *Kayhan Hava'i*, 30 January 1991.

32. *Kayhan Hava'i*, 12 December 1990.

33. 'Post War Era?' (Editorial); *Kayhan Hava'i*, 27 February 1991.

34. *Kuwait News Agency*, 5 May 1991; BBC/*SWB*/*ME*, 7 May 1991.

35. *Jumhoori Islami*, 19 January 1991; *Kayhan Hava'i*, 23 January 1991.

36. *Kayhan Hava'i*, 12 December 1990.

37. *Kayhan Hava'i*, 5 December 1990.

38. *Kayhan Hava'i*, 12 December 1990.

39. Mohajerani, the Legal and Parliamentary vice-President, during an interview on the Iranian TV, on 28 February 1991; BBC/*SWB*/*ME*, 4 March 1991.

40. *AFP*, 7 February 1991; BBC/*SWB*/*ME*, 9 February 1991.

41. Hooshmand Mirfakhraie, 'Miscalculation and Strategic Naivety in the Iraq-Kuwait Crisis', *The Iranian Journal of International Affairs*, Vol. II, Number 4, Winter 1990/1991, p. 561.

42. Commentary, Tehran Radio, 28 February; BBC/*SWB*/*ME*, 14 March 1991; and 12 March 1991; BBC/*SWB*/*ME*, 14 March 1991.

43. Commentary, Tehran Radio, 4 April 1991; BBC/*SWB*/*ME*, 6 April 1991.

44. Commentary, Tehran Radio, 6 March 1991; BBC/*SWB*/*ME*, 8 March 1991.

45. Iran's permanent representative to the United Nations, and a former member of the Supreme Defence Council, Kamal Kharrazi, in a conference on the Gulf Security at RIIA in London on 9 May 1991, expressed the need for a wider concept of security; BBC/*SWB/ME*, 13 May 1991.

7

The Soviet Involvement

James Gow

The most significant single feature of the Gulf crisis was what the Soviet Union did not do. It did not block American-led efforts to use United Nations mechanisms against Iraq. Whereas in 1958, when the new Ba'athist revolutionary, pro-Soviet régime gained power in Baghdad, Khrushchev had told the United States not to attempt to use force against Iraq (a characteristic attitude during the Cold War), in 1990 Gorbachev did not. Instead, the Soviet Union lent its support and worked co-operatively with the United States in opposition to Iraq's invasion of Kuwait. The Soviet approach to the crisis was a consistent continuation of the foreign and security policies promoted by Mikhail Gorbachev. There were, nonetheless, differences between the Soviet and American approaches. Those differences, as will be shown, were conditioned by the Soviet interpretation of the co-operative approach to international problems and by internal factors which constrained the leadership's room for manoeuvre: it could neither co-operate fully if it wished, nor impose significantly limitations on Washington when the two had different interpretations of co-operation.

Perestroika and Soviet External Policy

In the Gorbachev era, Soviet external policy was determined by domestic concerns. A pre-condition of internal reform was a secure international environment.[1] At the same time, there appeared to be a genuine desire for increased international co-operation at the heart of Gorbachev's 'new thinking'. This embraced a desire to increase the role played by international institutions, particularly the United Nations, in dealing with international problems.[2] One feature of particular relevance was the conclusion that the most likely cause of a clash with the West was involvement in regional disputes.

Emphasis, it was decided, should be placed on superpower co-operation in finding solutions acceptable to all the parties involved.[3]

The emphasis in Gorbachev's 'new thinking' was on the East-West axis, particularly on the relationship with the United States. However, there had also been significant, if lesser, developments in Soviet relationships with Third World countries. In the Middle East,[4] the major change was found in the Soviet Union's improving relations with Israel, with which diplomatic links had been broken in 1967. However, links with other Middle Eastern states had undergone improvement as well. Egypt, which had cut diplomatic links with the Soviet Union in 1981, was the subject of Soviet activity which produced a rapid *rapprochement*. There had been a period of improved relations with Iran, culminating only five days before Iraq invaded Kuwait, with the Iranian President, Ali Akbar Rafsanjani, making a call for the Soviets to be brought into closer co-operation with OPEC. Finally, the conservative Gulf states had also been courted. Diplomatic links had been established with Oman and the United Arab Emirates in 1985, and in 1988 with Qatar. However, efforts to woo Saudi Arabia had not led to the forming of official ties.

All this was in addition to long-standing links with Kuwait. The two countries had known fairly good relations since diplomatic links had been established in 1963 – much earlier than with any of the other conservative-Arab Gulf states. During the Iran-Iraq war, the Soviet Union had offered to give Kuwaiti ships escort. After the Americans re-flagged Kuwaiti ships, the Soviets leased three oil tankers to Kuwait in 1987, despite Iranian efforts to sink such vessels in the Gulf. Moreover, in 1988, Kuwait had signed an arms purchase agreement with the Soviet Union. Finally, at the time of the invasion, there were 900 Soviet citizens in Kuwait.

Despite a Treaty of Friendship and Co-operation signed in 1972, the Soviet-Iraqi relationship, both before and after that event, had been problematic.[5] Although the Soviets had initially supported the Ba'athist revolution in Iraq, there were a number of disagreements and disappointments in the following decades. In the political domain, the relationship was always strained. In part, this was due to Moscow's awkwardness in dealing with a régime which was, in essence, both anti-communist and anti-Kurdish. The Iraqi Communist Party was predominantly composed of Kurds; this made it a double enemy for the Ba'ath régime in Baghdad. Finally, during the Iran-Iraq war, the Soviet Union, although a long-time supplier of arms to Iraq, also supplied Iran at certain stages. The Soviets, clearly uneasy about the war, wavered between support of their uncertain Iraqi ally, which was renewing connections with the US, and strengthened relations with Iran. Soviet discomfort provided the impetus to its contribution at the UN in bringing the Iran-Iraq war to an end.

Iraq fell into both the categories of Soviet military involvement in the Third World identified by MccGwire – catch-all competition with the United States and China for influence; the need for an operational infrastructure to sustain Soviet strategy in the event of World war.[6] However, although the Soviet Union built Gulf naval facilities and also air-bases which would provide that infrastructure, it did not obtain use of the ports until 1968 – and on only one occasion (an airlift to Ethiopia) was permission given to use an airfield. The military aspects of the relationship with Iraq had been somewhat disappointing. Nonetheless, they were maintained and there was a sizeable contingent of Soviet military specialists in Iraq which grew from 1300 in 1967 to around 5000 in 1990. For this reason alone, Iraq, despite the unevenness of the relationship, was the Soviet Union's principal ally in the region.

The Iraqi Invasion, International Co-operation and Mediation

The initial Soviet response to the Iraqi invasion was determined by 'new thinking'. On 2 August, a Foreign Ministry statement rejected the Iraqi occupation of Kuwait and reiterated that the Soviet Union believed that 'no contentious issues, no matter how complicated, justify the use of force.'[7] Soviet policy was immediately aligned with that of the United States (US). The co-operative approach which was to characterise the crisis – especially in its initial phase – was conditioned by the already existing policies of 'new thinking', including collaboration with the US. It was also catalysed by the fact that the top foreign affairs men in both countries were already actively practising co-operation at the time of the invasion.

Soviet Foreign Minister Eduard Shevardnadze was with US Secretary of State James Baker at Irkutsk on 2 August when Iraq invaded Kuwait. They were able immediately to establish the basis for the co-operation which characterised the following months. On 3 August, they issued a joint statement calling on the international community to take practical steps in response. Soviet backing for the American line was underscored by a call for 'the immediate and unconditional withdrawal of Iraqi troops from Kuwaiti territory,' and the assertion that the 'sovereignty, national independence and territorial integrity of Kuwait must be fully restored and defended.'[8]

The two countries' rejection of Iraq's action was channelled through the United Nations. In the first week of the crisis, two Security Council resolutions, first demanding Iraqi withdrawal and then calling for mandatory sanctions, seemed to give the UN new life. Soviet support for the Americans in the United Nations coincided nicely with two pillars of the new era: co-operation with the US and strengthening of the UN.

There were many sceptics in the West who either distrusted Gorbachev's intentions or did not believe he could deliver with regard to *perestroika* and 'new thinking'. Doubts about 'new thinking' were particularly strong *vis à vis* the Middle East where critics argued that, even under Gorbachev, Soviet policy in the Middle East had not shown change, but rather has been characterised by continuity.[9] Soviet behaviour throughout the crisis, but most of all in the crucial early stages, demonstrated that there had indeed been change.

The Soviet Union might have behaved traditionally: it could have supported Iraq, it could have remained non-committal and it certainly could have opposed the deployment of US troops in the Middle East. It did none of these things. Accepting the deployment of American troops in Saudi Arabia went against the grain of all earlier Soviet policy in the region – to keep the Americans out. This matter was particularly sensitive, given the proximity of the Gulf to the Soviet Union's southern borders. However, the Soviets were satisfied with American assurances that troops would be withdrawn at the earliest opportunity. In the past, the Americans had often judged Soviet support for anti-American régimes in the Third World as an obstacle to US assistance in helping the Soviet Union over its economic ills. Soviet support for the US line added to the credibility of 'new thinking'.

Soviet support for the United States improved the country's image in the West as an international actor. This was confirmed in the supportive speeches of both Bush and Baker. The USSR's general acquiesence in the first months of the crisis gained it Western goodwill and increased the prospects of obtaining economic assistance. A senior State Department spokesman declared the US to be 'exceptionally pleased with the Soviet role'; 'Without the current Soviet position, the whole color [*sic*] of the problem would be totally different'.[10]

The central plank of policy in this opening phase was good relations with the Americans – as it had been throughout the era of 'new thinking'. The Gulf crisis provided an opportunity to confirm the new relationship and the post-Cold War order. In this crisis, senior figures emphasised, much depended on 'Soviet-American solidarity, on parallel or joint activity, on mutual support.'[11] In this connection, the Soviets provided the Americans with information on weaponry which had been sold to Iraq. This was more a symbolic gesture of the new co-operation between the two countries, rather than a real help; as some Soviets readily pointed out, the CIA almost certainly knew more already. Support for US policy was most significant at the UN. Baker made it particularly clear that Soviet support was essential in the passage of UN resolutions. Whereas opposition would have prevented concerted international action through the

UN, Soviet support made it much easier for the Americans to persuade other countries to join the endeavour.

Indeed, the Soviet Union used the crisis to strengthen the position of the United Nations in world politics – one of the key aims of Gorbachev's 'new thinking'. The Soviets voted unhesitatingly for three UN resolutions which called on Iraq to withdraw its troops, imposed an immediate economic and military embargo on the new Kuwaiti 'puppet' government and condemned and invalidated Iraq's subsequent annexation of Kuwait. The emphasis on the UN helped preserve some of the standing that the Soviet Union had clearly been losing in recent years as it retreated from superpowerdom. The UN legitimacy sought by the anti-Iraqi coalition gave the USSR a more significant role in the course of events than would otherwise have been the case unless it had committed an armed force. In a sense, the Soviet Union was able to have two pieces of cake and eat them both: through co-operation with the US and breathing new life into the UN, it was carrying out the principles of 'new thinking'; at the same time, it was retaining prestige and a principal role.

The Soviets were also trying to manage a third piece of cake. Moscow sought to gain Western approval, do what was right and still maintain links with Iraq. There were good economic reasons for wanting to keep contact with Iraq. The USSR was owed US \$5bn and stood to lose \$6bn if the contracts for services of Soviet military specialists in Iraq were broken.[12] Shevardnadze noted that \$800m worth of oil would be lost due to reduced shipments from Iraq.[13] This might have been compensated for by increased income from Soviet oil sales at a higher price. However, economic interest in Iraq had to be calculated against the possibility that debts would not be repaid and, more importantly, economic interests along the Soviet Union's primary foreign policy nexus with the West. There had to be some consideration of the impact that higher prices might have on the West. Western economies hit by high oil prices would find it increasingly difficult to give the Soviet Union the aid it sought.[14] (Very soon, of course, the oil price stabilised.)

The Soviet Union looked to play an intermediary role in the resolution of the crisis for which, as Vladimir Belyakov for one noted, it was well suited.[15] This was based on the country's long-standing ties with Iraq, its long-term good relationship with Kuwait, its emerging contacts with Saudi Arabia and its common interest with the United States. Policy was based on the premise that the Soviets had to be able to talk to both sides if they were to play a role in finding a solution.

In other regards, whilst always giving priority to its relationship with the US, the Soviet Union tried to plough a middle furrow. For example, although the USSR voted in the Security Council to employ coercion to enforce the embargo, it also abstained on a Cuban proposal to allow a free flow of food and medicine into Iraq. The Soviets also offered *de facto* compliance with Iraq's absorption of Kuwait by evacuating the embassy building there. However, in principle, it was insisted, the embassy remained open.[16] Finally, the Soviet Union did not cancel its Treaty of Friendship and Co-operation with Iraq. But, neither did it really honour it; its support for the Security Council vote allowing for the use of force can hardly be taken as a measure to secure Iraq.

The USSR not only maintained links with Iraq – and therefore a channel of communication – but also improved its relations with many of the less radical Arab régimes. The Soviet Union had been encouraging improvements in its contacts with the Gulf states in order to complete diplomatic ties with them. On 17 September, diplomatic relations were restored between the USSR and Saudi Arabia after a fifty two year break. Eleven days later, links were established for the first time with Bahrain.

The Soviet Foreign Minister wanted it to be clear that his people 'were and remain friends of the Arabs.'[17] This applied not only to the Arabs of the Gulf. The Soviets appealed to other Arabs by sharing with Iraq and several Arab states the view that any resolution of the Gulf conflict had to deal with the Arab-Israeli conflict as well. The long-standing Soviet proposal for an international Middle East peace conference (which would involve the Palestinian problem) was resurrected by Shevardnadze. However, this was not overemphasised. The Soviet position oscillated, with Foreign Ministry spokesman Gennadii Gerasimov saying that the situation in Kuwait could not be tied to other matters in the region.[18]

Overall, Soviet policy from August to December left the USSR well placed to build on its relations in almost all quarters if the crisis had a peaceful outcome and yet unlikely to be damaged by a messy war. However, its situation was not as healthy as it might have been. The prospect was limited by internal divisions and pressures about the nature and course of Soviet policy, particularly on the vexed question of the use of force. Ultimately, the pressures engendered shifted the emphasis of Soviet policy and caused the resignation of Shevardnadze.

Using Force and Shevardnadze's Resignation

The first sign of a significant difference in the Soviet leadership was Gorbachev's introduction of a special envoy, Evegenii Primakov, to visit Iraq, Europe and the United States during October. Primakov was both a close advisor to the President and an expert in Middle Eastern policy, who had had contacts with Saddam Hussein since

1969. Primakov's appointment followed criticism from 'Arabists' that policy on Iraq had been formed without reference to them; the team involved in negotiations with the West on European questions had automatically shifted to co-operating with the Americans on the Middle East.

Primakov's introduction represented friction in the Soviet leadership and a snub for the foreign ministry. Shevardnadze had declared his willingness to visit Iraq a month earlier. The Foreign Ministry believed that sending Primakov would signal a split to Saddam Hussein. That split, which would be perceived to be within both the Soviet leadership and, by extension, the Soviet-American alliance, would allow Saddam Hussein to think there were options open to him.

The special envoy's involvement showed that there was clearly a conviction in some quarters that the Soviet Union, in the person of Primakov, could persuade Saddam Hussein to withdraw from Kuwait – or at a minimum to release all hostages. Gorbachev and Primakov thought they were in a position to hold sway with the Iraqi leader. Shevardnadze was not convinced of this. He did not believe his country could seriously affect Iraq more than any other given the way the Soviets had initially and wholly sided with the United States; he was more concerned about how Soviet behaviour in the crisis affected the USSR's standing in other parts of the world.

Primakov's second visit to Baghdad brought considerable optimism. He convinced and persuaded Gorbachev that the Iraqi leader was ready to see the light. Reports circulated that Saddam was now prepared to release all hostages and was moderating his stance on Kuwait – which softening was taken to be a precursor to withdrawal. However, Primakov had evidently either misunderstood or been 'stiffed'. Saddam neither released Soviet citizens as promised nor showed any sign of withdrawal.

The outcome of this visit led Gorbachev to pass the initiative back to the Foreign Ministry. On 14 November, two deputy foreign ministers were sent on a Middle Eastern tour which did not include Baghdad. Another indication was the sudden replacement of Gennadii Gerasimov as (in effect) the Soviet Union's public relations officer. Head of Information at the Foreign Ministry, Gerasimov had been widely perceived as Gorbachev's personal spokesman. In that guise, he had made statements seemingly contradicting Shevardnadze, particularly in the initial phase of the crisis when the Foreign Ministry was keen to link the crisis to Middle Eastern problems in general. Moreover, Gerasimov's successor, Vitalii Churkin, was a close aide of Shevardnadze.

Primakov's mission to act as go-between and to seek a political solution was a counterweight to calls for the use of force to be sanctioned. There was obviously a difference between the President and his Foreign Minister on the country's role in the crisis. The possible use of force had become an issue at the end of September when Shevardnadze had warned Iraq that the UN could be empowered to use force and found himself unable to rule out a resort to military means; he even warned that in extreme circumstances, USSR would participate in UN approved military action, although in principle it would be better to rule out the military option.[19]

Gorbachev, on the other hand, refused to acknowledge any possibility of using force, suggesting that to do so would represent a return to the old ways.[20] The Foreign Minister had voiced his opposition to the speed and scale of the US military build-up in the early stages of the crisis. This had been guided by worries (not necessarily his own) about the proximity of the force to the Soviet Union's southern borders. Shevardnadze later, though, made several statements indicating a harder line which might allow for force to be employed. He believed that it was necessary to shadow the US. His understanding was that only a tough joint stand could prevent the Americans from becoming the dominant force in the region. To this end (and complementing the policy of enhancing the role of the UN), he secured a partial resurrection of the long dormant Military Staff Committee of the Security Council – although this did not lead very far.

Gorbachev was content to see US-Soviet co-operation at its new level. But he regarded a hard-line policy and a resort to war as outside the scope of the new ways.[21] The use of force ran counter to the precepts of 'new thinking' – and Gorbachev was clearly attached to many of its values. If the use of force was not an acceptable entry in the modern lexicon of international relations, then the precept applied also to the US and the coalition it was assembling in the desert. Gorbachev met President Bush in Paris at the time of the signing of the Charter of Paris. Despite indications from Shevardnadze and Primakov that the Soviet Union was beginning to regard the possible use of force as a necessary feature of the UN Gulf strategy,[22] Gorbachev remained reluctant publicly to sanction it.

Moreover, in practical terms, a decision on force would disturb the balancing act the USSR had performed between the US and Iraq throughout the crisis. It would also increase the President's vulnerability to criticism from conservative and military circles, as well as from Soviet Muslims. Most of all, any decision to admit the use of force would present the Soviet leader with a dilemma: to add Soviet troops to those in the Gulf or to permit a military action without Soviet participation.

The related questions of military deployment and military use cast a shadow over Soviet policy from the beginning of the crisis. First, there had been a naval blockade to reinforce UN sanctions on Iraq.

Foreign Ministry spokesman Iuri Gremitski said on 9 August that, at that stage, there was no question of the USSR participating in a multinational force or sea blockade outside the jurisdiction of the United Nations. Soviet naval vessels deployed from the Indian Ocean. Symbolically the presence of Soviet ships was important in the West, although it was not clear to what extent they were active in supporting the blockade. The ships were said to be protecting Soviet maritime traffic, although Baker said Shevardnadze had told him the ships were for use in the international blockade. Soviet reluctance to participate more fully was justified on the grounds that they were simply not equipped for this sort of operation.

The army, scarred by its involvement in Afghanistan and in dissident republics, was reluctant to get embroiled in what it feared would be a messy foreign adventure – an adventure, moreover, against a state that the military still essentially thought of as an ally. Shevardnadze was made well aware of this feeling in the military by an army political officer and People's Deputy, Nikolai Sergeevich Petrushenko. He and his colleagues, he advised, were struggling to adapt to the Foreign Ministry's ever-changing views.[23] Nonetheless, the Soviet Union would quite obviously lose even more of its influence and superpower status if it were not to commit troops. It could not reasonably expect to influence US policy and strategy in any serious way if it did not have any troops involved. Moreover, its international standing had always been based essentially on its military might.

One critic mocked Shevardnadze, after his resignation, for having been the architect of Soviet withdrawal from Afghanistan, on the one hand, and then having become a noisy militarist out of a wish to 'show that our country is still a great power.' He pointed out that, in fact, military might had been the Soviet Union's only means of maintaining world status and that it was the former foreign minister who had been primarily responsible for undermining that status by leading the policy of military retreat. Now, he wrote, 'we are losing international authority faster than we are destroying missiles.'[24]

Opposition to the use of force united both new and old thinkers. Where the military had trouble keeping up with the Foreign Ministry, the liberals, on the one hand, opposed the use of force in principle, and on the other, saw it as a recipe for disaster. This meant that if there were military action, the Soviet Union would be better off out of it. One commentary in the liberal paper *Komsomolskaia Pravda* urged the Soviet Union to do 'nothing'. The crisis, it was said, had enabled the country to improve its standing internationally by influencing events in the UN. This was particularly true of its position with regard to Arab countries. 'If we blindly follow US policy we shall continue playing second fiddle at best or pay for our mistakes with the lives of Soviet people at worst.'[25] With enormous objections from radicals and conservatives, there was little chance that the Soviet Union would (indeed could) send troops to the Gulf.

The reality of this was underlined by the legal position with regard to the deployment of forces outside the country's borders. Such a move was only possible with the approval of the Supreme Soviet; such approval was not going to be possible with all sides opposed to it. The President could only commit troops without reference to the Supreme Soviet if the country were subject to an act of external aggression. Any serious attempt to deploy troops would have antagonised many constituencies on all sides and aggravated the internal divisions which were already weakening the Soviet Union in all senses.

The common point of opinion between radicals and conservatives in the Soviet Union was the non-commitment of force. Shevardnadze's real fault was to suggest that the Soviet military might go to the Gulf, at least symbolically. Shevardnadze, by suggesting that his country might send some troops and by signing the UN resolution sanctioning the use of force and setting the Iraqis a 15 January deadline, alienated the larger part of the Soviet élite. However, for setting the deadline, he had the somewhat reluctant support of his President.

The Soviets did seem to persuade the Americans to set 15 not 1 January as the deadline. This, allowed the Soviets to have some influence on events as Resolution 678 on the use of force was debated in the United Nations at the end of November. It also gave them a last hope of achieving a political solution. Gorbachev and Shevardnadze had gained a 'pause for peace'. However, sanction of the use of force also indicated that the bottom line of Soviet policy was keeping in line with the Americans. This was more important than principles of 'new thinking' such as the non-use of force, important though that clearly appeared to be for the Soviet President.

By mid-December, Shevardnadze was besieged from all sides, in particular by the conservatives, who launched an all-out attack on his foreign policy, lambasting his 'pro-Americanism'. Whilst defending himself against charges which seemed to make him out to be the chief architect of military developments in the Gulf, he did warn the Supreme Soviet that circumstances might arise in which the executive might be forced to act without consulting the parliament.[26] This seemed to indicate that he and Gorbachev might order the deployment of troops, by-passing the Supreme Soviet as they did so. But the President did not back his foreign minister. This left Shevardnadze little option but to resign.

Shevardnadze's removal did not cue a change in policy. The central principles of 'new thinking' – non-confrontation and non-interference in other countries' affairs would remain intact. However, there were expected to be some changes in the content of foreign policy which could not remain 'as it was'.[27] What those changes would be was open to question as Soviet policy was somewhat adrift during a crucial month leading up to the appointment of a Foreign Minister, Aleksandr Bessmertnykh, and the 15 January deadline by which Iraq had to withdraw from Kuwait or risk a US-led offensive.

War and the New Foreign Minister

Shevardnadze's resignation and the pressures which caused it worried the Americans, who showed signs of losing faith in Gorbachev and US-Soviet co-operation. That Washington had come to doubt its recent trust in Moscow was evident as the US-led offensive approached. Soviet pleas for time to attempt to achieve an eleventh hour diplomatic resolution of the crisis were rejected. So too was a request for 48 hours notice of any assault; the Soviets were given only one hour's notice. That notice was relayed to the Soviet embassy in Baghdad which was reported to have informed the Iraqis.

When the attack came, the Soviet Union was taken by surprise. It was also pushed very much into the background for two weeks as the US-led air assault on Iraq was loosed. As the war built up, Soviet worries about the proximity of activities to their southern borders increased, especially as the US use of bases in Turkey grew. The Soviets were greatly concerned that a vicious war was being carried out in what they saw as their own back yard. Soviet Armed Forces in the Transcaucasus were put on full alert and air defence there was strengthened. However, the Soviet Union's principal response was diplomatic.

Diplomatic activity to try and create a consensus to end the conflict now became intense. This reflected Gorbachev's need to dissociate himself from the US position in order to show both Soviet Muslims and the Arab world that the Soviet Union wanted to be distanced from military actions which seemed to be beyond the terms of the UN resolution. Bessmertnykh, the new Foreign Minister, made it clear that apart from the obvious importance of contacts with the US, the Soviet Union was concentrating its relations with countries 'directly adjacent to our state.'[28]

Within the USSR, support for Iraq and protest against the prosecution of the war were growing. There was a series of demonstrations outside the US embassy in Moscow. One Muslim leader warned that the war had 'given rise to deep pain in the hearts of Muslims.'[29] There was a vote in Uzbekistan to send volunteers to fight for Saddam Hussein. As he struggled to prevent the Soviet Union from collapsing, Gorbachev's calculations had to include popular opinion in the Muslim republics.

There were other pressures from within the Soviet Union. The longer the war went without a cease-fire, the stronger became the voices of the hard-line conservatives for the Soviet authorities to distance themselves from the US conduct of the war and even from their policy. The rise of the conservatives, signalled in Shevardnadze's ouster, was further proven by the use of armed force in the Baltic republics in January, where there were fifteen deaths. This put further strain on relations with the US, although some awareness of Gorbachev's being hostage to the conservatives added to the American need not to encounter Soviet opposition in the Gulf and tempered criticism.

Domestically, the conservatives were generating pressure on the Gulf issue.[30] Doubts were cast on American aims and Gorbachev described relations as fragile. American mistrust was evident in the detention by US and Spanish naval forces of a Soviet merchant vessel said to be carrying arms to Jordan. There were also renewed allegations that Soviet military advisors were still inside Iraq, although these were denied.

In US behaviour (particularly prosecution of the war – seemingly – beyond the UN resolutions) Gorbachev saw that neither Shevardnadze's support of the US nor their joint faith in the UN was enough: the Soviet Union needed to have its own profile in international affairs in order to show that it did not approve of what many thought to be a misuse of the UN and if it were not to be marginalised. These considerations and pressures meant that Gorbachev, whilst continuing to support the UN policy, was under pressure to give Soviet policy a new profile and to press for peace. This was also the task of the new foreign minister.

Two weeks into his new job, Bessmertnykh was able to make his first impact. On 29 January, he and Baker issued a joint statement. The statement appeared to be a new initiative for peace and, certainly, a softening of the American position. 'The ministers continue to believe that a cessation of the hostilities would be possible if Iraq would make an unequivocal commitment to withdraw from Kuwait. They also believe that such a commitment must be backed by immediate concrete steps leading to full compliance with the Security Council's resolutions.' They continued to affirm their agreement to promote jointly Arab-Israeli peace and regional stability in the aftermath of the Persian Gulf crisis. This was essentially a reworking of the French proposal on the eve of the launching of coalition military action. It represented a US softening because it took Saddam's statement of intent to be enough. Previously, only the start of withdrawal would have satisfied the Bush Administration.

The Americans quickly made noises to the effect that there was no shift of position. Their discomfort was eased by Saddam Hussein who failed to produce an unequivocal commitment to order a retreat from Kuwait. It would be another two weeks before the Iraqi leader showed any sign of constructive concession. Even then, there remained considerable ambiguity about his intention. In the meantime, the Baker-Bessmertnykh proposal went on to the back burner, to be reheated in the months after the war had ceased.

A consequence of this and another product of conservative pressure on the leadership was the renewal of Primakov's mandate. He was again dispatched to Baghdad on 12 February in the hope of securing a deal which would avert a ground war. He was also able to take with him the possibility of certain Soviet guarantees in the event of a withdrawal.

The initiative emerged from a series of contacts between Iraq and the USSR. The key was Iraq's ambiguous statement of 15 February, which indicated that there could be some give in the Iraqi position at last. That statement itself had been prompted by Primakov's cajoling of the Iraqi leadership during his visit to Baghdad on 12 February. The initiative, as well as a concession to conservative pressure, also reflected the genuine concern of many inside and outside the Soviet Union, notably the Soviet leadership, that military activity was going beyond the mandate of Security Council Resolution 678. Gorbachev had already expressed such an opinion ten days earlier whilst affirming his country's support for the UN resolutions.

With the anti-Iraqi coalition all set to launch its ground offensive, Gorbachev attempted to provide Iraq with sufficient guarantees to enable it to surrender. Although details of the scheme were not released, they were understood to include an offer of Soviet protection of Iraq's existing borders, opposition to any attempts to punish either Saddam Hussein personally or his country, and a promise of future discussions on regional problems such as the occupied territories. The message should have been clear – accept this, or else. Although these could be interpreted as conditions, Primakov was insistent on American television that the essential part of the plan was unconditional withdrawal from Kuwait.[32]

This move put the Soviets in the limelight for a moment. Given the importance of Soviet support thus far in the crisis, Bush could not afford to dismiss the proposal. Although he said it was short of what was required, he was not in a position to reject it outright. To do so could have undermined US-Soviet cooperation not only in the Gulf, but in Europe and other parts of the world.

It was clearly felt in some quarters that the purpose of the initiative itself was to damage US-Soviet co-operation. The Arabist-Foreign

Ministry dispute became a slanging match. Men from the ministry told their American counterparts that Primakov was acting on his own, a 'wild card', although quite clearly the initiative had the President's backing. Officials, such as Sergei Tarasenko, a department chief, even announced why proposals for a peace plan to stave off the ground offensive should be unacceptable to Bush. He attacked Gorbachev and Primakov for not understanding that a totalitarian régime 'can only be liquidated'.[33]

Meanwhile, hawks in the United States condemned Soviet duplicity and suggested that the Soviet move was intended to undermine the American stand. For them, Gorbachev's objective was to obstruct the coalition's total victory. However, that victory was not to be delayed. After a momentary pause to see what happened, the ground offensive was unleashed and within days the fighting was over.

After the War

The American-led coalition scored a stunning victory. This left the Soviets somewhat in the shadows, especially after their efforts to avert the ground campaign. The US attitude was demonstrated by Bush's reference not to its superpower ally, but to a 'significant major country'.[34] In his victory address to Congress, Bush did not mention the Soviet role. The importance of the Soviet Union's role in allowing events to shape the way they did was forgotten. Only a US success was now in mind and the memory of what seemed like Soviet efforts to hamper it.

The decline and imminent demise of the Soviet Union appeared to be confirmed in the post-war phase when it became clear that Washington might sometimes need Soviet support still, but had little respect for a fading power, it was thought. Belief in the possibilities of co-operation had been exaggerated, not only in terms of Soviet capabilities, it seemed, but also of American commitment. American belief in a new world order, many thought, was less a question of the co-operation envisaged in 'new thinking', but of a *pax Americana* which they were happy to see the Soviets define as a new world order and support.

Once there was a cease-fire, Soviet-American relations picked up. Soviet leaders began to claim some credit for the successful outcome of the crisis. On 28 February, Bessmertnykh described 'the result of the collective effort of all the states which took part in seeking a settlement . . . including the US, other members of the coalition and the Soviet Union.'[35] He said it was a triumph for the entire international community, rather than any particular states: 'Each country which participated in the settlement of this crisis can claim part of the success. No party can claim the success single-handedly.'[36] Vitalii

Ignatenko, Gorbachev's spokesman, declared that the 'entire world community, and not only the men who fought on the battlefields, has scored a huge victory'.[37]

Despite the fact of the USSR's key role, none of this had much impact. However, as initial elation settled, it emerged that the US-Soviet relationship was salvageable; the relationship with the Americans remained the central plank of Soviet policy. The Soviets had had little choice but to back the Americans, according to Bessmertnykh: as the Cold War ended, it was important to avoid a precedent where 'a big country swallows up another one whilst bearing no responsibility to the world community.'[38] Bessmertnykh censured Soviet critics who had challenged the Gulf policy. He also made clear that he believed US-Soviet relations had withstood the test of the crisis.

As the months progressed, Soviet-American co-operation in the Middle East was renewed. Baker and Bessmertnykh worked jointly to prosecute a peace programme for the Middle East, although the running was again left to the Americans. Co-operation was found in other quarters. The Soviets also assisted in providing an air bridge for operations to supply the Kurds in northern Iraq. However, they avoided being drawn too closely into that post-war crisis. This was due to sensitivities about obvious meddling inside the boundaries of a sovereign state, sensitivities which reflected the Soviet Union's own concern about its problems with rebellious republics and peoples.

These internal traumas remained the Soviet Union's principal concern. The military destruction of Iraq accentuated them. A large body of opinion in the Soviet Union had previously rushed to accept some kind of integration with the West on the understanding that America could do no wrong. These people were unhappy at what they perceived to be efforts by Gorbachev to frustrate the coalition's victory. Others who had embraced the concepts of co-operative security, were disappointed with the way the United Nations' resolutions seemed to have been overridden by United States priorities from a different agenda. Most of all, conservatives and military critics were alarmed.

The US victory, especially, its manner, caused a Soviet military rethink and gave grounds for pressures to increase defence spending. The Soviets were well aware that the Americans had been using the conflict, in part, as a testing and learning experience. The Soviets themselves were also using it to much the same ends, as a flow of statements and analyses from Soviet institutes testified.[39] It seemed possible that there would be an attempt to reverse the changes in doctrine which had permitted the whole era of *perestroika* and 'new thinking'. 'Defensive' or 'non-offensive' defence was coming to be regarded as an impossible model for defence: how could Soviet

Armed Forces plan to fight an in-depth defensive war for five days, as was foreseen, when the American display in the Gulf suggested that within five days there might be little defensive and no counter-offensive capability remaining? The American suppression of and penetration of Soviet-made air defence systems also gave pause for heavy thought.

Although, the asymmetrical co-operation evident in handling of the crisis augured the possible resolution of regional conflicts, the Gulf confirmed that the days of the Soviet Union as a superpower were over. Shevardnadze's policy of managed withdrawal was transposed by the Gulf crisis into collapse. By abandoning competition with the US in favour of support for American positions, Moscow left itself with few options for influencing events. The domestic weakness which had been a prompt for 'new thinking' and the internal divisions resulting from it, severely limited Moscow's scope. Domestic divisions had prevented the Kremlin from pursuing co-operation fully if it wished; internal debility meant that it was not strong enough to limit Washington when the two had different interpretations of co-operation. Moscow's future appeared increasingly to be confined to minor amendment of American policy – not only in the Middle East, but everywhere – as the decline of the Soviet's role as a superpower increasingly became the demise of the Soviet Union itself.

Notes

1. See Alex Pravda, 'Introduction: Linkages between Soviet Domestic and Foreign Policy under Gorbachev', Tsuyoshi Hasegawa and Alex Pravda, eds., *Perestroika: Soviet Domestic and Foreign Policies*, (Sage for the RIIA, London, 1990, p.3).
2. Michael MccGwire, *Perestroika and Soviet National Security*, (The Brookings Institution, Washington D.C., 1991, pp.228–9).
3. See Margot Light, 'Soviet Policy in the Third World', *International Affairs*, 67, 2, 1991, p.270.
4. On Soviet Policy in the Middle East, see Galia Golan, *Soviet Policies in the Middle East: From World War II to Gorbachev*, (C.U.P., 1990, pp.258–90).
5. See Golan, *op. cit.*, p.158ff.
6. MccGwire, *op. cit.*, p.133.
7. *TASS*, 2 August 1990.
8. *TASS*, 9 August 1990.
9. See, for example, Robert O. Freedman, *Moscow and the Middle East: Soviet Policy Since the Invasion of Afghanistan*, (Cambridge University Press, Cambridge and New York, 1991).
10. Quoted in *International Herald Tribune*, 21 September 1991.
11. *Krasnaia Zvezda*, 2 October 1990.
12. *Izvestiia*, 4 September 1991.

13. *TASS*, 11 September 1990.
14. See Lev Strzhizzhovskii, 'Neprostoi Vopros', *Pravda*, 17 August 1990.
15. *Pravda*, 25 August 1991.
16. *The Independent*, 25 August 1990.
17. Quoted in *Le Monde*, 27 August 1990.
18. *The Financial Times*, 7 September 1991.
19. *The Guardian*, 26 September; *IHT* 10–11 November 1990; Richard Weitz, 'The Gulf Conflict and the USSR's Changing International Position' *Report on the USSR*, 12 October 1990.
20. See for example his speech during a visit to Spain, *Pravda*, 26 October 1990.
21. *Pravda*, 29 October 1991.
22. Primakov, whilst still favouring talk rather than force, accepted that force might now become necessary. He qualified this by counselling that if force were threatened it should be used promptly: if use of force were introduced it should not be an idle threat – otherwise the wrong signals would be given to Baghdad. *IHT*, 16 November 1990.
23. *Izvestiia*, 16 October 1990.
24. Aleksandr Gol'ts 'A Khvatit li nam posylok', *Krasnaia Zvezda*, 4 January 1991.
25. A Vasiliev, 'Should we send our boys to the Arab desert?', *Komsomolskaia Pravda*, 25 October 1990.
26. Judith Perrera, 'Shevardnadze's impossible position', *Middle East International (MEI)*, 11 January 1991.
27. Gol'ts, *loc. cit.*
28. *Pravda* 31 January 1991.
29. Shaik al-Islam Allashukur Pasha Zade. quoted by Judith Perrera, 'Anxious for peace', *MEI*, 8 February 1991.
30. *The Wall Street Journal Europe*, 22 February 1991 carried a survey of critical articles in the Soviet press.
31. *Pravda*, 13 February 1991. Some Western reports put the number of Soviet specialists in Iraq at 4,000. The Soviets officially had 193 'military specialists' there, the last of whom left on 10 January 1991; however, 111 Soviet civilians were said to have stayed in Iraq of their own volition. *Krasnaia Zvezda*, 12 February 1991, removing some of the mystery around these specialists, said that few of these were military officers; most were civilian engineers and technicians.
32. Jules Kogan, 'The end game', *MEI*, 22 February 1991,
33. Quoted by Dev Muraka, 'A winter of discontent', *The Middle East*, April 1991, p.24.
34. Muraka, *loc. cit.*, p.24.
35. *Izvestiia*, 1 March 1991.
36. *The Guardian*, 1 March 1991.
37. *The Daily Telegraph*, 1 March 1991.
38. Quoted by Judith Perrera, 'Caught by surprise', *MEI*, 25 January 1991.
39. Mary C Fitzgerald, 'Soviet Armed Forces after the Gulf War: Demise of the Defensive Doctrine?', *Report on the USSR*, 19 April 1991.

8

The Military Coalition

Julian Thompson

26 nations eventually provided forces for the international coalition against Iraq's invasion of Kuwait. Contributions ranged from the massive United States effort to small specialist support units from Central Europe. Of those 26, some took no part in the campaign to expel Iraq from Kuwait, but their presence was a welcome demonstration of the scale of international opposition to Iraq's aggression.

An array of potential and actual problems invariably arises during each coalition war. It has been so since antiquity. With the onset of peace, the difficulties are often forgotten, only to re-surface the next time. There seem to be two significant sources of friction common to all coalitions. Three of the major wars of this century – the First and Second World Wars (fought by coalitions on both sides), and the Korean War – were no exceptions. The causes of friction must be understood and anticipated; and 'lubrication' must be provided if the coalition is to operate efficiently.

The first cause of friction is that the nation providing the largest overall contribution will insist on having a casting vote in grand strategical decisions. Similarly, the nation with the largest forces in a particular theatre of operations, will usually, although not always, have the most influence on the conduct of the war in that theatre. Lesser members may feel that they are being dragged along on the coat-tails of the bigger powers, and indulge in unwelcome unilateral action to assert their independence.

The second cause is the effect of domestic pressures and national aspirations on each coalition member. These will colour its perceptions of the plans and actions of the other partners; its willingness to fall in with them, its degree of commitment; and may even lead to its conducting its own strategy in defiance of other members.

The efficacy of the lubrication depends on the extent to which there is co-ordination within the coalition at the grand strategic,

strategic and operational levels; it also depends on the organisation and process by which co-ordination is achieved. If the framework for co-ordination is in place before war breaks out, so much the better. In the First World War, co-ordination on both sides, at all levels, varied from rudimentary to non-existent. The United States and United Kingdom conceived a highly successful system in the Second World War. Although the defence of South Korea was *de jure* conducted under United Nations auspices, command was mandated to the United States who provided overwhelmingly the greatest contribution in men and materiel. The American commander-in-chief took his orders from Washington, not from the United Nations. But there was still a need to consult other members of the coalition on certain key issues; either bi-or multi-laterally, depending on the circumstances.

In the Gulf, the United States provided far the greatest force level, and *de facto* authority was vested in Washington, but without mandated United Nations command. The potential for friction existed in full measure, and the lubrication had to be effective.

Force Contributions

The international response to the Iraqi invasion of Kuwait in the early hours of 2 August 1990 was swift. The United Nations Security Council met before dawn New York time, nine hours later. The upshot was United Nations Resolution 660, condemning Iraq's invasion, passed by fourteen out of the fifteen members of the Council (Yemen abstained). The problem facing the international community was how to translate words into action, once it became clear that Iraq had no intention of withdrawing from Kuwait. The first stage was the imposition of sanctions, endorsed by United Nations Resolution 661 on 6 August. The sanctions were to be enforced by an international naval blockade.

Some non-Arab countries, notably the United States and Britain, already had naval forces in the Gulf, Arabian Sea, and Red Sea. They were soon to be joined by others, starting with the French on 8 August. The internationalisation of the naval forces in the region, immediately raised the question of command and control, and rules of engagement (ROE). The United States Secretary of State, James Baker, put his finger on the problem when he said, 'any blockade in the Gulf will need a traffic cop'[1].

As well as increasing naval forces in the area, the United States and Britain deployed fighter aircraft to Saudi Arabia and other friendly states in the region: Oman, Bahrain, and the Emirates. More United States Navy carrier battle groups (CBGs) were also ordered to sail for the area, providing a significant addition to the air order of battle.

The threat to Saudi Arabia and the Gulf States led President Bush to 'draw a line in the sand' with ground troops.[2] The United States 82nd Airborne Division deployed by air to Dhahran, soon to be followed by Marines from the United States amphibious group already in the Indian Ocean.

By 21 September 24 countries had made force commitments, including 12 Arab-Islamic nations. These ranged from 27 ships, 100,000 ground troops, and 600 combat aircraft from the United States, to 2,000 Afghan mujahadeen.[3] By December these figures had risen considerably, with more on the way; leading to an eventual total of 580,000 ground troops, 3,485 tanks, 2,400 combat aircraft, and more than 120 ships. The United States provided the greatest numbers with 400,000 ground troops, 2,100 tanks, 1,900 combat aircraft, and over 50 warships. The combined Arab-Islamic forces consisted of 150,000 ground troops, 1,150 tanks, 380 combat aircraft, and 35 warships. Of the 14 non-Arab nations, other than the United States, the only major force contributions were from Britain and France. Britain fielded 35,000 ground troops, 163 tanks, 96 combat aircraft, and 26 warships and fleet auxiliaries (RFA) (a total of 11 destroyers and frigates, with a maximum of 8 on station during hand-over periods in the run-up to hostilities and throughout the war, 5 mine-counter-measure vessels (MCMV) with one support ship, and 11 RFAs). France provided 5,500 ground troops, 72 tanks, 42 combat aircraft, and 8 warships.[4,5]

Regular Forces or Conscripts

The vast majority of non-Arab/Muslim forces deployed to the Gulf consisted of regulars. There are many advantages in deploying regular troops, and particularly in operations such as those conducted in the Gulf, especially if prolonged over several months. The composition of each national contingent, regular or conscript, conditioned the way individual nations fitted into the coalition.

Shuttle Diplomacy

From the beginning of the crisis, there was much shuttle diplomacy, mainly, but not exclusively, by the United States Secretary of State. Space precludes an account of what became an almost unceasing flow of envoys, both official and unofficial, in and out of the capitals of all the players and important bystanders. A major purpose of United States diplomacy was to encourage more nations into the fold, while ensuring the continued participation of those who had already signed up; a second was striving to keep Israel from attacking Iraq. This diplomatic process, which gathered momentum in the six months leading to the outbreak of hostilities, continued after the war started, and persisted until it ended.

Build-up, Deployment and Logistics

The build-up of United States forces in particular was impressive. Although the airlift was prodigious, 85 per cent of the United States warfighting materiel was lifted by sea. Of this massive United States sealift, 94 per cent of the total cargo moved to support their forces in the Gulf region went by strategic sea lift ship.[6] The first United States Military Sealift Command (MATS) ship to arrive in Saudi Arabia carried more equipment than all the airlift to that date.[7] However, it is worth noting that all the British logistic lift to support the deployed British combat aircraft, and until 7th Armoured Brigade deployed, was by the Royal Air Force air transport force. Until that point, no charter aircraft or ships were used.

Some idea of the overall logistic effort can be gauged from the figures for the one British armoured division in Saudi Arabia. By the time the land war started, 1126 flights and 142 ships (carrying 80 per cent of the equipment and stores required) had moved 35,504 passengers, 13,500 vehicles, 46,000 tonnes of ammunition, and 2,000 twenty foot containers.[8]

The deployment into Saudi Arabia was a 'Red Carpet' operation: by invitation and without the problems of having to seize beachheads, ports and airfields first. However, there were major logistic problems caused by lack of a communications infrastructure of the sophistication that one would find in Western Europe. For example, once formations moved to the positions from where the ground offensive would be launched, over 350 kilometres from ports, the equivalent of three corps found themselves sharing one main supply route (MSR), the Tapline Road (MSR DODGE). Traffic was nose-to-tail, and it was a striking tribute to the total air supremacy achieved by the Coalition air forces, that an MSR so close to Iraqi-occupied Kuwait, and the Saudi/Iraq border, could be so continually congested with impunity.

Stocks for 1st British Armoured Division alone consisting of nearly 18,000 tonnes of ammunition, over 7 million litres of fuel, and over 6,000 tonnes of other items, were moved along a route involving a round trip of over 700 kilometres[9]. The British were competing for road space on MSR DODGE with more than twelve other divisions, ten other brigades, and corps and army troops. The congestion would have been even greater had the British not reduced the distance that fuel had to be lifted by some 100 kilometres, by building a pipeline over the desert (PLOD), from Jubayl to An Nu'ayriyah. PLOD had the capacity to pump 130,000 litres per hour.[10]

In this context it is important that joint force commanders who are not soldiers remember that land force logistics have to be lifted to the 'customers' on a daily basis, possibly more frequently, depending on the tempo of operations and expenditure of combat supplies. These 'customers' may be moving many miles a day over difficult terrain. Although maritime forces also have to supply the moving user, their logistics are carried in self-contained packages, supply ships and oilers, with the same mobility as the warships.

The British Royal Air Force found it necessary to establish an in-Theatre air-supply system to cope with the distances involved (the Arabian Peninsular is the same size as Western Europe). To this end, seven C-130 aircraft, were permanently deployed in Saudi Arabia throughout both phases of the operation. These provided a 'milk run' round air bases, flying in spares, and other urgently needed stores. All supplies were flown into Riyadh, where bulk was broken, before redistribution using the C-130s. They were tasked nationally.

The naval effort to ensure the protection of allied shipping in the Red Sea, and approaches to the Gulf ports was not fully compre-hended by the media or the public. As well as maintaining the blockade (over 7100 merchant ships challenged and some 900 boarded by the United States Navy alone), defence in depth of reinforcement shipping and sea control operations were continuous from August 1990 to the end of February 1991.

COMMAND AND CONTROL AND OPERATIONS

Command and control during the build-up, and before operations began, was a key issue at several levels of command and in all three elements; sea, air, and land. It became even more important to have good procedures, understood and practised by all, established when the fighting started.

National and Theatre Level Command and Control

The Commander United States Central Command (CENTCOM), Lieutenant General (later General) Schwarzkopf deployed to Saudi Arabia early during the build-up. Initially, all forces in Saudi Arabia were under Saudi command. This situation was to persist throughout the period of the operation known as DESERT SHIELD, the defen-sive and build-up phase, which lasted until the start of the air war in the early hours of 17 January 1991. At this stage the name for the operation was changed to DESERT STORM. Throughout, CENTCOM reported direct to the United States Joint Chiefs of Staff (JCS(US), who in their turn reported to the President. The Saudis were involved in the planning from the outset.

Four United States component headquarters from CENTCOM also deployed early: Special Operations Command (SOCOM), Army (ARCENT), Air Force (AFCENT), Navy (NAVCENT), and Marines (MARCENT). Before DESERT STORM, the Saudi Joint Force Command (JFC), in command of all Arab Forces, joined these four under CENTCOM. (See diagram at Annex A). Before operations began, ARCENT changed its name to Third US Army.

As far as the United States forces were concerned, this structure was ideal, since all components, sea, land, air, and marines, reported to CENTCOM, and not on a single-service basis back to their various authorities in the United States. Thereby the opportunity for individual services to play cap-badge politics was reduced to the minimum.

Other than the Arab Forces through JFC, the only nation who co-operated fully with CENTCOM were the British. For political reasons, the French did not initially accept United States command, although their military commanders were in favour of such an arrangement. When the French Minister of Defence changed, the French put their land forces under TACON 3rd US Army, and their air component was tasked by AFCENT. The British command structure is of interest, not only because the United Kingdom provided the third largest force after the United States and Saudi Arabia, but, more importantly, the British had learned from the past, and the command structure provided a model for use in coalition operations.

The British Command Structure

The diagram at Annex A shows how the British fitted into the overall command picture. Full command of all British forces was retained by the Ministry of Defence.[11] Joint Headquarters (JHQ) at High Wycombe, the Headquarters of Air Chief Marshall Sir Patrick Hine, Commander-in-Chief Strike Command and United Kingdom Air, had Operational Command of Operation GRANBY, the British name for the Gulf operation. This headquarters became well equipped and organised to fulfil this function.

British Forces Middle East (BFME), at Riyadh, was a three star headquarters, commanded by Lieutenant General Sir Peter de la Billiere (COMBFME). He had Operational Control of all British forces in the Theatre. In this role he had total responsibility for all British forces, but was not concerned with the detail of day-to-day operations. He influenced the operational level planning before the fighting started, and managed relations with the Americans and the Saudis throughout. British officers on the CENTCOM planning staff ensured that national interests and capabilities were taken into account during the formulation of plans. This close partnership also operated at the force component level.

As soon as COMBFME judged the time was right, he 'chopped' British ground forces to TACON of CENTCOM as shown in the diagram. COMBFME also gave the Commander British Naval Forces the authority to 'chop' ships to TACON of NAVCENT as required. In the event, only some British ships were formally 'chopped' to CENTCOM, but all co-operated fully (TACON in all but name). A similar command arrangement was agreed for the British air component. The British air component commander and his planners worked so closely alongside AFCENT, that both air forces operated as one.

Headquarters BFME acted as the conduit for all national operational and policy matters between the force components in-theatre and the United Kingdom. This relieved the component commanders from involvement in these areas with their respective single-service commands, or the Joint Headquarters (JHQ) in the United Kingdom, allowing them to concentrate on the task in hand. The three British services in the Theatre could communicate with their own single-service authorities in the United Kingdom or Germany on non-controversial subjects, such as administration, provided they kept HQ BFME informed. Moreover, the British chain of command was an improvement on the command system for the Falklands campaign of 1982, where the lack of an overall commander in the Theatre led to misunderstanding and friction.[12]

It is always important to establish as early as possible the question of who is the critical commander of each national contingent. Almost invariably this is the senior national commander forward in the Theatre of Operations, in a position to assess the operational requirement – for the British, General de la Billiere. For example, soon after arriving, he recognised the need to deploy a complete British armoured division. The critical national commander and his staff must move into the Theatre as quickly as possible, otherwise planning of in-theatre matters will continue to be conducted from headquarters at the home base. This, with the best will in the world, is liable to lead to serious mistakes and delays simply because the planners are not completely *au fait* with local conditions or the specific problems facing commanders on the ground. This concept seems to be more readily understood by land forces than naval or air forces. Furthermore, in a multi-national situation, it is of the first importance that national contingents should have an overall commander of sufficient status to represent the national case and guard national interests hour by hour – as General de la Billiere did so brilliantly thoughout operation GRANBY. The commander who is to carry out the operation must make the plan. When the national in-theatre commander is handing off land, sea or air components to other headquarters, the relevant national component commander and his staff must go forward and start planning as soon as possible. There is a temptation for the planning and work associated with the deployment to the theatre to obscure the purpose of the operation: the 'get you in service' becomes the be-all and end-all at the expense of operational thinking and planning right up to the highest level.

It is important that national theatre assets are put under the national theatre commander from the outset. Initially the British Force Maintenance Area (FMA), was under command 7th Armoured Brigade, and then under 1st British Armoured Division, but this was changed after the Division moved away from its initial deployment area. As the Division became immersed in operations, the GOC could not be responsible for a logistic, or any other asset, several hundred kilometres away.

Naval Operations

With the exception of the British, the 14 national naval forces in the Gulf, Red Sea, and Arabian Sea, operated under their own national command throughout. Only the United States and British navies took part in active operations in the northern Gulf. Naval operations in the northern Gulf were principally in support of the threatened amphibious landing, which was part of the overall deception plan. They consisted of shore bombardment, minesweeping, and the destruction of Iraqi naval craft. The role of the escorts in the northern Gulf during this phase was to protect the amphibious ships, gunfire ships and MCMVs from land or sea-launched missiles. Strikes against the Iraqi coastal navy, including captured Kuwaiti Exocet-fitted craft, were successfully prosecuted by fixed-wing aircraft and by helicopters armed with air-to-surface missiles. The British Navy's Lynx helicopters, armed with sea Skua, were particularly successful.

Some 1200 Iraqi mines were laid in ten areas around the coastline of Kuwait. These mines, and the difficulty of achieving tactical surprise on so limited a coastline, led CENTCOM to decide not to make an amphibious landing in the opening phase of ground operations. However, to make the amphibious threat credible, mine counter-measures and naval gunfire operations were vigorously pressed home. The effort involved would not have been wasted if an amphibious operation had been required in a later stage of the land campaign: if CENTCOM had required reinforcement of ground operations, or as a third thrust to complement the outflanking move and push through Kuwait. Although the landing was never attempted, two marine brigades and the amphibious ships, tied down three or four Iraqi divisions guarding the coast. This greatly eased the task of the two marine divisions who spearheaded the attack into Kuwait from the south (see Annex C)

The United States Navy soon discovered that they had insufficient modern MCMVs capable of clearing the sophisticated mines laid by the Iraqis. This task fell mainly to the British, who were the only other Allied navy engaged in mineclearing while the war was in progress. The mine threat demonstrated how a nation with a small navy can seriously disrupt the plans of even the most powerful states lacking adequate mine clearing vessels and equipment.

Procedures

From the start of the blockade, operating areas were allocated to each national naval group, but no common Rules of Engagement (ROE) were agreed. When attempts were made merely to co-ordinate forces conducting the blockade, the French reserved the right not to comply. On the outbreak of hostilities, all but the USN and the British continued to operate in their own areas. The only employment for the ships from the remaining 12 nations was to blockade. Possibly a satisfactory state of affairs for the countries concerned; it practically guaranteed that their ships would not be involved in any fighting. On the other hand, although by this stage, the blockading task was minimal, at least their presence was a demonstration of international solidarity.

However, had the air, surface, and sub-surface threats been higher, such a loose arrangement would have been highly dangerous. Any one of these threats, let alone a combination of two or more, requires well understood, practised, and above all, common, procedures. Without these, attacks will penetrate the defences without warning, sectors will be left uncovered, and 'Blue on Blue', a euphemism for shooting at one's own side, will be an ever-present hazard.

NATO Procedures

Ships from nations who are members of the NATO Alliance, had common procedures and tactical publications. The latter, Allied Tactical Publications (ATPs), cover an array of procedures from signalling and manoeuvring, to resupply at sea (RAS) techniques. Some could be passed to allies such as the Australian Navy (France, who is not a member of the military alliance, has access to all ATPs). Furthermore, many NATO navies, and the French and the Australians, possess Link 11. This allows the tactical picture, including the threats, to be passed instantly by electronic means to all ships in a task force.

In one respect, the British are unique, as Royal Navy Type 42 frigates were designed to integrate with United States Navy air defence systems, for the battle against the Soviet Navy in the North Atlantic. In the Gulf, the Type 42s were integrated into the US Navy's anti-air warning defence in the forward anti-air screen. In situations such as the Gulf war, where there were two classes of naval performer, 'players' and 'non-players', the encryption keys in the Link 11 can be so fitted as to prevent non-players acquiring the players' picture. Even had the political will existed for the non-players to participate, it is questionable whether many of their ships would have been acceptable to the US Navy for use in screen operations, because of technical shortcomings.

Despite the agreement within NATO, that the 'members of the Alliance should contribute [to the coalition in the Gulf] each in their own way', with NATO providing only a 'forum for close consultation', it was clear that at sea, in the air and to a lesser degree on land, NATO procedures provided the glue which helped bind together an important part of the coalition forces.

Western European Union Maritime Forces

The importance and success of the use of NATO procedures had implications for the Western European Union maritime contribution and its level of participation. Although individual nations decided the level of their contributions and the scale of their participation, the WEU subsequently acted as a kind of sponsor. However, as we have seen, it was NATO procedures that underpinned the operations. They have been arrived at over many years of painstaking committee work, exercises and, on occasions, a good deal of give and take on the part of NATO members, some of whom did not agree initially with what was being proposed. When NATO is re-shaped to take account of the changed security situation in Europe, the procedures should be retained. Suggestions that NATO should be scrapped wholesale, would amount to throwing the baby out with the bath water.[13] However, the adoption of procedures is one thing, full participation in operations is another. It should not pass unnoticed that in the Gulf the only ships of the WEU fleet that took part in active operations were British.[14]

It is often politically easier to commit naval forces than land or air forces; land borders and air space do not have to be crossed. Ships tend to be out of sight and out of mind. In the Gulf War, as has already been noted, they could be positioned to avoid being attacked. In these circumstances nations can gain kudos from participations without much chance of serious damage.

This can create problems. There may be a profusion of unnecessary ships. Nations with little experience of far-flung deployments, and inadequate logistic systems, may be hard-pressed to maintain a presence if the operation is prolonged for more than a few months. To keep two warships on station well away from home waters, demands a minimum of four more ships, possibly six, in the pipeline, depending on distances and serviceability. To this must be added a fleet train of oilers and supply ships.

Air Operations

The deployment of air forces into the Gulf from countries outside the region also posed problems of command and control. Altogether, six Arabian peninsular, and six non-Arab nations provided combat aircraft. No combat aircraft were deployed by other Arab nations. In addition combat aircraft operated in and from Turkey. When air forces deployed, they were grouped to begin with under what was then called Allied Forces. The British worked hard to get out of this grouping, because they knew that their capabilities were well suited to operating under United States command and control arrangements. They soon succeeded, but were the only air force to do so, or indeed to appear to wish to make this move.

Air Space Management

From the very first day of DESERT SHIELD, tight air space management was essential. To begin with, there were difficulties: factional interests had to be settled and national pride soothed. Eventually, air space control was achieved by dividing the Gulf and adjacent areas into 6 zones: the Red Sea, South, West, Central, East, and Gulf. Airborne Warning and Control aircraft (AWACs) operated control, and Combat Air Patrols (CAPs), were flown 24 hours a day throughout DESERT SHIELD and STORM, and well after the cease-fire.

There was not one 'Blue on Blue' in the air despite 110,000 sorties flown during the war, and about the same number during the crisis period before. This excellent record was achieved by three measures. First, a large number of aircraft were re-equipped with new Identification Friend or Foe equipment (IFF), to make them compatible with US radars in AWACs and air defence systems. Second, a great deal of procedural work on ROEs was initiated. Last, but not least, all air operations for the Theatre, over land or sea, were tasked by the airtasking organisation in Riyadh. As the war progressed, the lack of an Iraqi air threat allowed the air space management system to operate in a more relaxed fashion than would normally be the case.

The Air Offensive

The aim of Coalition air operations was to force Iraq out of Kuwait or, failing that to 'shape the battlefield' and weaken the Iraqi forces, in preparation for the ground operation.[15] Never before has an air offensive, linked to a blockade, come so close to winning a war on its own. But in the end, a ground offensive was required. For example, although supplies to Kuwait were reduced by 50 per cent, the line of communication was not cut.[16] Indeed, it was the threat of a ground offensive that caused Saddam Hussein to attempt a belated cease-fire.

The Naval Air Contribution

The United States Navy actually opened the Allied air offensive by firing Sea Launched Cruise Missiles (SLCM) from ships in the Gulf and Red Sea. Eventually, some 291 cruise missiles were launched from battleships, cruisers, some destroyers and submarines. Cruise missiles were also fired from submarines in the Arabian Sea and the Mediterranean. Aircraft from the six United States CBGs carried out 23 per cent of all United States ground attack missions in Iraq, in addition to flying defence of the CBGs and seaborne lines of communication.

Sortie Rates

A significant difference between British and French sortie rates was caused by the need for the French to clear every sortie with their authorities in France. The British total (6,100) was two-and-a-half times greater than that of the French – a classic example of the importance of delegating powers to the commander on the spot, giving him authority to act within the confines of national policy and ROE.

Force Packaging

Each night several force packages formed up in radio silence. The basic ingredients of a force package are shown in the diagram at Annex B. The purpose of a force package is to penetrate the air defences by concentrating firepower and mass in time and space. The strike force is preceded by a fighter sweep, and Wild Weasel air-defence suppression aircraft. Fighters provide escorts on the flanks and rear. AWACs, JSTARs, and Early Warning Aircraft fly race-track patterns on the flanks of the strike, but keep back from the enemy air defence zone. Further back, tankers fly race-track patterns, to top up the strike after take-off, and to re-fuel, if necessary, on the homeward leg.

Although shallow strikes by A-10s, Jaguars, and attack helicopters could be carried out without force packaging, as could missions by stealth aircraft, any attempt at deep strike without force packaging risked disaster – as the Italians discovered when five out of a force of six Tornados failed to top up with fuel from the tanker; the sixth aircraft went on alone, and was shot down. Middle air operations are easier to force package. It would be difficult to envisage a force package without the United States Air Force. Equally, attempting an air offensive against a well equipped enemy air defence system without force packaging would result in very heavy, possibly unsustainable, losses – unless stealth aircraft were used.

The air operations in this war, proved conclusively that it is no good having a second-best air force. Not only its technology, but its training and doctrine must be of the highest standard possible.

As with naval operations, NATO procedures were used successfully.

Land Operations

Concept of Operations

The concept of operations was based on the appreciation of the ground and the Iraqi layout and capability. The Iraqi Army was deployed in three layers:

> ▶ Infantry, mainly conscripts along the coast and the border with Saudi Arabia, were well dug in behind a large obstacle belt. Their combat effectiveness had been reduced by at least 50 per cent by 24 February, the start of the land offensive[17].
> ▶ The tactical reserves equipped with T 55 tanks sited behind, and in places among the front-line troops. Their main role to block an attack from the south or the coast. It was assessed that their combat effectiveness had been reduced by 50–75 per cent. But they still posed a major threat. Fortunately, they were not expecting an attack from their flanks or rear[18].
> ▶ The theatre reserve provided by the Republican Guard Divisions sited in Iraq, and poised to counter-attack, or withdraw.

General Schwarzkopf recognised that the coast, the marshy Euphrates-Tigris valleys, and the Iraqi's own defences, berms and minefields, could constitute a trap for the Iraqi Army, provided: one, that he could destroy the bridges across the Euphrates, Tigris and their tributaries; two, he could keep the Iraqis looking south and east; and three, could carry out a wide out-flanking movement to the west.

The key to realising these three lay in deception. Space does not permit a detailed description of the methods used. They included:

▶ All training being designed to suggest a massive attack from Saudi Arabia directly north into Kuwait.

▶ The move of logistic materiel to the west was delayed as long as possible.

▶ Radio deception.

▶ Much publicity given to the activities of 1st British Armoured Division with MARCENT on the coastal flank, including a television report showing British artillery firing near the sea.

▶ Artillery raids on the area of the Wadi al Batin, combined with probing attacks by 1st US Cavalry Division.

Command and Control of the Land Battle

Command and control of the land battle was made possible because all contingents who played important roles were large enough, division size or above, to be given major objectives and independent axes. Multi-national mixed forces were avoided, and hence all the problems caused by differences in language, battle drills, and procedures – both operational and logistic. Command was exercised in the usual manner by operations orders, briefings of commanders, and when the battle started, by radio orders and face-to-face contact. Codeworded phase lines and objectives were further aids to control of a fast-moving advance, enabling axes to be changed with the minimum of fuss.

Liaison officers were exchanged between national formations and United States superior headquarters. In the case of the British 1st Armoured Division, at the request of the GOC, additional staff officers were sent from the United Kingdom to work in US VIIth Corps Headquarters. This enabled a British input to be included in plans from the outset.

The period before the land campaign started was put to good use in training and formation exercises. A large scale armoured and heliborne attack can not be conducted by semi-trained formations with any degree of confidence.

LESSONS FOR THE FUTURE

It is unlikely that operations as large as DESERT SHIELD and DESERT STORM will be mounted again in the foreseeable future. However there may well be a need at some time for a smaller mix of nationalities and forces to participate in an operation outside the present NATO area. Space does not permit any discussion of the possible threats or the types of response. Indeed, a cynic might well say that it would be a nugatory exercise anyway. If the British experience is anything to go by, only about three of the numerous operations in which British forces were engaged since 1945 were covered by contingency plans, let alone foreseen. Let us therefore assume that there will be operations which are limited in scope as suggested above. In the Gulf War, the Coalition forces had time to prepare. Because the Coalition had the initiative, they had a golden opportunity to sort out two vital functions: command and control and logistics. There was also precious time for a third which might or might not apply in future operations: training. It is as well to remember that in the Falklands operation, the only training that could be carried out before the troops were committed to battle was confined to what was possible on board ship *en route* to the area of conflict plus a little small arms practice on Ascension Island. Readiness is often emphasised in words but the harsh reality of its importance in quick reaction tasks is understood by few and all too seldom is anything positive done about it. It was as well, in 1982, that those who were ready were put in to bat.

In the Gulf there were no agreed command and control arrangements when the coalition forces deployed. Time was needed to iron out problem areas, and carry out the fitting of special equipment, such as common IFF.

Logistics in the Gulf were made easier because it was a 'Red Carpet' operation. Plenty of fuel was available in-country. Airfields and ports were modern and well equipped. Future operations may not be so blessed. There were logistic difficulties caused by lack of roads, wear and tear on vehicles and equipment, and other features of operating in the desert, such as the need to supply water in large quantities over long distances. But again, there was time to establish the best methods of tackling these problems, and to avoid learning on the job – in the middle of a battle. Because time may not be vouchsafed again, there is a need for coherent doctrines for logistic organisations at a national level, for use in operations outside the NATO area.

The basis for the success of DESERT STORM was the well understood and practised procedures, exercised over a number of years under the NATO Alliance. In the past, there had been more joint operation and integration at sea and in the air than on land.[19] But even on land, common methods and terminology had been hammered out. The 'learning curve' was not steep, except perhaps in the essential, but low-level, tactical art of living and fighting in the desert. Here again, it was only some, like the British, who needed to reacquire these skills.

It might be thought that some preparation for future operations could be achieved through contingency planning but, for the reasons given above, this would probably prove a waste of time. It might be better to examine likely tasks and prepare force mixes to meet each situation. Following this would be the need to work on common procedures such as interoperability of equipment and weapons and, above all, of command and control, communications and intelligence. But wait, have we not heard all this many times in the NATO context? Yes, and it was difficult enough even under the threat of attack by the Soviet Union. It seems unlikely that any grouping other than NATO, or the WEU underpinned by NATO procedures, would make any progress in essential areas of military coalition.

The WEU must also tackle the question of force participation and counter the tendency to 'ante up' the force that suits the producer, rather than that required by the customer, or the job. It is too much to expect that nations will follow the NATO precedent and agree in advance to the commitment of specific forces. But the shopping list can be prepared in advance, to speed up the staff-work, perhaps by double-hatted NATO staffs.

It is also unlikely that any large-scale operation against a well equipped, numerous, and determined enemy would ever be mounted without at least United States participation, and probably leadership. This emphasises the value of using procedures that are culled from NATO.

It also underlines the need to understand the lessons of coalition warfare that have been learned, or rather relearned. Above all, this means the reality of coalitions, that the nation providing the biggest contribution will invariably have the major say in how the war is conducted – the corollary being that nations wishing to influence events, are better placed if they make a significant contribution to the coalition in terms of *military force*. As the military historian John Terraine has said:

> '. . . . the small print of coalitions may be searched until eternity without ever finding a clause which says that one ally should do all the dying while the other hands him his ammunition and makes admiring noises from a distance.'[20]

Or, as the then Chief of the Imperial General Staff of the British Army in 1943 judged:

> 'We have not really arrived at the best strategy, but I suppose that when working with allies, compromises, with all their evils, become inevitable.'[21]

Whatever scale or type of operation is envisaged, there will be a need for: strategic and tactical mobility, in the air, at sea, and on the battlefield; first class, state of the art equipment, including the most modern combat aircraft, helicopters, vehicles, and ships (not forgetting MCMVs); and last, but not least, well trained, regular troops.

The means of mobility must take into account the possibility that ports and airfields may have to be seized first. This requires an amphibious and air assault capability supported by equipment which allows supply over beaches, and into airstrips and rudimentary ports.

Force levels must be right, so that national components can operate as a self-contained team, avoiding multinational force mixes below the level of military practicability. In land force terms, this means division, or at a pinch, brigade group. Mixed units look good politically, they are military nonsense.

Planning must be carried out by the commander who is to implement the plan. He and his staff must move forward as early as practicable.

It is important to avoid mono-directionalism. Fixed ideas about how and where future operations might occur, often borne of resource driven defence policy, may result in doctrine and equipment which reduce operational flexibility.

Some of the friction in multinational operations will be greatly reduced if three principles are followed:

▶ There must be a common object.
▶ There must be equity in the allocation of tasks. The perception of equity is more important than the facts.[20]
▶ There must be good will at all levels. This includes not insisting on invoking the fine print of the command and control doctrine at the expense of common sense and getting the job done.

Finally, relationships within a grouping of allies will be better if all recognise that domestic pressures will always play a part in the attitudes of each member of a coalition. Carping is likely to increase the friction. Cheerful acceptance, at least in public, may produce more co-operation.

Much was learned, or relearned, about the operation of military coalitions in DESERT SHIELD and DESERT STORM. No war provides a blue-print for the next. But it is of considerable assistance if there is at least a body of lessons, and an outline doctrine, to avoid constantly reinventing the wheel.

Annexes to Chapter 8

ANNEX 'A'

DESERT STORM: COMMAND ORGANISATION

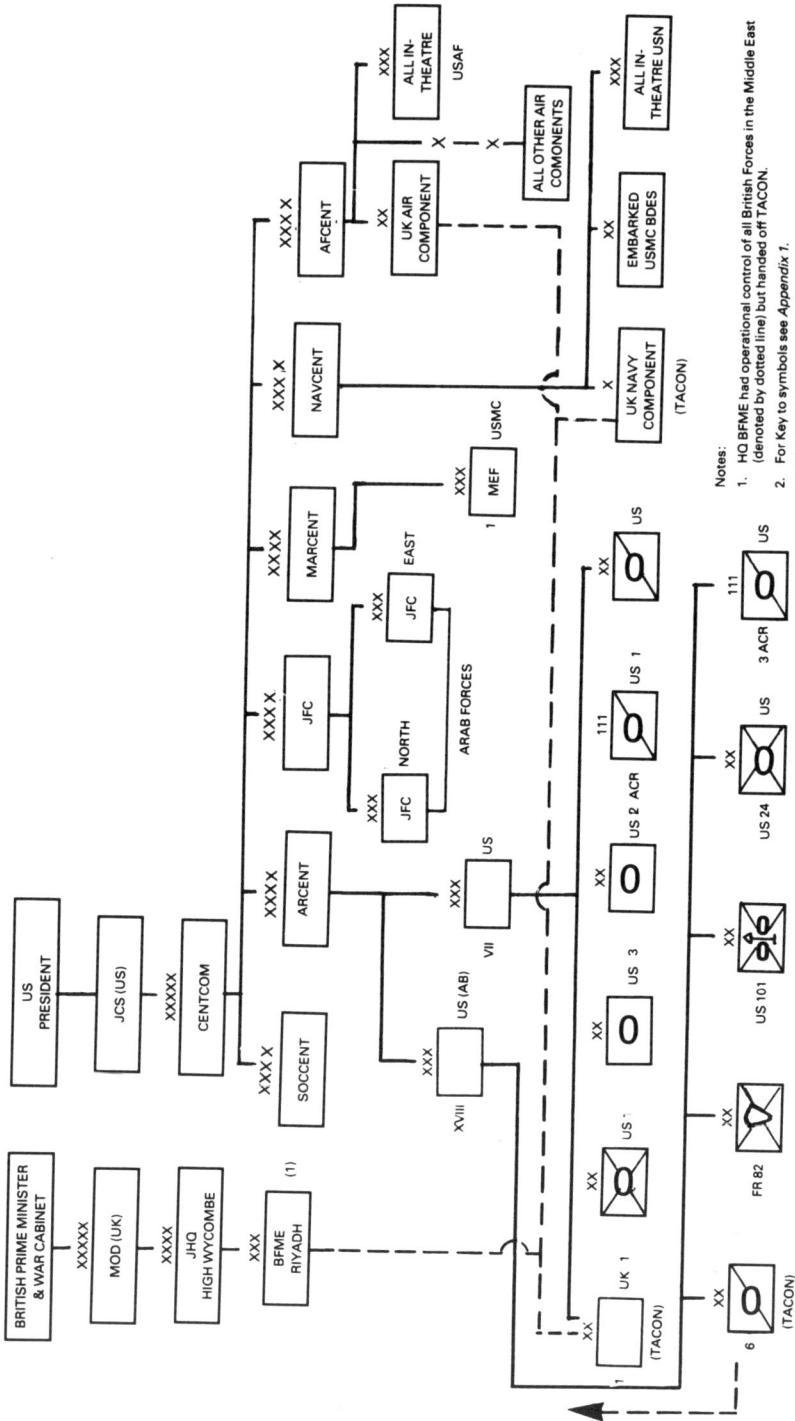

US PRESIDENT

JCS (US)

XXXXX CENTCOM

BRITISH PRIME MINISTER & WAR CABINET

XXXXX MOD (UK)

XXXX JHQ HIGH WYCOMBE

BFME RIYADH (1)

XXXX X SOCCENT

XXXX ARCENT

XXXX JFC

XXXX MARCENT

XXX X NAVCENT

XXXX X AFCENT

XXX ALL IN-THEATRE USAF

XX UK AIR COMPONENT

ALL OTHER AIR COMONENTS

XXX ALL IN-THEATRE USN

XX EMBARKED USMC BDES

X UK NAVY COMPONENT (TACON)

XXX JFC NORTH

XXX JFC EAST

ARAB FORCES

XXX 1 MEF USMC

XXX US (AB) XVIII

XXX US VII

XX US

XX US 1

XX US 3

XX US 2 ACR

XX 111 US 1

XXX 111 3 ACR US

XX US 24

XX US 101

XX FR 82

XX UK 1 (TACON)

XX 6 (TACON)

Notes:

1. HQ BFME had operational control of all British Forces in the Middle East (denoted by dotted line) but handed off TACON.

2. For Key to symbols see *Appendix 1*.

3. For short Glossary see *Appendix 2*.

Appendix 1

The XXs above the formation signs indicate either the size of the formation or the level of command.

XXXXX

Five star headquarters eg MOD (UK) or
Army Group Headquarters at CENTCOM.

XXXX

Four star level of command.

XXX

Three star level of command, in land forces a corps, or
headquarters with three star commander.

XX

Two star level of command, in land forces a division.

X

Brigade

III

Regiment (Colonel's command) (US)

Appendix 2 – Glossary

AB	Airborne
ACR	Armoured Cavalry Regiment
AFCENT	United States Air Force CentCom.
ARCENT	Army CentCom; all US Army under Centcom.
Bdes	Brigades.
BFME	British Forces Middle East, an overall term covering all British Forces deployed to the Middle East for DESERT STORM and SHIELD.
CENTCOM	Central Command, a United States command with responsibility for operations outside the Continental United States.
JCS(US)	Marines presided over by a Chairman, in this case heads of United States Army, Navy, Air Force and Joint Chiefs of Staff United States; the professional General Colin Powell.
JFC	Joint Force Command; the Saudi Command comprising all coalition land forces other than the US, UK and France.
JHQ	Joint Headquarters.
MARCENT	United States Marines, CentCom.
MEF	Marine Expeditionary Force. A United States Marine formation, configured for the task. Usually a minimum of a division with its own air wing. In this case a corps of two divisions with two air wings.
MOD(UK)	Ministry of Defence United Kingdom.
NAVCENT	United States Navy CentCom.
SOCCENT	Special Operations Command CentCom, responsible for all Special Operations, by all services.
TACON	Tactical Control – see Note 11.
USAF	United States Air Force.
USMC	United States Marine Corps.

FORCE PACKAGING

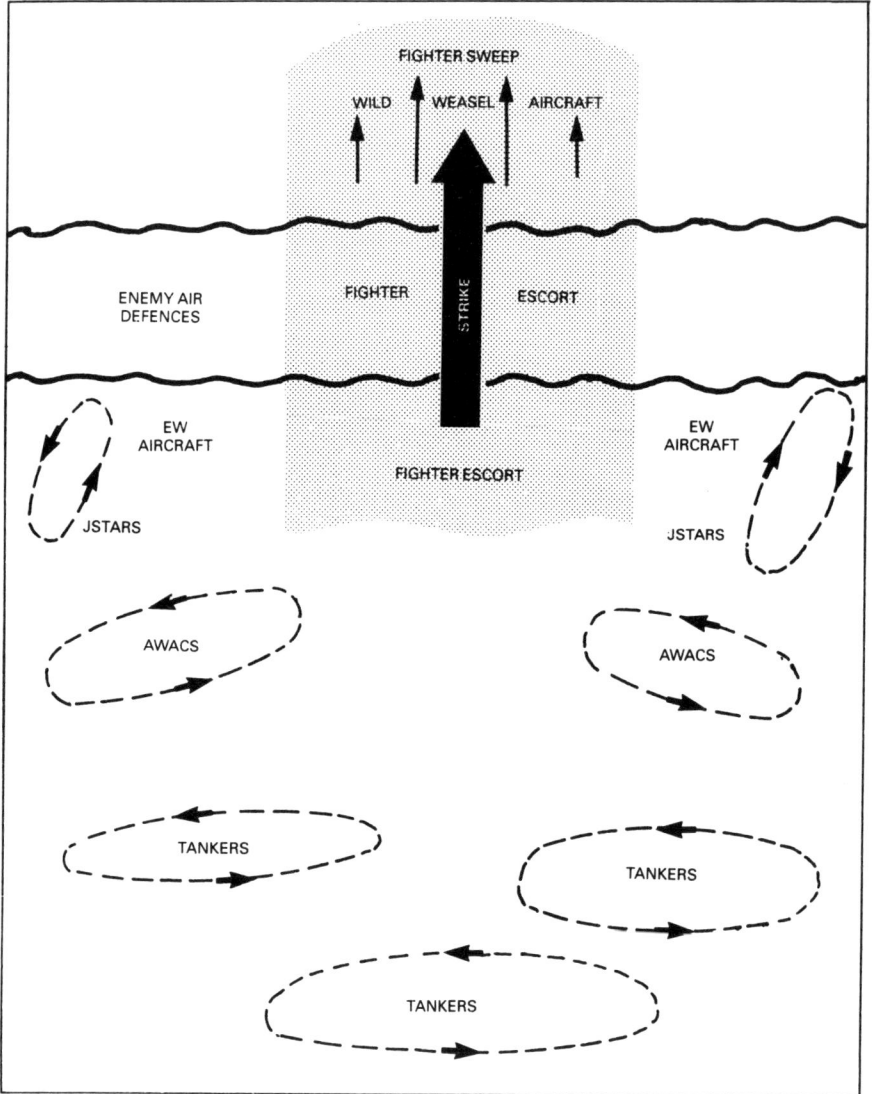

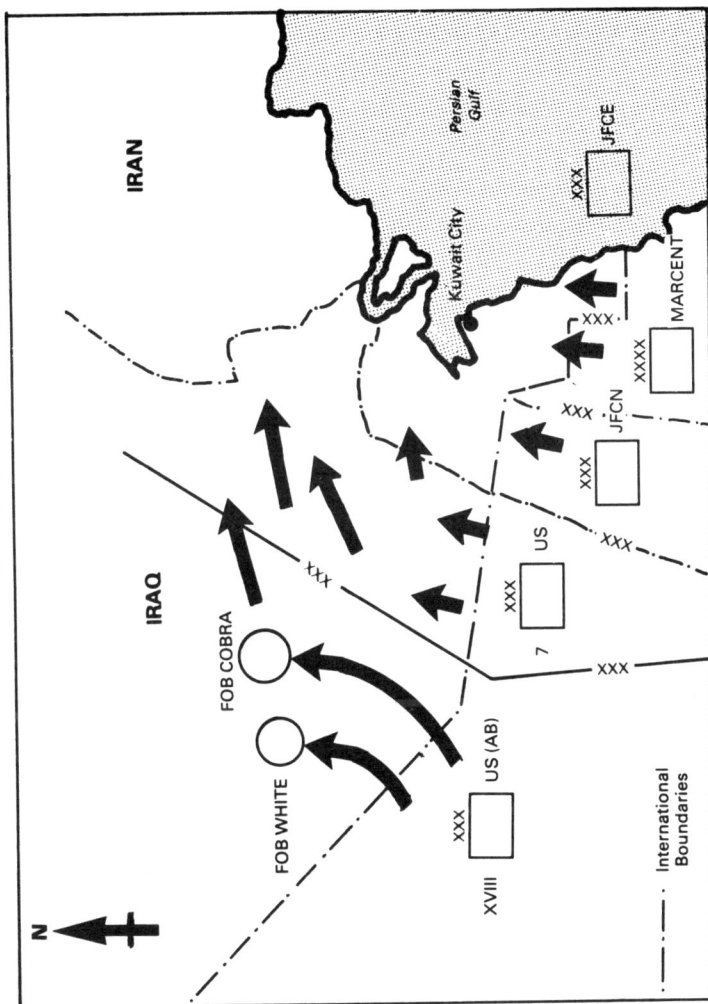

ANNEX 'C'

OPERATION DESERT STORM:- OUTLINE DEPLOYMENT
(Not to scale)

Notes

1. J H A Thompson. The *Observer* 26 August 1990.
2. *Daily Telegraph*, 8 August 1990.
3. Royal United Services Institute (RUSI) for Defence Studies, Gulf Force-level Update dated 21 September 1990.
4. RUSI Gulf Force-level Update dated 30 November 1990.
5. Draft of *OPERATION GRANBY*: An Account of the Gulf Crisis 1990–91, and the British Contribution to the Liberation of Kuwait, Army Code 71512. (abbreviated to *OP GRANBY DRAFT* hereafter). Where there is conflict between this document and the RUSI Gulf Force-level updates, the figures in the *OP GRANBY DRAFT* are used. The figures in the RUSI document do not take account of Battle Casualty Replacements (BCRs) and battalions sent out in early–mid January 1991, for prisoner of war handling. Aircraft figures also changed throughout the war because of casualties and reinforcements.
6. Vice Admiral Francis R Donovan USN, Commander Military Sealift Command, to the House Armed Services Committee, 19 February 1991.
7. Commander R I Money Royal Navy, Going the Distance; Sustaining Future Conflict, *RUSI Journal* Spring 1991. p31.
8. *Third Line Logistic Operations during Op GRANBY*, notes of presentation held by Logistics Team, British Army Staff College, Camberley. (referred to hereafter as Third Line Log Ops), p15. Of the 142 merchant ships chartered by the British for the Gulf, only eight were British flagged.
9. *OP GRANBY DRAFT*, pp3–5.
10. *Third Line Log OPs*, pp9–10.
11. The types of command status, as defined by NATO, are:

    Full Command – as implied by the term, the commander has full command over the formation of forces under his command. Full command applies only within national forces and covers every aspect of operations, administration and logistics. The Full Commander can hand operational command or operational control of the force, or part of it over to another commander (see below).

    Operational Command – the authority granted to a commander to assign missions or tasks to subordinate commanders, to deploy units, to reassign forces, and to retain or delegate operational and/or tactical control. It does not of itself include responsibility for logistics. Such authority can be delegated to an allied commander, but only if it is politically acceptable to a nation to allow him to use the assigned forces as he thinks fit. The Full Commander always retains the option to withdraw these forces, so consultation and trust between alliance partners is essential.

    Operational Control – the authority delegated to a commander to direct forces assigned to him to accomplish specific missions or tasks, which are usually limited by function, time, or location; to deploy the units concerned, and to retain or assign tactical control of those units. It does not include authority to assign separate employment of components of those units concerned, or change the task. It does not of itself include logistic responsibility.

    Tactical Control (TACON) – similar to operational control, but usually limited to one operation, or phase in an operation.

12. J H A Thompson, *The Lifeblood of War: Logistics and Armed Conflict*, Brassey's, 1991, pp261–61 & pp272–274.
13. The Right Honourable Alan Clark, MP, Minister of State for Defence, speaking at King's College London, proposed that the NATO Alliance should be broken up without further delay.
14. Dr W F Van Eekelen, Secretary General, Western European Union, speaking at the Royal United Services Institute for Defence Studies, on 14 May 1991.
15. *DRAFT OP GRANBY*, p4–1.
16. *DRAFT OP GRANBY*, p4–3.
17. *DRAFT OP GRANBY*, p5–3.
18. *DRAFT OP GRANBY*, p5–3.
19. United States practice is to produce an Operation Plan (OPPLAN), which is a debating document at staff level. The executive document is the Operation Order (OPORDER). The phases of the operation are implemented or amended as the battle unfolds by Fragmentary Orders (FRAGORDERS), disseminated in message form by radio or hand. This is different from the British custom, and from that of several other nations.
20. John Terraine, lecture to the RUSI June 1989, RUSI Journal Summer 1989, p61.
21. Terraine, *RUSI Journal* Summer 1989, p60.
22. A good example of this occurred towards the end of the land campaign. Main Headquarters VIIth US Corps ordered GOC 1st British Armoured Division to swing south from his axis to clear and open a new Corps/Army MSR running due north from the Iraq/Saudi border, parallel to the Wadi al Batin. Although the Corps Commander at his Tactical Headquarters, wanted the Division to continue eastwards. However, the GOC 1st British Armoured Division regarded this as a perfectly proper task, although disappointed to be pulled away from his eastwards advance. Headquarters 3rd US Army discussed this order with Corps Main Headquarters, expressing concern that under the terms of TACON, this was an improper employment of 1st British Armoured Division, and might cause resentment and repercussions in British circles at a high level. The order was countermanded.

9

The Economic Implications

Susan Willett

The international reprisals against Iraq for its invasion of Kuwait, have been heralded as evidence of a new world order based on international consensus and co-operation. A unique aspect of this newly found co-operation was the extent of 'burden sharing' to cover the costs of war. Capital-rich states such as the Gulf oil states, Germany and Japan funded military powers such as the United Kingdom, France and the United States to provide the fighting power to restore the *status quo* in Kuwait. The dichotomy, revealed by the burden-sharing process, between those countries with financial power and those with military power has raised some interesting issues about the new world order and international security.[1]

Estimates of the direct costs of the allied military operations in the Gulf have been put at between \$80bn–\$100bn.[2] The United States bore the lion's share of the military burden, providing 53 per cent of the ground troops, 80 per cent of the combat aircraft and roughly 60 per cent of the ships. In return, they received contributions of \$54bn resulting in an embarrassing revelation that the US made a profit out of the war.[3] The attention paid to counting the cost of the Gulf War and to the 'burden sharing' issue has obscured the broader economic dimensions of the Gulf crisis and the subtle way in which the war has redistributed resources and affected the global economy.

Primarily, the economic dimension of the Gulf crisis centred on the strategic importance of oil. The American Secretary of State, James Baker, left the allies in little doubt about the central role of oil in the crisis when he stated at a NATO meeting in August 1990:

> The stakes involved in the current crisis in the Gulf are very high for all of us around this table. Since 1949, every American president has said that the Gulf is a vital US and Western interest and that we could not allow any hostile power to gain a stranglehold over its energy resources. Now Saddam Hussein poses just such a threat. Given the

central importance of Gulf oil to the global economy, all of us here share an interest in thwarting this dictator's ambitions. We all have a critical stake in this.[4]

The dependence of the global community on oil gives emphasis to the notions of interdependence and economic security. However, it is questionable whether the global community has yet developed effective mechanisms to deal with threats to economic security. As this chapter argues, the cost of the war and the economic uncertainty it created effectively established the conditions for further economic insecurity for many nations of the world, not least for Eastern Europe and the Third World.

The alternative to using force was to continue with the United Nations sanctions policy and to seek a diplomatic resolution to the crisis, a course of action favoured by many UN member countries including the Soviet Union. But sanctions also come at a price. Without the effective management of global energy supplies and a fairer distribution of compensation for the economic effects of sanctions, the result is greater economic instability for the more vulnerable UN members.

The choice between going to war or pursuing sanctions was a political one, strongly influenced by military strategic considerations. The economic implications of that choice are only now being assessed. But if the UN is to recognise economic security as being equally significant as other forms of security, the question arises of how account should be taken of economic considerations when making decisions about collective action. In this respect, the Gulf War may have some important lessons to teach the global community.

In attempting to assess both the direct and indirect economic effects of the Gulf crisis it is necessary to attempt to answer three questions. Who has paid the price? In what form has the price been paid? And, whether or not other measures could have been taken to reduce the economic burden of the crisis?

Sanctions

Faced with the immediate crisis following Iraq's invasion of Kuwait, the United Nations Security Council voted unanimously on August 6th to impose economic sanctions against Iraq and to demand its unconditional withdrawal under the terms of Resolution 661. Sanctions against Iraq were designed to impose a maximum degree of political and economic isolation in order to destabilise the country and thereby force the Iraqis to withdraw from Kuwait.

The application of sanctions against Iraq represented the collective will of the world community against an instance of aggression at precisely the moment when the United Nations appeared capable of operating in the way its founders had hoped. In this sense, the Gulf crisis represented an ultimate test for both the use of sanctions and the institution of the United Nations. As the US Secretary of State himself put it:

> If these UN sanctions fail, despite enjoying such a rare unanimity of support, it is hard to imagine how any UN sanctions could ever succeed. The United Nations, as an institution will have suffered a mortal blow. We do not want this to happen. There is no need today to dwell on what may need to be done . . . But first we should give the sanctions time to work, and give ourselves time to see what also is needed to make them effective.[5]

There was much debate, in the lead up to war about how effective sanctions were likely to be in achieving Iraq's withdrawal from Kuwait. To a great degree, the effectiveness of sanctions, depends on the dependence of a nation on external trade and the extent of its internal self-sufficiency. The Iraqi economy was highly vulnerable to sanctions as it relied heavily on foreign sources of supply for food-stuffs – 80 per cent of the country's normal food consumption was imported – and basic industrial inputs and spare parts. In addition 95 per cent of its foreign exchange was earned from the sale of oil, so that even if there had been countries willing to flout sanctions, Iraq would have been unable to pay for its imports, once its existing financial resources were depleted.

One of the most important objectives of sanctions was to under-mine the Iraqi military machine, by depriving it of food, spare parts and fuel. In early December, the Director of the CIA told Congress that Iraq's military could maintain its current combat readiness for no more than nine months if economic sanctions continued to hold and that the ability of the Iraqi airforce to fly regular missions could decline within three months[6]. Indeed, the state of Iraqi frontline troops and the lack of effective resistance during the short but bloody land war, suggest that sanctions were in fact proving highly effective in undermining Iraq's military machine.

Despite the apparent effectiveness of sanctions, they were not given enough time to work. The military build up in Saudi Arabia, created a momentum of its own which appeared to undermine any diplomatic solution to the crisis. A number of arguments were put forward in an attempt to justify the abandonment of the UN sanc-tions policy in favour of the use of force. The chief of these were; first, that the international coalition was viewed as fragile and im-mediate action was needed to prevent it falling apart. Secondly, the weather conditions from November to March were favourable for military action after which time the heat and dust storms would make it impossible to use the military option, for another six months at least.

The persistence of such arguments and the political effort Baker engaged in during the autumn and winter of 1990 in raising support for the use of force, made it questionable whether there was in fact any desire on the part of the dominant actors in the crisis to find a diplomatic solution to an infringement of international law through the mechanisms of the United Nations.

What are the Costs of Sanctions and Who Pays?

Sanctions were applied for six months before the outbreak of war. During that time, a large number of nations, particularly the oil importing Third World countries, found themselves facing increased economic hardship. As Margaret Doxey, in her excellent analysis of sanctions notes, collective international action invariably places a disproportionate burden on those that are least able to carry it[7]. Although, in many historical cases, the costs of sanctions have been spread among a number of states, they are rarely spread evenly and certain countries are more vulnerable to the loss of trade or increase in commodity prices.

Early on in the application of sanctions against Iraq it was recognised that certain countries would face economic hardship as a result of UN actions. In recognition of the economic disruption this caused, the United States established a Gulf Financial Crisis Co-ordination Group (GFCCG) after the 22 September 1990 G-7 summit. The GFCCG met in early January, February and March 1991. Membership of the Fund included the US, the European Community, Japan and the three Gulf oil-producing states as well as Kuwait's government in exile.

The United States' attempt to deal with the consequences of sanctions was determined more by political considerations of maintaining cohesion in the military alliance against Iraq, particularly with respect to new-found and unlikely allies such as Syria and Egypt, than with any genuine concern for the economic hardships caused by sanctions. Those who suffered most were the frontline states Egypt and Turkey although Jordan, despite being the most highly vulnerable state, received very little assistance from the CFCCG because of King Hussein's tacit support for Iraq.

The Turkish government, estimated that the Gulf crisis cost it $5bn, in the 12 months from the beginning of the crisis. This sum included $1bn in lost exports to Iraq, about $400m in lost contracting and transport services, $300m in lost pipeline revenues, about $1bn to be paid in higher oil prices, (based on a price of $27 a barrel ($27/b)) and $700m in foregone Iraqi debt, net of Turkish debt servicing to Kuwait.[8] In addition, the Turkish treasury estimated that about $1bn was lost in earnings from tourism, around $400m in foreign investments, and about $200m in invisibles such as bank loans and workers' remittances.

According to Egyptian government estimates, Egypt was liable to lose $9bn – almost equivalent to half of Egypt's gross domestic product. This was undoubtedly an overestimate; ODI figures suggests a loss of $1bn corresponding to nearly 3 per cent of GDP. The losses include the loss of workers' remittances, the loss of income from the Suez Canal and a loss from tourism.[9]

The Jordanian economy was the most highly dependent upon Iraq, which took 50 per cent of its exports and supplied 90 per cent of its oil. The ODI estimated that Jordan stood to lose $1.8bn in 1990–1991 corresponding to 25 per cent of GNP. Loss of remittances amounted to $150m per annum while loss of savings and investment may have been as high as $8bn.[10] The GFCCG drive to raise compensation produced $13.5bn in commitments.

Economic Assistance for Frontline States

Contributions to the GFCCG totalled $13.5bn, of which:

► $8.8bn came from the Gulf States
► $2bn from Japan
► $2.2bn from European countries and EC

In addition to direct compensation the US and the Gulf states wrote off a significant amount of debt to Egypt, some $14bn of military loans. Compensation was also provided to Israel and Syria. Israel calculated its war costs at $3bn in lost tourism, industrial production, trade and direct damage. To cover this, it was expecting the US almost to double its annual aid contribution of around $3bn and also to write off its debt of $4.5bn. In addition, the Israeli government requested a further $10bn over the coming five years for the settlement of Soviet immigrants. Syria's token involvement in the military operations, brought it $1bn in aid from Saudi Arabia and a further $1.2bn from other Gulf states.

Impact on Other Economies

However, these countries were not the only economies to have suffered significant economic disruption as a result of the Gulf crisis. The indirect effects of the increase in oil prices, the loss of workers' remittances and the disruption in trade adversely affected countries as far afield as Sri Lanka and Romania. India, Pakistan, Bangladesh and the Philippines also lost substantial income from workers' remittances. In 1989 it was estimated that workers' remittances to developing countries amounted to £2.4bn.[11] In addition to the loss of revenue these countries had to pay for the repatriation of their citizens who had been working in Iraq and Kuwait. There were an estimated 190,000 Indian expatriates, 90,000 Bangladeshis, 45,000 Philippinos and 95,000 Sri Lankans and an unspecified number of Pakistanis stranded in Kuwait and Iraq. Many of these people fled the country, creating a refugee problem in neighbouring Jordan, which contributed further to the latter's economic crisis.[12]

Apart from the loss of trade and workers' remittances the main way in which economies were affected by the Gulf crisis was through oil price volatility. The immediate effect of sanctions against Iraq was to reduce the world supply of oil by 7.3 per cent or 4.5 million barrels a day – the combined output of both Iraq and Kuwait. The actual and potential curtailment of oil supply rapidly translated into oil price volatility. Within 48 hours of the Iraqi invasion of Kuwait world crude oil prices had increased from $18/b to $25/b, rising to $40/b in October when the price peaked as the fear of the imminent outbreak of war was transferred to the spot market in Amsterdam. Once the false alarm passed, however, the price settled at around $30/b until hostilities broke out on January 16th 1991.

'Psychology of the oil markets'

Although sanctions had an immediate effect on the global supply of oil, the OPEC countries were quick to substitute the shortfall in supplies, thus the price volatility of oil was more a reflection of the fear of the effect of war on the supplies of oil than a genuine disequilibrium between the global supply and demand for oil. The increase in the price of oil was attributable to hoarding and speculation, a phenomenon, referred to at the time by Sheik Yamani as the 'psychology of the oil markets', which was driven by short-term market perceptions.

The degree to which individual countries were affected by oil price volatility varied according to a number of factors, such as the degree of dependence on oil imports, the weight of oil consumption in total spending, and the general health of the economy. In the first five months of the crisis when the price of oil averaged out at about $30/b, the bigger a country's net oil imports the greater the loss of income when the price went up.

The hardest hit economies were the oil-importing Third World and Eastern European countries, all of which experienced considerable economic destabilisation. In contrast to reduced oil dependency in the OECD, many developing countries, especially in Latin America and the Far East, had come to use more energy per real dollar of GNP than in 1973 because of rapid industrialisation and urbanisation, greater use of motorised transport and subsidised energy prices. They thus found oil price increases even more disruptive than in earlier oil price shocks. The impact of higher oil prices was aggravated by slower growth in demand for their exports, higher interest rates and lower commodity prices.

A report commissioned from the Overseas Development Institute (ODI) by a number of leading charities identified at least 40 developing countries which suffered the equivalent of a natural disaster as a result of the economic consequences of the Gulf crisis[13]. The report stated that:

> At least 40 low and middle income countries suffer(ed) an impact of more than 1% of GNP: 16 of them over 2%, including countries as distant from the Gulf as Jamaica and Paraguay. The Indian States of Kerala and Gujarat, with a population together of over 70 million, would join them, if they were separate countries. The total direct cost for low income countries is at least $3.2bn, when lower middle income countries are included, it is at least $12bn.

Effect on the Third World

The effect on the Third World of the increase in the price of oil was particularly damaging in conjunction with the recession in the North, the debt crisis, falling prices for primary commodities, and in some cases internal conflict and drought. Table 1 shows the impact of the Gulf crisis on developing countries.

In relative terms the greatest losers were in sub-Saharan Africa. Without additional funds the consumption of oil in these countries fell with disastrous effect on the region's productive output which was 70 per cent dependent on oil. Years of austerity had already cut this region's oil import bill to a bare minimum. Further cuts in oil imports were translated into the closure of power stations, mines and factories. Transport was another obvious casualty. Cutbacks of this nature will transfer into slower growth in the future and result in a further slide in the living standards of some of the poorest peoples in the world.[14]

The ODI estimated that the sum necessary to compensate the 40 developing countries hit by the economic effects of the Gulf crisis was some $12bn, representing a relatively small amount in comparison with the estimated cost of the crisis put at between $80–$100bn. In dealing with this crisis the international community, more than in any other crisis invoked the articles of the United Nations. However the coalition did not implement Article 50 of the UN Charter which awards compensation to countries who are disadvantaged as a result

TABLE 1 IMPACT OF THE GULF CRISIS ON DEVELOPING COUNTRIES:
(Where impact is greater than 1 per cent of GNP)

Region	Country	Impact of Gulf Crisis as percentage GNP
Middle East	Jordan	25.3
	Turkey	4.5
	Egypt	2.9
	Yemen	10.4
North Africa	Morocco	1.8
South Asia	Bangladesh	1.2
	Pakistan	2.1
	Sri Lanka	3.7
East Asia	Papua New Guinea	1.8
	Philippines	1.5
	Thailand	1.5
Latin America	Costa Rica	1.5
& Caribbean	Dominican Rep.	2.7
	Honduras	1.3
	Jamaica	2.4
	Nicaragua	1.4
	Panama	1.4
	Paraguay	2.5
Sub-Saharan	Benin	2.2
Africa	Botswana	3.2
	Côte d'Ivoire	1.2
	Chad	2.5
	Ethiopia	1.9
	Kenya	1.4
	Lesotho	1.8
	Liberia	2.0
	Madagascar	1.9
	Mali	1.7
	Mauritania	1.2
	Mauritius	1.6
	Mozambique	1.7
	Rwanda	2.9
	Sudan	2.9
	Tanzania	2.6
	Zambia	1.1

Source: Overseas Development Institute, March 1991.

of Security Council decisions. The ODI report states in no uncertain terms:

> Sanctions and military action have brought harsh economic consequences to many developing countries. A political decision is needed to recognise these costs of the UN action as much as are the direct costs to the combatants and to implement Article 50.[15]

Just at a time when the global community appeared united in a common effort to improve global security, the Gulf crisis deflected the attention of the wealthy nations from the humanitarian needs of the world's poor. The enormous effort and resources put into sharing the burden of the costs of war and to gain political support for military action from the more reluctant participants such as China, the Soviet Union and France, was unavailable to those most adversely affected by the crisis. The fact that the main burden of economic sanctions was born by the least privileged sections of the world's population raises some difficult challenges to the use of collective sanctions. In particular, the further impoverishment of Third World oil-importing countries is counter-productive to many of the values which the United Nations seeks to promote, namely economic and social development and improvements in basic human rights. Although the negative effects of sanctions were recognised by the international institutions, the level of compensation and the search for solutions was minimal.

Despite this gloomy picture, there were some winners in the Third World, namely the oil producing states – Mexico, Venezuela, Iran, Indonesia and, of course, the oil producing Arab states. Mexico and Nigeria used their increased oil revenue to repay a significant part of their debts. Mexico's foreign reserves reached $10.3bn at the end of 1990, $3.4bn more than in 1989. This increase was largely derived from Mexico's $3bn windfall from higher oil prices.

And in Eastern Europe

Another part of the world to have been adversely affected by the Gulf crisis was Eastern Europe. Oil price increases coincided with the first time that Eastern European countries had to pay market prices in hard currency for their oil imports. Previously, most of these countries had had access to subsidised oil from the Soviet Union. However, Soviet oil production had been declining over the last three years. It was estimated to have fallen to about 585 million tonnes in 1990 compared with an output of 607 million in 1989 and 624 million in 1988. Oil exports declined by 17 million tonnes in 1989. As a result of the decline in oil production, the Soviet Union reneged on its contracts to the Eastern European countries who then faced a critical shortfall in oil supplies. Many Eastern European countries had intended to make up their shortfalls in orders from Iraq.[16]

Years of dependence on cheap Soviet oil, meant that the Eastern European countries failed to look for alternative energy supplies. To complicate matters the oil refineries in Eastern Europe had been designed to treat crude Soviet oil and were unable to use oil from other sources.

TABLE 2   USSR OIL EXPORTS TO EASTERN EUROPE 1989 (m tonnes)

Country	Total Shortfall	1990 Shortfall
Bulgaria	12.64	10–15%
Czechoslovakia	12.86	12%
E. Germany	20.13	na.
Hungary	7.79	22%
Poland	15.16	27–28%
Romania	3.95	na.
Yugoslavia	9.6	30%

Source: Financial Times, 13/9/90 September 1990.

Poland experienced a shortfall of 23 per cent in 1990. It had planned to import 3.8 million tonnes of oil from Iraq as part payment for contracts carried out in Iraq worth over $500m. Soviet oil deliveries to Czechoslovakia in July and August were cut by 15 per cent. The shortfall could have been met by Iraq's outstanding debt to Czechoslovakia, earned largely from arms exports. Hungary's supply of oil from the Soviet Union was reduced by 30 per cent in July 1990. The overall annual shortfall was estimated at 22 per cent. Bulgaria experienced a 10–15 per cent shortfall, it had planned to make up this shortfall in part from a 2.6 million tonne oil order from Iraq. Romania, which imported 3.9 million tonnes of Soviet crude in 1989 was not affected by Soviet cutbacks as it was able to substitute supplies from Iran and Saudi Arabia. However, Iraq continues to owe Romania more than $3bn. Hungary's supply of oil from the Soviet Union was reduced by 30 per cent in July 1990. The overall annual shortfall was estimated at 22 per cent. Yugoslavia also lost out as it had anticipated the delivery of 30 per cent of its crude oil from Iraq in 1990, in part payment for Iraq's outstanding debt of $3bn.

The oil shortage, the increase in oil prices, and the lack of hard currency have undoubtedly hindered the efforts at economic and political reconstruction in Eastern Europe. The IMF World Economic Outlook predicted that the economies of Eastern Europe would shrink by about 5.5 per cent, partly as a result of higher energy prices compounded by the high energy use in the region.[17] Despite calls for compensation to Eastern European countries, there was only a limited response by the international community.

As the crisis deepened and the march towards war became inevitable, the plight of Eastern Europe and the world's poorest nations was all but forgotten. Yet there had been at least one way in which the international community could have reduced the effect of sanctions without recourse to direct compensation. That would have been to take interventionary action in the oil market through the mechanism of the International Energy Agency (IEA), as had been argued in a Chatham House study in 1982, following the Iranian revolution.[18]

Estimated Cost of the War

Military action against Iraq was legitimised for a number of reasons, including the violation of international law, the threat to Western strategic interests and the threat to peace and stability in the Middle East. UN Resolution 678 clearly expressed the stated aim of international collective action, namely to force Iraq to withdraw from Kuwait. However, once military action had begun it became clear to all but the most blinkered of observers that the American intention was also to destroy Iraq's military capability and the economic infrastructure upon which the military depended. This objective engaged the Allies in an aerial campaign the scale of which had not been seen since the Second World War.

The allied reliance on high technology equipment and the high intensity of the conflict, made the Gulf War the most expensive war in history, on a day-to-day basis. The total cost of the war to the allied forces has been estimated at between $80–$100bn.[20] Even before hostilities broke out the deployment of military forces in the Gulf involved a considerable economic cost. Washington estimated that its pre-war military costs amounted to $8–9bn, while the UK's costs were put at $2bn (£1bn), of which £520m was accounted for within the 1990/91 defence budget[21].

Early estimates by the US Congress Budget Office of the costs of the war were put at between $28bn–86bn. Once the war ended, the Secretary of Budget declared that it had cost $61bn, a figure which Congress thought an exaggeration, because it was based upon the assumption that all lost materiel would be replaced. The most recent Congress Budget Office assessment of the costs puts the figure at $45bn.

The 1991 Statement on Defence Estimates put the costs of UK operations at £2.5bn. although the final figure had not yet been determined at time of writing since many decisions had to be made concerning the replenishment or repair of lost and damaged equipment. It is likely that the total bill, including munitions and equipment replacement, will come out at around £3.5–£4bn, these costs are likely to be spread over several years. It is expected that the bulk of the additional costs will be covered by the cash contributions pledged by other nations. Contributions received by Britain in 1990–91 totalled some £518m, with a further £1.5m pledged for 1991–92.

Burden Sharing

Anxieties about the economic burden of the cost of the war mobilised the US into a 'burden sharing' campaign. Following a fund-raising world tour in September 1990, James Baker secured a significant level of commitment to cover compensation for the frontline states and the costs of Operation DESERT SHIELD. The arguments the US used to extract financial commitments were an exact replica of the burden-sharing debate with both their NATO allies and Japan. Just as in the past, linkages between trade, money and security were explicit, as threats were made to restrict the US market or to withdraw armed forces from the territories of penny-pinching allies. This pressure continued after the Gulf war ended, as Congress tried to ensure the fulfilment of prior pledges. In March 1991, the Senate voted by an overwhelming majority to stop arms sales to defaulters and several legislative proposals were introduced in August 1991 to increase the import duties from countries that had not paid in full. The argument used to justify such pressure focused on the role of the US in protecting global oil supplies and the great dependence of Europe and especially Japan on Middle Eastern sources of supply.

After some initial reluctance to fund what was clearly seen as a mercenary army, the US received pledges of $53bn from Japan, Kuwait and Saudi Arabia, the United Arab Emirates and Germany. Contributions were in both cash and kind, the latter in the form of oil, food, water and equipment. Given that a large proportion of the donations were from the Gulf states, Baker can be said to have invented a unique method of recycling petro-dollars. The size of the donations led to an embarrassing situation for the US, which appears to have made a profit of at least $8bn from the war.

In contrast to the US initiative, Britain was slow to ask for contributions to its war effort. Only after war broke out, when an indication of the likely scale of costs became apparent did the government begin to make noises about burden sharing. In total the United Kingdom received pledges of just over £2bn. Unlike the US the UK did not made a profit. It is unlikely that the true cost of the war to the UK will ever be known, due to the government's reluctance to reveal a figure which might be politically unacceptable. Whatever the size of the extra burden on the defence budget, it will mean that either defence cuts are slowed down or internal efficiencies will have to be made.

Given the scale of foreign contributions to the United States and

TABLE 3   GULF CRISIS: MAIN FINANCIAL CONTRIBUTIONS
(to cost of the war, $bn)

	US	UK	of which, aid in kind totalled
Saudi Arabia	16.80	0.56	6.0
Kuwait	16.01	1.32	–
UAE	4.00	0.50	0.14
Germany	6.57	0.60	0.53
Italy	0.45	–	–
Japan	10.74	–	0.46
South Korea	0.37	–	0.02
Norway	–	0.175	–
EC		0.02	–
Total	54.94	3.175	7.15

Source: *International-Strategic-Studies: The Military Balance 1991–92*(1159/Brasseys).

United Kingdom war efforts the cost of the Gulf War to these economies has proved relatively marginal. But for both countries it is unlikely that they will be able to mount an operation on the scale of the Gulf war again. For despite optimism about the precedent set through burden-sharing in the Gulf War, it is doubtful whether the OECD countries with financial power will be so willing to see the international agenda set by those with military power. Both Germany and Japan were reluctant contributors. What is certain is that the war has forced them both to examine their foreign and defence policies and to see themselves as important actors on the global stage. The long-term ramifications of this process for the international balance of power is yet to manifest itself, but already there are signs that the role which these two countries will play may well be different from the traditional military approach to international relations adopted by the United States and the United Kingdom. For the oil rich countries such as Kuwait and Saudi Arabia who provided some 60 percent of the funding for the war, their economic power has been subtly and irreversibly weakened so that, at least in the medium-term, it is unlikely that they would be able to provide a similar scale of financial support.

The Indirect Costs of War

During the war there was much speculation in the press about the economic consequences of war. The economic uncertainty which the war generated contrasted greatly with one popular misconception –

that wars coincide with economic expansion. This notion is based upon the naive assumption that the increased defence expenditure generated by the Gulf would provide the stimulus to ease Western economies out of the growing recession. Simultaneously, an opposite sentiment was being expressed that the direct cost of the war would fuel inflation. Neither prognostication was borne out by the war in the Gulf.

In the first place, equipment replacement was unlikely to generate a sufficiently significant increase in procurement spending to act as a demand stimulus for the manufacturing sector. In both countries the general trend in defence spending was on a downward curve and there was no indication that the Gulf War had reversed that process.

Secondly, wars cause inflationary booms when they raise the demand for labour and goods beyond the capacity of economies to supply them. The war in the Gulf was fought with soldiers and equipment which had already been supplied and was thus unlikely to drain additional resources from the economies involved. With some of the costs of war being offset through burden sharing, the war simply delayed the slow down in defence spending which was already under way. A likely consequence of this could be a smaller than expected peace dividend, which would not cause the surge in demand that some observers anticipated.[22] Rather than through the direct cost of war, it was through its indirect effect on prices, markets and investor confidence that the Gulf War impacted on the global economy and in particular affected the developed market economies.

The Developed Market Economies

The Bank of England Quarterly Bulletin claimed that the uncertainty caused by the war, by undermining investor confidence, weakened share prices everywhere and had effects on relative demands for different currencies, arresting the weakening of the US dollar against the yen and the mark. In combination, these effects have contributed to the slowing down of global economic growth.[23] The May Bulletin stated that:

> Although there is little evidence of the Gulf crisis having direct output effects (except in the oil industry), confidence effects have contributed to the downward revisions to growth forecasts for the major overseas economies in 1991. The crisis has affected the progress of budgetary consolidation. Supplementary budgets to fund Gulf related expenditures have been approved in Japan and proposed in the US, while in Germany a package of tax increases has been adopted, largely to offset the rising cost of unification, but also to finance contributions to Gulf war effort. In France public expenditure is to be reduced partly to offset costs of funding the Gulf crisis.

The high price of oil contributed to a further decline in Japan's current account surplus which declined from $60bn in 1989 to $40bn in 1990[24]. This in turn affected the pattern of Japan's capital flows, resulting in Japanese banks' retrenchment from international business. As financial inflows in the US from Japan diminished so the US economy continued to slow down thereby reducing US government revenues. In addition to the influence on capital flows, the war affected specific sectors of the global economy, such as the airline and travel business, which suffered an unprecedented downturn in demand. This, in turn, dampened demand for aircraft replacement, causing considerable problems for the global aerospace industry.

The downturn in consumer confidence affecting retail sales led manufacturing and service companies to postpone investment decisions and lay-off large numbers of employees. The European OECD members experienced a drop in industrial production of some 1 percent between September and December 1990. In the UK, the recession deepened more than most forecasters had envisaged. GDP declined by over 2 percent and there was still, at the time of writing, little sign of recovery. Unemployment rose by 60,000 a month, in the three months to December 1990 and, by the second quarter of 1991, had risen to an average of 80,000 a month.[25]

The hopes that the ending of hostilities would restore consumer confidence and bring about an end to the recessions in the US and UK were short-lived. Feelings of patriotism and victory were not enough to reverse the deep economic malaise being experienced in both countries. Nor did the hope that the rebuilding of Kuwait would act as a much needed pump primer, come to fruition. Although the bill for the reconstruction of Kuwait was sizeable, (estimated at between $50–$100bn), payments for contracts were to be spread out over several years and were therefore unlikely to provide the immediate boost to demand required.

Damage to Middle Eastern Economies

Kuwait sustained considerable damage to its economy through the destruction of its oil wells and refineries and damage to its infrastructure. Early estimates of the cost of restoring Kuwait's oil production total some $20bn, $10bn for restoring oil production and another $10bn for repairing the damage to refineries[26]. It has been estimated that the destruction of the oil wells through fire, reduced Kuwaiti oil reserves by 10–15 percent, which represents a significant long-term loss to the economy. There was also a huge amount of reconstruction work involving the rebuilding of roads, hotels and so forth, estimated at about $20bn.

In addition to the cost of economic reconstruction, Kuwait took on huge financial commitments in the form of burden sharing – $16bn for US military support and a further $10bn for other coalition partners. The cost of these commitments combined with the extent of reconstruction have placed a strain even on Kuwait's vast assets, some $90bn in cash, bonds and equities. The Kuwaiti government was understandably reluctant to liquidise all their assets, for example their 9.8 percent stake in BP and a 25 percent share of the German chemical group Hoechst, in order to realise the capital for reinvestment, which was fortunate for those companies. Instead they were forced to borrow some $20bn against these assets and their future oil reserves[27]. The government also developed some innovative financial schemes to raise capital including the giving to foreign oil companies of equity stakes in exchange for help in restoring the petrochemical industry.

However, the Kuwaiti government used reconstruction as an opportunity to reshape its national economy. It looked to create a less populous country, reducing its expatriate labour force by about 1 million. This enforced economic hardship on those Third World communities who had been dependent on migrant workers' remittances from Kuwait. The plight of the Palestinian people was particularly tragic. Many Palestinians who had been resident in Kuwait for years, were denied access to work and deported from the country. The loss of income was a serious economic blow not only to the Kuwaiti Palestinians but to many of their community in the diaspora who were dependent on those fortunate enough to have regular incomes. The persecution of Palestinians in the aftermath of the war gave rise to concern amongst human rights organisations, who have condemned the Kuwaiti government.

Another far less quantifiable cost that the Gulf crisis incurred was the effect of the ecological disaster. Of about 1,000 oil wells in Kuwait 800 were damaged through fire. It was estimated that between 4–6 million barrels – worth up to $76m (£40m) – $114 (£60) – a day were being destroyed. The burning oil wells produced highly toxic black smoke, blocking out the sunlight and thereby reducing the temperature in parts of Kuwait by several degrees. The smoke contained high concentrations of hydrogen sulphide, which contributed to an outbreak of respiratory disorders. Medical experts could only guess at the long-term health problems which are bound to result from exposure to such toxic fumes.

The task of fighting the fires was enormous. Vast amounts of equipment had to be flown in from America and a huge number of pipes were laid to carry an estimated 100,000 to 150,000 tonnes of water needed to cool each well. The Texan teams brought in to fight the fires, had never encountered a disaster on the scale of that in Kuwait. The president of O'Brien, Goins, Simpson Inc., a Texan oil-field engineering company, estimated that the cost of just putting out the fires might be $2bn[28].

In addition to the oil well fires, there was the problem of the oil spill in the Straits of Hormuz which was threatening the delicate ecology of these inland sea waters. A thorough assessment of the damage produced a figure for the spill of 2m barrels. This was eight times the amount of crude oil spilled in the Exxon Valdez disaster and it polluted dozens of beaches along the Gulf coast.

The damage caused by a spill arises not so much from its size as from its location, the ease with which it can be dispersed and the environmental sensitivity of a region. The geography and climate of the Gulf – essentially a closed sea – make it especially vulnerable to oil pollution. Several endangered species faced an increased threat from the spillage, including whales and bottle-nosed dolphins. Marine turtles and rare crabs were also highly vulnerable. The Gulf's coral reefs (described as the 'rain forests of the sea') support hundreds of species of fauna and form a critical link in the marine food chain, which supports fish which in turn are a major source of food for the local human population. The marine life of the Gulf is also vitally linked to bird life. The area is a main pathway for bird migrations between Siberia and the winter nesting grounds in Eastern Africa. The shrimping and fishing industries were affected as well as the pearl industry which, before the discovery of oil, had sustained the Gulf economy for hundreds of years. Oil pollution also posed a threat to the supply of fresh water, from desalination plants (Saudi Arabia alone has at least 29 of these). All these factors affect the communities along the shores of the Gulf whose economic survival is linked to the health of the sea.

The Saudi Arabian economy was also facing considerable financial problems. Despite an estimated $33bn in oil revenues in 1991, the government faced a budget deficit of $50bn (not helped by its commitment of $16.5bn to cover US military costs). In the past, the Saudis had financed their deficits by internal borrowing but post crisis some foreign borrowing looked unavoidable. Borrowing from international financial markets opened up both the Saudi and Kuwaiti economies to foreign influence for the first time. In the long term, this may have a profound effect on the structure of economic development in the region.

Needless to say, the most adversely affected Middle Eastern economy was Iraq's. Coalition bombing and shelling destroyed much of the civilian infrastructure – roads, communications, electricity supplies, water and sewage systems and health care facilities were destroyed. A UN fact-finding mission to Iraq in March 1991 reported that:

The recent conflict has wrought near-apocalyptic results upon the economic infrastructure of what had been, until January 1991, a rather highly urbanised and mechanised society. Now, most means of modern life support have been destroyed or rendered tenuous. Iraq, has, for some time to come, been relegated to a pre-industrial age, but with all the disabilities of post-industrial dependency on an intensive use of energy and technology[29].

Reports by aid agencies revealed the health consequences of the immediate postwar damage to civilian infrastructure, the biggest health hazards being the lack of clean water and the breakdown of sewage systems which led to an increase in infectious diarrhoea, particularly among children. Medical Aid for Iraq estimated that in April 50 civilians were dying each day from waterborne diseases[30]. After a tour of Iraq in March 1991, Dr H J Geiger of US Physicians for Human Rights summarised the destruction of the country's civilian infrastructure as 'a bomb now, die later kind of war . . . This is a slow moving catastrophe of immense proportions[31].'

While the slow rebuilding of the infrastructure could gradually increase the availability of electrical power, access to clean water and disposal of sewage and waste in some of the larger cities, growing malnutrition, deteriorating health and lack of sanitation all increased the risks of epidemics and water-borne diseases throughout the region. Improvement in this situation was dependent on massive infrastructural repair which was beyond the capabilities of the Iraqi government while UN sanctions remained. The ability to rebuild Iraqi infrastructure and thus prevent the on-going human catastrophe was compounded by Kuwait's demand for war reparations.

The United Nations' Gulf war cease-fire resolution confirmed that Iraq was liable under international law for any direct loss, damage or injury to foreign governments, nationals and corporations as a result of its unlawful invasion and occupation of Kuwait. The resolution called for the creation of a fund from Iraq's oil revenues to provide compensation and a commission to administer it. As yet it has not been decided how much compensation should be paid, when it might be paid and who should decide who would get it. The answers to these questions were certain to play a large part in determining the economic future of post-war Iraq. Inevitably, the figure for total reparations would have to balance legitimate claims for compensation against what was needed for Iraq to survive and re-enter the world community. Charles Brower suggested that once a fixed sum was set, the fund could draw from Iraq's oil revenues at a specified rate until the total was reached. Alternatively, a percentage could be levied on Iraq's oil revenues for a stated number of years, possibly subject to review and potential modification as events dictated[32].

Whatever the mechanism and the final sum fixed, the result would be that, even with zero world inflation and the present level of oil prices, Iraq's oil exports would be mortgaged for at least 30 years to come, leaving Iraq unable to restore its economy to its pre-war levels of developments, although Bush hinted that the removal of Saddam Hussein might allow for a Marshall-style aid programme from the international community, coupled with debt relief. Without such a programme, Iraq will be condemned to economic misery for the many years to come which will undoubtedly contribute to further internal instability and strife. US diplomats are aware that Iraq must not be squeezed too harshly, that the kind of humiliation imposed on Germany through the Versailles Treaty must be avoided, as in the long run it could be counter-productive.

Conclusion

Given the scale of foreign contributions to the American and British war efforts, the cost of the Gulf War to those economies proved relatively marginal, particularly when compared to the economic burdens incurred by many Third World countries as a result of the crisis. However, both the US and UK have been adversely affected by the indirect effects of war. The structural weakness of both economies, which has been attributed to their high military spending, has been exposed by the global recession which was intensified by the war.

The burden of costs incurred as a result of the Gulf crisis has been unequally distributed and, through the combination of the direct and indirect costs, the North/South divide has been intensified. For example, the US was likely to receive direct inflows from the Middle East of between $50–$100bn, while many Third World countries have suffered large-scale reductions in their national wealth. In effect, the global economy has been altered in subtle but profound ways. Specifically, the war has led to a transformation of the previously insular economies of Saudi Arabia and Kuwait, forcing them to interface with the financial institutions of the West and in so doing opening them up to Western economic power and influence.

Despite the large transfers of capital to America, the economy has not benefited from the war, as the indirect costs were partly responsible for the present American recession. Moreover, if the US increases its spending on military equipment as a result of the Gulf War, then the influx of petro-dollars is likely to be absorbed by defence spending, rather than being channelled into domestic productive investment which lies at the root of economic malaise in the United States.

Governments throughout the world are being forced to grapple with a bewildering variety of economic problems which have arisen from, or have been exacerbated by the Gulf crisis. The fact that the main burden of international action against Iraq has been borne by the least privileged sections of the world's population raises some difficult challenges for the United Nations. In particular, the further impoverishment of the Third World and Eastern European oil-importing countries is destructive of many of the values which the United Nations seeks to promote, namely economic and social development and the improvements of basic human rights. Although this problem has been recognised, the level of compensation and the search for solutions has been minimal. But perhaps more importantly, the economic burden of the Gulf crisis could lead to greater global insecurity as the emiserisation of vulnerable economies precipitates instability and volatility. Such an outcome would undermine the very principles upon which the legitimacy of the Gulf War was based, namely for greater peace and security.

Rarely in the debate on how to deal with international or regional crises are the economic implications given the due consideration they deserve, in part because they are so incalculable (and perhaps also because those who suffer most do not have the strongest international voice). Given the general problem of knock-on economic consequences, we should realise that future recourse to such action will raise again the issue of the extra burdens placed on the poorest countries of the world. If they come to feel that the United Nations' actions result in greater hardship for them and economic advantage for the rich nations, they are likely to be wary of future calls to international action under the auspices of the United Nations.

Notes

1. Isabelle Grunberg, *Financial Power and Military Security in the New World Order: Burden Sharing in the Gulf War*, Paper presented to the British International Studies Association, Warwick Conference 16–18 December 1991.
2. *Financial Times* 30 October 1991.
3. The US Congressional Budget Office have estimated that the US cost of the war did not exceed $45bn, while contributions to the US effort amounted to a total of $53bn.
4. The text of the speech of Secretary of State Baker to the NATO Council on 13 August 1990 in Brussels is available from the United States Information Service, US Embassy.
5. Speech of Secretary of State Baker, *op. cit.*
6. *New York Times* 6 December 1990.
7. Margaret Doxey: *Economic Sanctions and International Enforcement*; (Royal Institute of International Affairs. Macmillan 1980).
8. *Financial Times* 20 September 1990.
9. Overseas Development Institute, *The Economic Impact of the Gulf*

Crisis on Third World Countries, Memorandum to the Foreign Affairs Select Committee, Jointly submitted by CAFOD, Christian Aid, CIIR, Oxfam, Save the Children Fund and World Development Movement, March 1991.

10. *Ibid.*
11. *Financial Times*, 12 September 1990.
12. *Independent*, 12 September 1990.
13. *The Economic Impact of the Gulf Crisis on Third World Countries* (published jointly by CAFOD, Christian Aid, CIIR, Oxfam, Save the Children Fund and the World Development Movement, available from Oxfam, 274 Banbury Rd, Oxford OX2 7DZ, March 1991).
14. See Leonard Doyle 'Gulf Stand-off will crush poor nations': *The Independent* 22/10/90.
15. ODI *op.cit.* p8.
16. Judy Dempsey, 'Lamps going dim in Eastern Europe', *Financial Times*, 13 September 1990.
17. International Monetary Fund, *op.cit.*
18. See D Badger and R Belgrave *Oil Supply and Price: What Went Right in 1980?* Energy Paper No 2. British Joint Energy Policy Programme, Policy Studies Institute (Royal Institute of International Affairs, 1982).
20. *Guardian*, 28 January 1991.
21. *Financial Times*, 23 January 1991.
22. T Barker, J P Dunne and R Smith, *Measuring the Peace Dividend in the United Kingdom*, (Journal of Peace Research, 1990).
23. *Bank of England Quarterly Bulletin* (Bank of England, Feb 1991)
24. *Ibid.*
25. *Bank of England Quarterly Bulletin* (Bank of England, May 1991).
26. *International Business Week*, 11 March 1991 p 26.
27. *Financial Times*, 8 March 1991.
28. *International Business Week*, *op.cit.*
29. *Report to the Secretary-General on Humanitarian Needs in Kuwait and Iraq in the Immediate Post-Crisis Environment*, by a mission led by Mr Martti Ahtisaari, Under Secretary General for Administration and Management, United Nations, 28 March 1991.
30. Quoted in *Counting the Human Cost of the Gulf War*; (MET Report, The Medical Educational Trust, June 1991). p13.
31. '*Iraq; Bomb Now, Die Later*' The Lancet, 20 April 1991.
32. Charles Brower; 'Settling Iraqi Reparations'; *Financial Times*; 11 April 1991. Charles Bower has been a judge of the Iran-United States Claims Tribunal at the Hague since 1984.

10

The Gulf War and the New World Order

Lawrence Freedman

The idea that the Gulf crisis was a test case for a 'new world order' was introduced almost as the Iraqi tanks rolled into Kuwait on 2 August 1990. The phrase itself did not play a prominent part in rationales for the US decision to commit forces to the defence of Saudi Arabia on 8 August, but in his speech to the American people explaining the decision President George Bush did convey the essential idea of a 'new era', which could be 'full of promise, an age of freedom, a time of peace for all peoples', and which would be put at risk if there was a failure to resist aggression.[1]

The creation of a new world order was not stated as an explicit American objective until 11 September 1990. In an address to Congress Bush restated what had become the four basic objectives of American policy – immediate and unconditional Iraqi withdrawal from Kuwait, restoration of Kuwait's legitimate government, assurance of security and stability in the Gulf, and protection of American citizens. He continued:

> We stand today at a unique and extraordinary moment. The crisis in the Persian Gulf, as grave as it is, also offers a rare opportunity to move toward an historic period of co-operation. Out of these troubled times, our fifth objective – a new world order – can emerge: a new era – freer from the threat of terror, stronger in the pursuit of justice, and more secure in the quest for peace. An era in which the nations of the world, East and West, North and South, can prosper and live in harmony.[2]

Immediately after the war Bush told Congress that hopes for an enduring peace had before been 'beyond the grasp of man', but 'now we can see a new world coming into view'. Later, Bush began to spell out his meaning of the 'New World Order' in a series of post-war speeches. In the first of these he offered the following definition:

> The New World Order does not mean surrendering our national sovereignty or forfeiting our interests. It really describes a responsibility imposed by our successes. It refers to new ways of working with other nations to deter aggression and to achieve stability, to achieve prosperity and, above all, to achieve peace. It springs from hopes for a world based on a shared commitment among nations large and small to a set of principles that undergird our relations – peaceful settlement of disputes, solidarity against aggression, reduced and controlled arsenals, and just treatment of all peoples.

He described the Gulf war as the first test of this new order. Its novel features were that a regional conflict did not serve as a proxy for superpower confrontation, the United Nations Security Council functioned as intended and nations from all around the world joined together against an aggressor. He acknowledged that the world was not moving into 'an era of perpetual peace'. Instead, 'The quest for the New World Order is in part a challenge to keep the dangers of disorder at bay.'[3]

Even from within the President's own formulations it is therefore possible to detect two versions of the new world order. The first and most optimistic and positive version of the concept offers the vision of the international community achieving its most cherished values of peace, stability, justice and prosperity. The second, and more moderate, version simply suggests that the international community is now better able to cope with challenges to its basic norms.

Naturally, the first version is the most vulnerable to charges of exaggerated ambition; soaring rhetoric can race ahead of reality. In the awkward weeks after the successful conclusion of the war, with President Saddam Hussein still in power and international attention focused on some of the more painful and discreditable aspects of the post-war condition of both Iraq and Kuwait and of American policy, the outcome appeared to fall far short of any vision of a better world.[4] Even with the second version, based on the four principles outlined in Bush's speech of 13 April, there are obvious difficulties. For example, the promise of just treatment for all peoples is problematic because it raises the fundamental question of how the tension between the rights of states (non-interference in internal affairs) is to be reconciled with the rights of individuals and of groups. It is also extremely ambitious because the definition of injustice is always controversial. At any given time there are numerous instances of injustice by any definition, and the self-determination of individual groups can be in direct conflict with one another. So, while a description of a new world order that excluded reference to injustice would be found wanting, once this is included then achievement is certain to fall far short of the reality. In any event, the problems of interpretation and enforcement in individual cases ensure a mixed achievement.

Most commentators dismissed the first version as rhetoric and came down in favour of the second. As Flora Lewis has put it, the rules of international behaviour that Bush has in mind may be needed, but this does not constitute a new world order – just a more orderly world. She also notes that one of the problems with Bush's phrase is that a call for 'order' from Washington 'chills practically everyone else', because it sounds suspiciously like a *Pax Americana*.[5]

An underlying theme in all the discussions is that the United States has now acquired a pre-eminent position in the international hierarchy. This situation has developed because of the precipitate decline of the Soviet Union. Bush himself has indicated that it is the new relationship with Moscow that creates the possibility for his new order. For many analysts, therefore, the new order's essential feature is not the values it is said to embody nor the principles upon which it is to be based, but that it has the United States at its centre. According to this view, the problem lies in an overestimation of American capabilities and its readiness to intervene when the next challenge arises.[6]

The optimistic version argues that the political transformations currently under way can be channelled into a generally harmonious and virtuous system of international relationships. The moderate version doubts this, but suggests that at the very least the new system of relationships can keep in check the disorderly and fissiparous tendencies associated with these transformations.

In effect, the debate is over the consequences of the West's victory in the Cold War rather than in the Gulf for the generality of international conflicts. A cynical interpretation of Bush's rhetoric is that this is the most recent example of a tendency that can be traced back to Woodrow Wilson's promotion of national self-determination and Franklin Roosevelt's promise of the 'Four Freedoms'. The language of idealism is employed in the service of the traditional preoccupations of power politics. Thus, William Pfaff argues that the new world order may simply add up to the United States making greater use of international institutions while pursuing its national interests. The question then becomes one of whether national interests are defined in a wide or narrow manner.[7]

While there is much to be said for the view that at issue is the use to be made of international institutions and norms by the United States, Pfaff overlooks the extent to which these institutions and the international system which they imperfectly reflect also shape American behaviour. The invocation of a new order does more than simply dignify old-fashioned power politics with an idealistic label.

A Pax Americana?

The basis for a *Pax Americana* lies in Washington's capacity to exert overwhelming military power and leadership over a multinational coalition. The fact that a 'unipolar' world is now taken seriously is an interesting commentary on fashions in punditry, given that 'declinism' was in vogue barely two years ago and that more sophisticated analysis assumed not that bipolarity would shrink into unipolarity, but would grow into multipolarity with new centres of power.

There were always a number of reasons to qualify the model of bipolarity, especially when the focus was on economic rather than raw military power, and there were many states who felt able to stand aside from East–West conflict. Now the model no longer works at all: while the Western pole has held, the Eastern pole has disintegrated. When at the end of the 1980s the Warsaw Pact collapsed, the states of Eastern Europe redefined their international position as they redefined their basic political and economic orientation. The Soviet Union still has many of the attributes of a superpower, including its nuclear capability. However, it is self-absorbed: its military is in internal upheaval and withdrawing from the European garrisons; the gap between its technology and that of the West is growing; and its international prestige generally is in decline.

While the United States is now the only 'super' power, it recognized in the Gulf that it was not *that* super. The Bush Administration took great economic risks in the Gulf war. It accepted the high costs of *Desert Shield* and a rise in the price of oil even though an economic recession was under way. If the war had gone badly the collapse in American economic confidence could have been dire, and this, in itself, indicates a good reason for not rushing into these sorts of activities in the future – especially against, rather than with, the rest of the international community. Even in the Gulf, it was necessary to pass the hat round to partners who were not able to contribute in other ways – Germany and Japan – and to the main beneficiaries of Western military action – Saudi Arabia and Kuwait. If the charge of being mercenary stung, it was not for long. It was as well that America's regional backers were wealthy.

Washington took the lead in the Gulf, but US capacity for action depended on co-operation from three other groups of states: those in the region who were threatened by Iraq; Western states who shared the risks and responsibilities of taking action against Iraq; and states unwilling or unable to take direct action but who were crucial in ensuring the passage of UN Security Council resolutions, China and the Soviet Union being the most important in this regard.

Western Europe

The level of consultation and co-ordination of policies among the Western powers remains remarkably high. This is important to bear in mind because so much of international politics up to 1945 was shaped by the competition for power and influence between these countries – especially the major European states of the UK, Germany and France. Even at the start of the 1990s, they could still look at the Middle East with very different perspectives. However, in the Gulf crisis the factors pulling them together turned out to be far more profound than those pushing them apart. This tends to be underestimated by those who see post-Cold War international politics reverting to the pattern of an earlier and cruder period of great power politics.[8]

The Gulf crisis found most Europeans in a reactive mode. It is supposed that if the Community had pushed harder on the linkage between the Kuwaiti and the Palestinian issues, then a breakthrough might have been achieved. This was vetoed at the start of 1991 by the British and Dutch. For those of this persuasion, the problem was therefore the unanimity requirement in the Council of Ministers.[9] Majority voting might have made a push on linkage possible, but there is no evidence that Saddam was interested in an international peace conference as a cover for withdrawal, nor that he was interested in courting Europe separately from the United States.[10] When France decided at the last minute to go it alone on this initiative, after the Council of Ministers had decided collectively not to do so, it reinforced suspicions that when high national interests are at stake there would be no respect for the disciplines of a common policy.

In terms of military operations, there was little choice but for the UK and France to place themselves under American command. The Western European Union distinguished itself in co-ordinating naval forces, but not in a particularly demanding situation. It seems to have done enough for it to be seen as the basis of a new European Defence Community (at least in its 'out-of-area' role), but there is little here to build on in terms of ground forces.

In addition, three other features are relevant. First, the European proposals tended to be for the type of forum in which Europe could act most naturally as a collectivity (e.g., international peace conferences, Conference on Security and Co-operation in the Mediterranean, etc.). Second, there is the extent to which the British and French posture was as much determined by their responsibilities as Permanent Members of the Security Council rather than of the European Council of Ministers. Third, the protracted and painful process by which an aid package was put together for Egypt, Jordan and Turkey was discouraging because it might be expected that the

European Community would be most geared to the economic dimensions of crisis management.

The Community's response to the Kurdish tragedy was less slow than that of the United States, and this provided an opportunity for an initiative. France set the tone with a demand that the plight of the Kurds be taken seriously, and this was followed by a British proposal for 'safe havens', unanimously adopted by the European Council. It also moved with unusual speed to agree an aid package.[11] However, again there were limits to what the Community could do on its own if the Americans had remained passive. Its role on this occasion appears to have been mainly to help resolve a deadlocked American debate.

If it is the case that military power may be less significant in the near future, then the Community's collective economic power should come into its own. Its first priority must therefore be to develop this economic power as an instrument of external policy, for if it fails here, there is little reason to expect it to succeed on the more ambitious plans for a collective defence policy. The test for this will come with developments in Central and Eastern Europe, where great problems are appearing and the Community will be expected to lead the West (as it is doing with the Group of 24).

This prognosis is therefore no different from what it would have been prior to the crisis. The supreme test for the European Community in its move to a common foreign policy lies in its capacity to cope with the aftermath of the implosion of communism in Europe and this will, in the first instance, require the sorting out of the relationship between its external commercial interests, its external political interests, and its internal development. In this sense, attempting to develop a common capacity to deal with a repetition of the Gulf crisis is a distraction.

The Soviet Union

The weakness of the Soviet Union was a key element in forging the anti-Iraq coalition. The USSR's economic troubles ensured a high stake in close and co-operative relations with the West. The coincidence of a visit by US Secretary of State James Baker to Moscow just as the crisis was breaking made possible a strong joint statement condemning Iraq's action and calling for an embargo on arms supplies to Iraq.[12] In early September, President Bush made a point of meeting President Mikhail Gorbachev in an emergency summit. Treating the Soviet Union as an important player reduced the risk of it acting as a 'spoiler' in the crisis. During the war, there were complaints in the Supreme Soviet over Moscow's support for a military campaign against a former client; the war was widely perceived as a pretext for the establishment of a Western military presence close to the Soviet Union's southern border.[13] Some in the ruling group saw the possibility of reasserting the Soviet Union's international role by using residual links with Iraq to forge a diplomatic breakthrough both before the war and in the flurry of activity preceding the ground offensive. It is an interesting question as to whether Gorbachev considered that he might be doing the United States a favour by developing an acceptable diplomatic alternative to what many expected to be a land battle that would be painful for coalition forces. At any rate, when Washington made it clear that it wanted nothing less than Saddam Hussein's agreement to all Security Council resolutions, Moscow did not complain about the collapse of its much-publicized initiative, and it put the blame for continued fighting on Saddam.

The importance of a good working relationship with Moscow was essential to the coalition's use of the Security Council. The Gulf war might not serve as a model for future international crisis management if there is a reversion to a more antagonistic East–West relationship. However, given the dire economic situation in the Soviet Union, even an authoritarian government in Moscow would require a degree of Western support. A return to a pre-Gorbachev hard line could not occur, because it would be impossible to retrieve the ground conceded since the end of 1989. Nor is it necessary to suppose that the readiness to allow the Security Council to work is simply a function of Soviet weakness. It did not hinder the British use of the Security Council during the 1982 Falklands War. Moreover, the current pattern of co-operation began in 1988, when efforts to bring the Iran–Iraq War to a close were initiated. Permanent membership of the Security Council flatters Soviet diplomacy, and if the Council ceased to operate effectively then it would risk further marginalization.

The risk is more of a growing disorder, as the Soviet economy deteriorates further. This could render co-operation with Moscow difficult in practical terms, and lead to a series of crises around the outer rim of the Soviet Union. This may mean that the Soviet Union will be much more implicated in future crises, which could hinder crisis diplomacy. It may also create a temptation to trade support in the Security Council for acquiesence in a crack-down in dissident Republics. This charge was made with regard to the Baltics during the Gulf war, although in the event Moscow did not use the international preoccupation with the Gulf as a cover for the imposition of martial law along the lines of the 1956 Suez Crisis and the crushing of the rebellion in Hungary.[14]

The United Nations

The hopes for a new world order have become closely associated with the United Nations largely through the experience of the Gulf war. When the concept was first mooted early in the crisis, the institutional implications were by no means clear. The President based American policy on the principle of non-aggression, not on support for the UN in itself. The initial economic and military moves were made after the Security Council had condemned the invasion, but before specific authority was obtained for strong measures. The principles of non-aggression could have been promoted using a much more general authority (i.e., Article 51 of the Charter which refers to self-defence). This was certainly considered at crucial points – especially with the move beyond the economic embargo to an enforced blockade. This was the turning point, for from then on the coalition forces had international blessing to engage in what would otherwise have been an act of war against Iraq. Confidence in the authority that could be gained through the use of the Security Council resolutions grew with each successful vote.[15]

While the use of the UN was encouraged through successful practice, the need to develop policy through a coalition of forces was evident from the start, and indeed was a precondition for the successful use of the Security Council. But holding together an international coalition required muting criticisms of the practices of particular states, and repairing relations with states whose past behaviour had made them subject to strong criticism. This was particularly true in the case of: China, which was in a position to veto Security Council resolutions and saw in the crisis an opportunity to end its post-Tiananmen Square isolation; Syria, condemned in the past for state terrorism but now valued as a radical member of the anti-Iraq coalition; and Iran, previously the *bête noire* of American policy, but now to be dissuaded from any alliance of convenience with its erstwhile Iraqi enemy. Many members of the coalition – including Kuwait and Saudi Arabia – had poor human-rights records. It was therefore impossible to sustain such a wide-ranging coalition on the basis of the highest political standards.

So while the stand taken was essentially principled in terms of its opposition to aggression, it is important to note that it was the unambiguous and vicious nature of the aggression that made it possible to forge such a coalition. The principle itself involved the rights of states. When the post-war attacks on Kurds and Shi'ites, which led to their desperate flight towards Turkey and Iran, raised the question of the rights of individuals or groups in the face of oppressive state action, it was much more difficult to generate a unified international policy. The Soviet Union and China both detected dangerous precedents in terms of interference in internal affairs, with their own Baltic and Tibetan situations in mind. As such situations are more likely than crude aggression to arise in the future, this may provide another indication of the limits of the United Nations to enforce principles. The sympathy in the West for the Kurds' plight prompted Western action irrespective of UN involvement, but the slow Security Council response was a drawback. This tragic episode stressed the need for clarification of the principles of outside intervention in support of oppressed peoples, if the methods applied in the Gulf were to serve as the basis for future international crisis management.

Implications for future crises

If the major challenge for the future proves to lie in regional conflicts, then some of the most important questions concern the influence of the Gulf experience on those tempted to commit aggression in the future. The post-mortems on the failure to appreciate the high risk of Iraqi aggression and to act accordingly reveal familiar failures in Western policy-making: the disbelief that so often appears in the face of imminent aggression, and only the shock of the occupation producing the measures that, had they been threatened, might have prevented the attack in the first place.[16]

The failures in Iraqi policy-making were much more serious. Any suggestion that the Gulf war will exercise a benign influence on the conduct of international affairs will depend on its lessons being taken to heart by other would-be aggressors. The sweeping victory in the Gulf undermined any notion that the Third World can now compete with the West in the military sphere. Whatever high-technology systems have been acquired by Third World states, the ability to defeat formidable military capabilities with sophisticated intelligence, command and control, and training is still lacking. This gap was obscured so long as American military encounters with the Third World involved jungle or urban conflicts in politically complex situations such as Vietnam or Lebanon. Victories in Grenada and Panama or the bombing of Tripoli did not really count because of the weak nature of the opposition. Even then, there were elements of incompetence in the American performance, which led to the argument that a focus on the procurement of major weapons systems had diminished the ability to grasp the fundamentals of the military art. There is now no question that in regular warfare the West and the Third World are in different classes, and that this difference is most marked with respect to the United States because of the sheer size and range of its military establishment. It is hard to imagine any Third World leader picking over the details of the Gulf war and working out how much better he would have done had he been in Saddam's position. It is going to be a long time before any Third World leader challenges American military power on anything approaching American terms.

A second, hopeful possibility is that there will be a reduced tendency in the future to miscalculate a Western response to flagrant aggression. Saddam Hussein made the classic error of assuming that pre-occupation quietude in the West would translate into post-occupation quiescence. This grew out of a failure to recognize that an act of aggression is an issue in itself, and not simply a more daring means of resolving an otherwise intractable dispute.

The example of a substantial regional power attempting to advance itself in an international environment that it understands imperfectly is reminiscent in a number of critical respects of the Argentine occupation of the Falklands, which resulted in the successful British campaign to retake the Islands. The two cases had many elements in common: an American statement of a lack of interest in the substance of regional disputes being interpreted as indifference to the resolution of this dispute by armed force; the availability of a military option that had been developed in secret for some time; a conviction that speedy, decisive action would present the world community with a *fait accompli* and, possibly, a similar belief that a limited gain could be extracted from dramatic action by combining an occupation with a promise of early withdrawal; and surprise when the aggression was followed by a serious military response from the West.[17]

Saddam seemed to believe that the crucial American vulnerability was the fear of casualties catalysed by the trauma of Vietnam. This vulnerability was probably exaggerated, but in any case it has now been lessened as a result of the United States experiencing so few casualties in the Gulf.

However, while the Gulf experience should help to deter those contemplating blatant aggression, it does not provide clear evidence of how the West will respond to more complex situations. Even in the face of considerable public disquiet over the Kurds, President Bush went out of his way to insist that the US would not get involved in an Iraqi civil war.[18] Memories of the debacle in Beirut from 1983–4 (in which a single terror bomb produced twice the casualties incurred during both *Desert Shield* and *Desert Storm*) exercise a powerful influence in Washington.

In many Third World conflicts, there are no obvious Western interests other than the protection of nationals. With the East–West conflict itself no longer a factor, the temptation for the US and other Western states to become directly involved in Third World conflicts to prevent a Soviet 'gain' has declined. Oil, however, infused every aspect of the Gulf crisis. It helps explain why Iraq invaded Kuwait and why the Gulf states could subsidize Western armies. Low oil prices followed the successful conclusion of the war; high prices could have followed failure (although not necessarily if the aggression had been ignored). It is nonetheless doubtful that even oil would have stimulated Western action if a major point of principle had not been involved as well.

There is always a basis for a cynical analysis of political behaviour, but this can underestimate the need in democracies to provide rationales with which both the élite and the general population can feel comfortable, and also its importance in any sort of consensus-building in the UN. It was the point of principle that made *Desert Storm* a 'just war'. It is hard to imagine the West allowing itself to be seen in the future, as it was in the past, ready to fight an unjust war.

Furthermore, if the deterrent effect of the Gulf war does persuade radical Third World states to be more wary of provoking American power, then blatant challenges to international order may be few and far between. Apart from conflicts in the Central American 'backyard', the main result of recent developments may be that far fewer occasions arise in which the US needs to throw its military weight about. The post-Cold War process of military contraction will also continue.

The Middle East

The most demanding challenges for future international crisis management are as likely to come in the future as in the past from the Middle East. This is an extraordinarily complex political system, composed of an unstable mixture of religion, natural resources and raw military power. In the attempts that were made to resolve the Gulf crisis before actual hostilities began, the only acknowledgment of this complexity was the crude linkage between the Gulf crisis and the Palestinian problem. However, this is but one linkage among many. Saddam Hussein's own list of the regional problems to be addressed before consideration be given to Kuwait included the Syrian position in Lebanon and Israel's in the West Bank.

As the Gulf conflict progressed, other connections emerged – Iraq's long-standing feuds with both Syria and Iran, as well as the Turkish interest in Iraq's handling of its Kurdish minority. Many states have claims against each other. Even Saudi Arabia has in the past claimed some Kuwaiti territory. Within individual states can be found deep social tensions – between secular and fundamentalist Islam, between Shi'ites and Sunnis, conservatives and radicals, the super-wealthy and the miserably poor.

This complexity is responsible for some of the region's most puzzling features. Political leaders in the area continually have to balance one set of concerns against another, with alliances and enmities shifting in an effort to ensure that in handling one threat a new one is not created.

The Gulf war has provided a huge shock to this system. The states closest to Iraq all had reason to fear its growing strength. The exception to this was Jordan, whose Palestinian population saw Iraqi strength as the best available challenge to Israel. The others – Iran, Syria, Turkey, Egypt, Saudi Arabia, the small Emirates as well as Israel – found a common cause in cutting Iraq down to size, even though they then became worried that if it were diminished too much a power vacuum would be created which another might exploit to enhance its own regional position. This is why so much importance was attached during the war to promises to keep Iraq intact afterwards.

Even if Saddam Hussein does survive in power, the comprehensive nature of Iraq's defeat has undermined his credibility and power for the foreseeable future. The extent to which this is likely to make a practical difference depends on whether Iraq was in the regional ascendance to the degree that was so widely assumed prior to the war.

The assumption of regional ascendance followed the war with Iran. Iraq benefited from that war in every sense but the one for which it initiated the conflict. It did not achieve its main objectives, but it at least thwarted Tehran's designs, which explicitly extended to the overthrow of Saddam and his regime. In keeping Iran in check, Iraq was seen by the majority of Arab states and by the West to be serving their interests. Iran's size and location meant that it was far more important than Iraq in strategic terms, but Iran's fundamentalism rendered it inaccessible.

In keeping Iranian fundamentalism at bay, Iraq earned gratitude – as well as credits and arms. The US tilted in its direction towards the end of the war, when Iran was seen as a threat to freedom of the seas. French distrust of Syrian policy in Lebanon provided another reason to back Iraq. Its apparent strength then began to attract other support. Jordan saw it as a potential counter to the threat of an aggressive Israel. The PLO saw in Saddam a new, well-connected patron developing the means to neutralize Israel's capabilities for mass destruction.

It remains an important question as to whether this sort of support served as the basis for a long-term Iraqi ascendance or whether it simply fed Saddam's illusions. By 1990, there was evidence that elements of this support were evaporating. First, the resolution of the power struggle in Tehran in favour of moderate elements created a Western interest in improved relations with Iran. Iran, after all, was still of greater economic and strategic importance than Iraq. Second, the growing unacceptability of Saddam's regime was putting its good relations with the West in jeopardy. The treatment of the Kurds, the execution of the journalist Farzad Bazoft, the tell-tale signs of an interest in developing different types of weapons of mass destruction had all eaten away at the readiness of Western governments to support Saddam. A crisis was brewing even before Iraq invaded Kuwait. Third, Saddam was finding it difficult to pay his bills. This was leading the French to reconsider their arms-transfer relationship with Iraq. The economic basis to Saddam's power was threatened by the heavy debt burden left over from the war with Iran and the lack of any obvious material benefit from the so-called 'victory' over Iran. This dire economic position, combined with irritation at the oil pricing policy of Kuwait and other Gulf states, provided a powerful motive for the invasion.[19]

This left as the remaining basis of Saddam's regional support the combination of his championship of the Arab cause against Israel and his accumulation of raw military power which, at least in some key elements, was considered tried and tested. With Syria preoccupied in Lebanon and suffering from the decline of its Soviet patron, Iraq was well placed to take up the leadership of radical Arab nationalism. This was therefore becoming a growing feature of Iraqi rhetoric. Coupled with Jordanian weakness, there was reason to expect some sort of Iraqi clash with Israel.

While it is unlikely that Kuwait was annexed simply in order to bolster Saddam's general leadership of the Arab world, his readiness to speak out on behalf of the Palestinians was one of his strongest cards. Had his annexation succeeded, he would have been a power to be reckoned with in all aspects of Middle Eastern affairs and, given the nature of his ascent, a source of chronic insecurity to his neighbours.

The crisis itself encouraged an exaggeration of Iraqi military power. The coalition leaders stressed the Iraqi danger in order to mobilize public opinion against this 'new Hitler'. Opponents of direct military action stressed Iraqi strength to warn of a 'new Vietnam', while Saddam himself was pleased to encourage lurid descriptions of his military might to deter the coalition and to raise his profile as the 'new Saladin'.

It would be to detract from the allied campaign to suggest that the eventual sweeping victory reflected the extent to which Iraqi military power was built solely on myth. As can be seen in the war with Iran and in the recent civil war, within their own class the Iraqi armed forces are capable and ruthlessly directed. However, from early on in the crisis, informed analysts questioned Iraq's capacity to cope with a true world-class power. Prudence made it necessary to assume that the Iraqis would exploit the tactical advantages of a well-prepared defence much more effectively than was the case. The most fearful component of the Iraqi armed forces, which exercised a considerable influence as no more than a putative threat, were the elements of a capability for mass destruction – ballistic missiles and chemical, biological and nuclear weapons. There is no doubt of Saddam's determination to equip himself in this regard. Exactly how far he had got is not yet clear, but less progress may have been made in the nuclear and biological spheres than feared, and Iraq's chemical capability was less functional than supposed. Iraq's missile arsenal turned out to be more extensive in numbers and range than anticipated. Whether this added up – as Saddam claimed – to a counter to Israeli nuclear capability is doubtful. At any rate, this programme has now been set back. Iraq's economic and military weakness means that it cannot play, for the time being, a leading role in Middle Eastern power politics.

The most critical feature of the shifting balance of power in the region is the prominent role currently being played by the United States and, to a lesser extent, the UK and France. The willingness to draw in these external powers, with their mixed records in Middle Eastern affairs, is testament to the extent to which the old system had got out of kilter.

Over the past few years Soviet influence has declined markedly, and so it no longer drives US policy nor that of the regional powers. This is why President Hafez Assad of Syria is far more interested in good relations with the US than he would have been otherwise. This is also the factor which has denied Saddam the traditional escape route for defeated Arab leaders – prompt military and economic assistance from Moscow.

There is therefore no external power capable of balancing Western influence in the region. Indeed, it would not be surprising if Arab leaders soon started to cultivate the EC in an attempt at least to offset what might otherwise be seen as an over-commanding American position.[20]

It would be unnatural if such a dramatic change in the regional power structure was not viewed with misgivings. It is widely suspected – and not only in the Islamic world – that the West seeks to use its new position to help sustain its wealthy conservative 'puppets', block any resolution of the Arab–Israeli conflict, and keep oil prices low.

The new position is also producing misgivings in the West. There is little interest in setting up a permanent military presence in the Gulf. Experience of the volatility of the area warns against attempts to sort out the generality of regional conflicts. James Baker and UK Foreign Secretary Douglas Hurd have both indicated that the preferred position for the West should be to back local initiatives along the lines of the Damascus Declaration,[21] rather than rush forward with its own designs.

Yet the expectations of a leading Western role are now well established. Despite their attempts to do so, the coalition powers were not able simply to abandon the Kurds to their fate. Arab governments are suggesting that the United States will need to deliver Israel at an early peace conference in return for their co-operation during the Gulf crisis.

The shake-up in the Middle East will lead to opportunities for creative diplomacy. The working relationships established in recent months and the engagement of senior policy-makers mean that they can be exploited. It might be remembered that the last serious breakthroughs in the Arab–Israeli dispute followed the October 1973 War. If progress is to be made this time, it will require sensitivity to the changing nature of the Middle East's complex political system rather than grand plans and gestures.

Can Syria and Israel reach a settlement on the Golan Heights? Will this require progress on the Palestinian question first? If so, how can the Israelis be persuaded to speak to any serious representatives of the Palestinians? Who can speak for the Palestinians: the discredited leadership of the PLO, the newly elected representatives from the West Bank, or King Hussein of Jordan? Would it help or hinder to bring the USSR into this process?

There is no local power in the Middle East that can pull all these strands together. The West has no alternative but to take an active part. The challenge for the future, therefore, is to use enhanced influence constructively without being tempted into excessive promises or commitments.

Conclusion

The makings of a new world order exist, but not necessarily the grand and elevated design suggested in some American rhetoric. It has two critical features: first, the pre-eminent position of the US and other Western powers within the international system; and, second, the series of precedents created during the Gulf crisis for collective international action against flagrant violations of international law. These precedents were generated as a result of the unambiguous nature of the Iraqi action which provided no scope for equivocation. There were no grey areas which could be seized upon by the faint-hearted to justify inaction.

A more engaged Western role in the generality of international conflicts and even in enforcing the principle of non-aggression does not depend on the UN, although for the moment that is available as an instrument for legitimizing as well as shaping policy. Whether it will be available in the future is just one of the many issues raised by the uncertain development of the Soviet Union.

Because the point of principle was so important in this case, the principle itself has now been emphasized, which will make it harder to turn a blind eye to blatant examples of aggression in the future. It may even be that the reluctant involvement in Iraq's internal affairs necessitated by Saddam's oppression of those opposing his regime is setting further precedents.

The movement away from the assertion of the rights of states to the rights of individuals and groups is controversial. Nonetheless, it is hard to see how such a movement can be avoided if the Gulf experience is to be a building block for the future and there is to be some collective response to the widely expected disorders in various regions of the world.

The experience of the past year should alert Western policy-makers to the difficulties they may face if they seek to limit their international commitments on the basis that they must not interfere in the internal affairs of other states. In Central and Eastern Europe, if nowhere else, it is prudent to expect the development of crises which cannot be contained. These crises will provide some of the most crucial tests for any new world order. If the view is taken that the principles raised by intervention are too controversial and that the conflicts which see minorities being persecuted are too compli-cated to deserve entanglement, the new world order may have gone as far as it can go in demonstrating a readiness to enforce the principle of non-aggression. This may seem modest, but, given twentieth-century history, it is an achievement not to be dismissed lightly.

Notes

1. Text of Speech by President George Bush, *Financial Times*, 9 August 1990.
2. President George Bush, Address to Congress, 11 September 1990 (US Information Service).
3. President George Bush, Speech at Air University, Maxwell Air Force Base, 13 April 1991 (US Information Service).
4. See, for example, Jim Hoagland, 'The New Order Starts with a Betrayal-as-Usual', *International Herald Tribune* (hereafter *IHT*), 4 April 1991; Theo Sommer, 'A World Beyond Order and Control', *The Guardian*, 15 April 1991.
5. Flora Lewis, 'A More Orderly World, Not a "New World Order" ', *IHT*, 18 February 1991. A similar but more pessimistic argument is found in Stanley Hoffmann, 'Watch Out for a New World Disorder' and 'A State's Internal Conditions are Outsiders' Business', in *IHT*, 26,

27 February 1991.

6. See, for example, the various contributors to 'A New World Order?', *Newsweek*, 11 March 1991. Edward Mortimer discusses the concept largely in terms of the shifting relations between the US and the USSR in 'Judgement of History', *Financial Times*, 18 January 1991.

7. William Pfaff, 'A Dose of Realpolitik in This "New Order" ', *IHT*, 23–4 March 1991. See also his 'More Likely, a New World Disorder after This War', *IHT*, 30 January 1991.

8. For example, John J. Mearsheimer, 'Back to the Future: Instability in Europe after the Cold War', *International Security*, vol. 15, no. 1, Summer 1990.

9. *The Independent*, 5 January 1991.

10. Iraqi Foreign Minister Tariq Aziz rebuffed Jacques Poos of Luxembourg in early January 1991 when this was suggested.

11. The plan was put forward by British Prime Minister John Major, to the Luxembourg summit of European leaders on 8 April 1991. See *Financial Times*, 9 April 1991.

12. See US–Soviet Joint Statement, *Financial Times*, 5 August 1991.

13. See *Financial Times*, 8 February 1991.

14. On 13 January 1991, the presidents of the three Baltic Republics plus Boris Yeltsin, the Russian leader, called on the UN deadline for Iraq to leave Kuwait to be extended so that urgent attention could be given to the Baltic confrontation. *Financial Times*, 14 January 1991.

15. There were 12 resolutions covering all aspects of the crisis in 1990, culminating in Resolution 678 of 29 November authorizing the 'use of all necessary means' to implement previous resolutions. It was only in this last resolution that one of the Permanent Members (China) abstained. Those resolutions, which were largely condemnatory of Iraqi actions, were generally unanimous. In those which authorized action against Iraq, Cuba and Yemen tended to abstain or vote against. The Permanent Members worked together in the temporary and permanent cease-fire resolutions of 1991 (686 on 2 March and 687 on 3 April respectively).

16. See, for example, Pierre Salinger with Eric Laurent, *Secret Dossier: The Hidden Agenda Behind the Gulf War: An Insider View of the Countdown to the Crisis* (London: Penguin Books, 1991).

17. On the Falklands case see Lawrence Freedman and Virginia Gamba-Stonehouse, *Signals of War: The Falklands Conflict of 1982* (London: Faber, 1990).

18. Bush observed that 'I do not want one single soldier or airman shoved into a civil war in Iraq that's been going on for ages'. *IHT*, 15 April 1991.

19. See Efraim Karsh and Inari Rautsi, *Saddam Hussein: A Political Biography* (London: Brassey's, 1991), Chapter 9.

20. The question of European Community participation in the peace process soon became an issue during the Baker 'shuttle', with Israel hostile to its involvement and the Arabs keen. *The Guardian*, 18 April 1991.

21. On 6 March the foreign ministers of Egypt, Syria and the six states of the Gulf Co-operation Council (GCC) agreed on a joint formula for

peace and security in the area, including military contingents from the two non-GCC countries. See 'A New Arab Order for the Middle East', *Newsbrief* (Royal United Services Institute, April 1991).

Index